NO CHARGE FOR WINE & [...]

All Articles in this List are correctly described as required by the Merchandise Marks Act 50 & 51 Vic. Cap. 28.

..., 1896.

Branch:—1a, UPPER BAKER STRE[...]

THE
VICTORIA WINE COMPANY.

Head Office, Warehouses & Vaults: 8 to 10, OSBORN STREET, LONDON, E.

Bottled & Cask Beer Stores: JOHN STREET, CHURCH LANE, E.

LONDON BRANCHES.

BAYSWATER: 24a, Hereford Road
BELSIZE PARK: 26, England's Lane
BRIXTON HILL: No. 104
BROCKLEY: 85, Brockley Road
BROCKLEY: 291, Brockley Road
BROMPTON: 65, Fulham Road
BROMPTON: 279, Fulham Road
CAMDEN TOWN: 69, Camden Road
CHELSEA: 123, King's Road
CLAPHAM ROAD: No. 374
COMMERCIAL ROAD (East): Nos. 161 & 163
CROUCH END: 50, The Broadway
FINSBURY PARK: 87, Stroud Green Road

HACKNEY: 380, Mare Street
HAMPSTEAD (West): 5, Deanington Parade, West End Lane
HAMPSTEAD ROAD: No. 115
HAMPSTEAD (South): 15, Goldhurst Terrace, Finchley Road
HAMPSTEAD: 62, High Street
HOLLOWAY: 113, Holloway Road
KENSINGTON: 147, Earl's Court Road
KENSINGTON: 6, Maclise Road
KENSINGTON: 13, Stratford Road
KENSINGTON: 123, Warwick Road
KENSINGTON (West): 1, Charleville Road

KENSINGTON: 4, Moreton Terrace, Old Brompton Road
KENSINGTON (South): 152, Cromwell Road
KENTISH TOWN ROAD: No. 175a
KILBURN: 213, Belsize Road
KILBURN: 313, High Road
MAIDA VALE: 2, Bristol Gardens
NOTTING HILL: Percy House, 32, St. Lawrence Road
NOTTING HILL GATE: 32, Pembridge Rd.
OLD KENT ROAD: No 691
PADDINGTON: 3, Praed Street
PECKHAM: 111b, Queen's Road

PECKHAM RYE: No. 19
PIMLICO: 136, Tachbrook Street
PIMLICO: 160a, Ebury Street
POPLAR: Bank Bldgs., 187, East India Rd.
PORTMAN SQUARE: 65, George Street
REGENT'S PARK: 1a, Upper Baker Street
ST. JOHN'S WOOD: 19, Circus Road
SHEPHERD'S BUSH: 338, Uxbridge Road
SHEPHERD'S BUSH: 35, Goldhawk Road
STOKE NEWINGTON: 64, Green Lanes
STRATFORD: 124, The Grove
WALHAM GREEN: 454, Fulham Road
WHITECHAPEL: 8, Osborn Street

COUNTRY BRANCHES.

ANERLEY: 93, Penge Road
BALHAM: 65, Bedford Hill
BALHAM HILL: 5, Grand Parade
BLACKHEATH: 21, Tranquil Vale
BRENTFORD (New): 186, High Street
BRIGHTON: 33, New Road
BROMLEY (Kent): 80, High Street
CROYDON (West): 136, North End
CROYDON (East): 87, George Street
CRYSTAL PALACE: 94, Anerley Road
DULWICH (West): 5, Croxted Road

EALING: 2, The Mall
EALING DEAN: 138, Uxbridge Road
FOREST HILL: 59, Park Road
GRAVESEND: 169, Windmill Street
HOUNSLOW: 251, High Street
LADYWELL: 225, High Street, Lewisham
LEE: 184, High Road
LEE: 17, Burnt Ash Hill
NORBITON: 180, London Road
NORWOOD (Upper): 7, Central Hill
PENGE: 52, Oakfield Road

PUTNEY: 160, Upper Richmond Road
RICHMOND: 73, George Street
SOUTHEND: London House, 38, High St.
STREATHAM: 119, High Road
SURBITON: Victoria Road
SUTTON (Surrey): 132, High Street
SYDENHAM: 54, Kirkdale
TOOTING: 23, Upper Tooting Road
TOTTENHAM: 560, High Road
TULSE HILL (Upper): No. 1

TULSE HILL: 94, Norwood Road
TURNHAM GREEN: 2, Bank Buildings, Broadway
WANDSWORTH: 68, East Hill
WANDSWORTH: 46, West Hill
WANDSWORTH (New): 11, Battersea Rise
WILLESDEN: 2, The Mall, High Street, Harlesden
WIMBLEDON: 10, Ridgway
WIMBLEDON: 51, The Broadway

Bankers:—LONDON & WESTMINSTER BANK

Days of Delivery in London—W. & N.W., Mondays & Thursdays; E. & N., Tuesdays & Fridays; S.E. & S.W., Wednesdays & Saturdays.

THE VICTORIA WINE COMPANY beg to call attention to the annexed List of Prices. The increasing business of the Company (shown by their holding more licenses than any firm in the Kingdom) has led to the opening of a number of Branches where Wine from ½-pint upwards, and single bottles of Spirits, Beers, Mineral Waters, &c., can be obtained; and as the principle of cash payment is strictly adhered to, a very low rate of profit has to be paid by the customer. Should any Wines or Spirits bought of the Company not be approved, the same, on application, will be exchanged free of expense, or the money returned, provided the bottles be unopened.

NEW SPANISH TREATY.—The Company have pleasure in notifying that through this Treaty they are again enabled to introduce a Pure Foreign Port and Sherry at One Shilling per Bottle. They have also improved the qualities of their other Sherries, and have made several important additions to list, thus giving their customers the full benefit of the Treaty.

Brand on Cork.	SPANISH PORTS.	Per Doz.	Per Bot.	Brand on Cork.	SHERRIES.	Per Doz.	Per Bot.
Victoria Wine Co.*	PORT *, Spanish Port, remarkably good value	12/	1/	Victoria Wine Co.*	SHERRY pure Spanish Sherry, remarkably good value	12/	1/
Victoria Wine Co. 1	PORT No. 1, do. pure and wholesome, with Port character	15/	1/3	Victoria Wine Co. 1	SHERRY No. 1, a good, pure, wholesome Wine	15/	1/3
				Victoria Wine Co. 2	SHERRY No. 2, full-flavoured, soft old Wine	18/	1/6
	PORTS FROM OPORTO.			Victoria Wine Co. 2*	SHERRY No. 2*, golden, this Wine is richer in flavour than the above	18/	1/6
	All the following Port Wines are the produce of the Douro District, and are guaranteed:—			Victoria Wine Co. 3	SHERRY No. 3, delicate, pale, slightly rich Wine	24/	2/
Victoria Wine Co. 2	PORT No. 2, rich soft Wine, great body and flavour	18/	1/6	Victoria Wine Co. 3*	SHERRY No. 3*, golden, a very old Wine	24/	2/
Victoria Wine Co. 2*	PORT No. 2*, a fruity generous Wine, nice flavour	21/	1/9	Victoria Wine Co. 3d	SHERRY No. 3d, a delicate pale dry Wine, recommended	24/	2/
Victoria Wine Co. 3	PORT No. 3, very fruity, specially adapted for invalids	24/	2/				
Victoria Wine Co. 3*	PORT No. 3*, a drier Wine than the above, will much improve in bottle	27/	2/3	Victoria Wine Co. 4	SHERRY No. 4, old, pale, possessing a splendid flavour	30/	2/6
				Victoria Wine Co. 4*	SHERRY No. 4*, golden; this is rich in character	30/	2/6
Victoria Wine Co. 3a	PORT No. 3a, fine old, tawny, matured, Martinez, Gassiot & Co.'s shipping	28/	2/4	Victoria Wine Co. 4d	SHERRY No. 4d, pale, superior, dry Wine, recommended	30/	2/6
Victoria Wine Co. 4	PORT No. 4, fine Wine, rich, soft and delicate	30/	2/6				
Victoria Wine Co. 4*	PORT No. 4*, this Wine has fine aroma, is stouter than the above	33/	2/9	Victoria Wine Co. 5	SHERRY No. 5, Oloroso; elegant, rich, soft	36/	3/
Victoria Wine Co. 4d	PORT No. 4d, splendid body and bouquet, dry	30/	2/6	Victoria Wine Co. 5*	SHERRY No. 5*, very fine, golden Wine, rich in character, and strongly recommended for the use of invalids	36/	3/
Victoria Wine Co. 5	PORT No. 5, old, rich, fit for any gentleman's table	36/	3/				
Victoria Wine Co. 5a	PORT No. 5a, this old Wine has fine silky flavour and finish	39/	3/3	Victoria Wine Co. 5d	SHERRY No. 5d, a very pale, dry, elegant, fine Wine, with excellent aroma	36/	3/
Victoria Wine Co. 5d	PORT No. 5d, this beautiful dry Wine is unequalled at the price	36/	3/	Victoria Wine Co. 6	SHERRY No. 6, Amoroso; a beautiful pale Sherry, possessing a splendid, soft, rich, nutty flavour	44/	3/8
Victoria Wine Co. 6	PORT No. 6, very old, light coloured and dry; great aroma and flavour	44/	3/8	Victoria Wine Co. 6d	SHERRY No. 6d, a very superior, and very dry, delicate Amontillado Pasado	44/	3 8
Victoria Wine Co. 6*	PORT No. 6*, a full-bodied Wine, with great character; very soft and delicate on the palate	44/	3/8	Victoria Wine Co. 7	SHERRY No. 7, gold colour, of a rich mellow flavour	36/	3/
Victoria Wine Co.**	PORT * *, a Wine of rare and special quality	48/	4/	Victoria Wine Co. 8	SHERRY No. 8, brown colour, very old, has great body and flavour, with dryness	36/	3/
Victoria Wine Co. 7	PORT No. 7, very light, old and dry, a really magnificent Wine	54/	4/6				
Victoria Wine Co. 7*	PORT No. 7*, with medium colour and splendid bouquet; has a rich soft silky flavour	54/	4/6	Victoria Wine Co. 9	SHERRY No. 9, very old brown, has magnificent body and flavour	44/	3/8
Victoria Wine Co. 8	PORT No. 8, White Port; a most delicious Wine; rich golden, delicate flavour	41/	3/5	Victoria Wine Co. 12*	SHERRY No. 12*, Montilla; the natural Wine of Spain, having had no additional spirit whatever; extremely suitable for dinner use	14/	1/2
Victoria Wine Co. 10	PORT No. 10, a truly grand, soft, luscious Wine	40/	3/4				
Victoria Wine Co. 10*	PORT No. 10*, dry in character, with magnificent aroma and full colour	36/	3/	Victoria Wine Co. 14	SHERRY No. 14, a very pale, beautiful Wine, has a mellow, exquisite flavour	48/	4/
Victoria Wine Co.11* Seal on Cork.	PORT No. 11*, very grand young Vintage Wine; will turn out exceedingly fine in bottle	30/	2/6	Victoria Wine Co. 15	SHERRY No. 15, a selected old pale Wine, singularly delicate, with magnificent bouquet	60/	5/
Victoria Wine Co. Green Seal	PORT No. 5*, old crusted, 2 years in bottle	36/	3/	Victoria Wine Co. 16	SHERRY No. 16, Amontillado; of very finest quality procurable	70/	5/10
Victoria Wine Co. Red Seal	PORT No. 11, old crusted, 3 years in bottle; matured in the wood, and carefully bottled	42/	3/6				
Victoria Wine Co. Black Seal	PORT No. 12, old crusted, 5 years in bottle; a good generous Wine, medium colour, and fine flavour	49/	4/1		**New Spanish Treaty.**—The reduction in the Duty has enabled The Victoria Wine Company to select, for those who prefer a Wine light in alcohol, some very fine parcels of Sherries below 30 degrees which, being Pale and nutty Wines, they can strongly recommend.		
Victoria Wine Co. Yellow Seal	PORT No. 13, old crusted, 8 years in bottle; a Wine of great elegance; has great softness and character, full of wing	59/	4/11				
White Seal Brand on Cork.	PORT No. 13*, a superb Wine, 10 years in bottle	70/	5/10	Victoria Wine Co. 3a	NATURAL MONTILLA, pale, light and elegant	16/	1/4
Alto Douro	PORT No. 14, Alto Douro; recommended for invalids; it is shipped especially to the Victoria Wine Co.	42/	3/6	Victoria Wine Co. 3b	MONTILLA ESPECIAL, a most delicate Wine, suitable for dinner purposes, rather drier than above	20/	1/8
Victoria Wine Co. 15	PORT No. 15, the finest quality of Port Wine that can be produced shipped to the Victoria Wine Co. by Messrs. Martinez, Gassiot & Co., of Oporto, under the mark of ◇◇◇◇	48/	4/	Victoria Wine Co. 3b	PALO, a very high-class dinner or dessert Wine	25/	2/1
				Victoria Wine Co. 5b	FINO SECO, a fine flavoured, pale, dry Wine	28/	2/4
				Victoria Wine Co. 5b	DELICIOSO, a soft, nutty Wine, with great flavour	32/	2/8

Attention is called to Port No. 3, being specially adapted for Invalids, 24/- per dozen, 2/- per bottle.

NO CHARGE FOR WINE & SPIRIT BOTTLES.

WINE
FOR SALE

WINE FOR SALE

Victoria Wine and the Liquor Trade

1860-1984

ASA BRIGGS

THE UNIVERSITY OF CHICAGO PRESS

The University of Chicago Press, Chicago 60637
B. T. Batsford Ltd., London W1H 0AH
© 1985 by Asa Briggs
All rights reserved. Published 1985

Typeset by Servis Filmsetting Ltd, Manchester
and printed in Great Britain by Anchor Brendon Ltd, Tiptree, Essex

Library of Congress Cataloging-in-Publication Data

Briggs, Asa, 1921 - Wine for Sale.

    Includes index.
    1. Victoria Wine (Firm) - History.
    2. Wine Industry - Great Britain - History.
    I. Title.
    HD9381.9.V5B75   1986   338.7'6632'00941   85-20877

ISBN 0 226 07485 4

94 93 92 91 90 89 88 87 86 85   54321

Contents

List of Illustrations

Between pages 184 and 185
A transport problem, 1916
Horse-drawn delivery carts, Harveys, Bristol, 1920
Austin 10 delivery van, mid-1930s
Modern delivery van
Christmas advertisement, 1880
W. Glendenning's 1931 Christmas list
W. Glendenning's 1932 Christmas list
1933 Victoria Wine and Tyler's price lists
Victoria Wine price lists from the 1930s
A wartime price list, 1940

Back endpaper
Part of Victoria Wine wine list and wine selector, 1983

List of Tables

Acknowledgements

I am deeply grateful to all the people in Victoria Wine, including many who have retired from the business, who have helped me to write this book. It would be invidious to try to select names, but without the bold initiative of Eric Colwell and the imagination and organisation of Evelyn Ellis it would never have appeared.

Outside Victoria Wine my greatest debt is to Susan Hard who has braved every kind of relevant archive and tackled every kind of question in her search. John Arlott, as knowledgeable about all aspects of wine as about all aspects of cricket, read the text, and wrote the foreword, which I greatly appreciate. Dr Bryan Wilson, Fellow of All Souls, an old friend, read the proofs. He has taught me much about wine and continues to do so. My secretary, Margaret Stevens, has made it possible for me to prepare legible texts and, equally important, a legible index. Billett Potter has kindly given me access to his collection of wine lists. I am greatly indebted, finally, to Anthony Seward who has seen the book through the press.

I hope that this is the kind of exploratory study which will not remain the only one of its kind. The relationship between history and social history is a crucial relationship in understanding contemporary culture and the limits to it.

Worcester College, Oxford
June 1985   *Asa Briggs*

Foreword
by John Arlott

The story of Victoria Wine has three quite separate strands and, for all that Lord Briggs has skilfully interwoven them into their true historic pattern, each has a quite separate social significance.

The first, of course, is the commercial success of William Winch Hughes in starting from scratch and selling drink to the ordinary man through a type of shop presentation which then, as now, met the requirement of that customer quite admirably.

In the early days of this story and, indeed, for some years afterwards, wine shops tended to be of two kinds. The traditional wine merchant served an almost exclusively upper-class clientele, for good wine was comparatively dear, and knowledge of it confined to a narrow segment of the community. At the other end of the scale were the dram shops, sleazy establishments where alcohol per ha'penny was the criterion.

The triumph of Victoria Wine has always been to tread an immaculate middle path. They have ensured that the ordinary man has neither been overawed by their shops, nor ashamed to be seen going into them.

In the countries that produce wine it is accepted as part of everyday life. Britain though is not at heart, nor in fact, a wine-producing, nor even – yet – truly a wine-drinking country. Governments have constantly fenced the trade round with obstacles and burdens; above all, taxation has made wine exaggeratedly dearer than it need be. William Winch Hughes and his successors met these problems and, to the best of their considerable abilities, smoothed the path for their customers.

Paucity of information makes Mr Hughes a shadowy figure. Nevertheless, the shop fronts which preserve his business name impinge on many more consciousnesses than more ostentatious memorials to men, whose

3

characters have been described in detail.

In a later phase, as the post-1945 section of the history quite strikingly demonstrates, the firm fell into the developing financial and commercial pattern of the modern world, moving out from the limitations of a single business into mergers, takeovers and amalgamations. Crucially, though, it retained identity; not only has its name survived where those of other incorporated firms disappeared, but William Winch Hughes's original purpose has been maintained. Even though it has become 'the shop window of the largest drinks group in Europe', Victoria remains the shop where the ordinary man can buy drink. That has involved, essentially, skilful keeping in step, never either out of date or way out: a rare commercial sympathy.

Crucially, Victoria have kept in historic step with the growth of general wine-drinking in this country, especially over the last thirty years when it has extended beyond even the reasonable ambitions of the trade itself.

The factors that have persuaded a steadily growing proportion of the British population to turn to wine are numerous. In early days war service and business travel; then surely, the strongest influence – continental package holidays for people who had not previously gone overseas; but also, not to be forgotten, secondhand influences such as going out to a meal or a wine bar with a convert – all have played their part.

Compensating in business terms for the decline in public house trade, yet competing with the supermarkets by virtue of a wider range and choice of stocks, the Victoria shops have both reflected and assisted the wider popular interest in wine, for the continuingly valid reason that they are easy to shop in. They have fitted into a social pattern in which a vastly greater number of wine books, wine tours, tutored tastings and, simply, general discussion have increased knowledge, information and, above all, enthusiasm for the one kind of drink which fosters wide and deep interest.

The British public has long suffered financially from the fact that they are not a wine-producing people. They have, though, reaped one great advantage. The wine-producing countries are invariably – indeed, almost compulsorily – parochial, concentrating on their own wines. Britain, though, is the wine market-place of the world. No other country has so many shops offering such a wide choice; Victoria offers wines from no less than 20 different countries (amongst which France, with 25 separate and distinct wine regions, counts simply as one). This reflects

4

not merely the expansion of a business, but its integral share in an aspect of British social life which the reader can sense developing through Lord Briggs's pages.

Alderney   John Arlott
Channel Islands
June 1985

CHAPTER ONE

Introduction: A Business in its Social Setting

'From the earliest ages of mankind wine has been drunk,' wrote a student of French wines in 1865, 'and it is only reasonable to suppose that everything is known respecting it'.[1] If that were true, there would be no need for a further book on the subject. Drinking wine could continue very happily – as it usually does – without reading about it. Yet there were striking changes within the half-century after 1865 both in the growing of grapes and in the retailing of wine, not to speak of its consumption, and there have been bigger changes still in the quarter-century before this book was written.

The year 1865 is of special significance in this book, for it was then that William Winch Hughes started the Victoria Wine Company, the oldest 'wine chain' in the country. His first store was in Mark Lane in the City of London, and within only a few years he had 50 shops scattered over a wide area. By 1879 there were 63 shops; and when he died in 1886, there were 98 from Norwich to Bristol, and from Birmingham to Brighton.

Whatever Hughes had been selling, such a business achievement would have been outstanding, for there were few retailing chain stores of any kind at this time. Indeed, John James Sainsbury did not open his second store until 1876; Jesse Boot of Nottingham did not start his chemists' chain until 1884; Marks and Spencer did not form their partnership in Leeds until 1894.[2] As one of Hughes's obituary writers put it at the time, 'when we think of the number of employees, of the vast expense, and of the constant supervision it must require, and when we

---

[1] W.R. Smee, *French Wines at One Penny Per Bottle Customs Duty*, 2nd edn. (1865), p. 11.
[2] For another branch of drink sales in London, see the interesting and important article by P.J. Atkins, 'The Retail Milk Trade in London, *c*.1790–1914' in the *Economic History Review*, Vol. 33 (1980).

finally recollect that it was practically the creation of one man, we must confess that Mr Hughes's business career was no ordinary achievement.'[3]

As it was, the fact that William Winch Hughes was selling wines in his chain stores rather than some quite different range of products was even more remarkable, for there had long been economic, social, political and cultural barriers to the drinking of wine in Britain. For the early nineteenth-century clergyman wit, the Rev. Sydney Smith, 'Beer and Britannia' were 'inseparable ideas': wine, even port wine, came far behind. And the image of the wine trade in the mid-nineteenth century was very different from that of the trade in beer: it was traditionalist rather than commercial. There were, however, changes of fashions. The novelist Anthony Trollope, with his keen eye for the distinctive attributes of occupation as well as for the idiosyncrasies of personality, drew a sharp distinction between an English wine merchant, Mr Prettyman, 'a handsome old gentleman with grey hair, always well dressed, who goes about London in a pill box brougham, by which he is known to all men who know anything,' and a newcomer wine-dealer, Alphonse de Finadieu, who knocks at the door, hands in his card, and asks the householder whether he has tasted his champagne.

The former, for Trollope, was what every wine merchant should be: the latter was an upstart. Prettyman talked about his wine 'with a modest humour, but with gentle sarcasm.' He was 'always the fine gentleman, though he never drops the wine merchant.' Moreover, he sent in his bills only once a year. Alphonse de Finadieu both expected to be paid quickly and left you with a headache. 'Wholesome beer or whisky-and-water are beverages which a man may swallow, and rise to his next day's work in comfort. But wine from the cellars of Alphonse de Finadieu is a sin not to be forgiven.' 'It is safer to stick to Prettyman,' Trollope concluded, 'and give few dinners and wines of less costly names.'[4]

William Winch Hughes had nothing in common either with Mr Prettyman or with Alphonse de Finadieu. Nor was he looking for the same kinds of client. His idea was to sell for cash wine in shops to people who would never be visited by any existing wine merchant. When he was asked in 1879 how the kind of business he conducted was carried on before he entered the scene in 1865, he replied simply, 'there was no one ever sold wine at so low price to the public as I do.'[5] Hughes wanted to

[3] *Ridley and Company's Monthly Wine and Spirit Trade Circular*, 11 September 1886.
[4] A. Trollope, 'The Wine Merchant' in *Pall Mall Gazette*, 26 August 1880.
[5] *Minutes of Evidence to the House of Commons Select Committee on Wine Duties* (1879).

reach not a select clientèle, but the widest possible drinking public. No one had quite thought in those terms before. The contrast in pricing policy is well brought out in a mid-Victorian observation in the 1850s that the prices of a wine merchant were no more questioned than the fees of a doctor. Hughes wanted the wine business to have more of the characteristics of a trade and less of a profession.

Yet for Hughes to start his business at all, there had to be a new set of conditions for the international wine trade, which had languished in the early nineteenth century. The early history of Victoria Wine is inextricably bound up, therefore, with the history of the reduction of the duty on French wines – by W.E. Gladstone, then Chancellor of the Exchequer – in 1860. Gladstone forecast that large numbers of people who had not drunk French wines before would drink them if heavy duties, long imposed, were reduced; and with characteristic determination he persuaded Parliament that he was right, so that on 29 February 1860 the duty on wines of all descriptions was reduced to three shillings per gallon. 'There is a power of unbounded supply of wine if you will only alter your law', Gladstone explained, 'and there is a power, I won't say of unbounded demand, but of an enormously increased demand, for this most useful and valuable product.'[6]

On 1 January 1861 there was a further change when the uniform rate of three shillings per gallon was superseded by the imposition of a scale of duties, based on degrees of strength, ranging from one shilling per gallon on wines containing less than 18 degrees of alcohol to 2s 11d per gallon on wines containing 45 degrees of alcohol. Finally, there was a further downward revision according to scale in April 1862. Equally important, Gladstone turned to the economics of distribution as well as of taxation. His 'single bottle' Act of 1861 enabled any shopkeeper not expressly excluded by statute to obtain an off-licence for selling wine and any owner or manager of an 'eating house' to take out an annually renewable licence for wine consumption on the premises. His object, he told a fellow Liberal M.P., was 'first, to open some new and cleaner channels for consumption, secondly not to create a new monopoly.'[7]

Remarkably little has been written by professional historians about wine in Britain in the nineteenth century, less, indeed, than about wine in

---

[6] Hansard, *Parliamentary Debates*, 10 February 1860.
[7] Letter of W.E. Gladstone to Edward Baines, 24 February 1860 (Gladstone Papers, British Museum).

the fourteenth and fifteenth centuries, or, of course, the twentieth.[8] Yet at the moment of reducing the duties, Gladstone in his impressive speech spanned the history of wine over the centuries. He also struck, as was his wont, at rooted national prejudices:

> There is a notion gone abroad that there is something fixed and unchanging in an Englishman's taste with respect to wine. You find a great number of people who believe, like an article of Christian faith, that an Englishman is not born to drink French wines ... Endeavour to pour the French wine down his throat, but he still will regret it ... What they maintain is absolutely the reverse of the truth, for nothing is more certain than the taste of English people at one time for French wine. In earlier periods of our history French wine was the great article of consumption here. Taste is not an immutable, but a mutable thing.[9]

Without the intervention of the Liberal leader, Gladstone, William Winch Hughes, who was a stout Tory, would never have prospered. Yet Hughes did not deal only in French wines. Indeed, in his early lists he was offering wines from Australia and California as well as wines from Europe. And, more important still, from the start he was selling beer and spirits as well as wine. Gladstone wanted to reduce the trade in beer and spirits by increasing the trade in wine: Hughes wanted to increase his own share in both. He would never have been able to start his business on the lines that he followed had it not been for the changes in fiscal policy in 1860, yet he might not have prospered as he did had the changes of 1860 produced all the results expected of them.

As for Gladstone, he did not succeed in making wine the regular drink either of the middle classes or the working classes, the two huge groups to which he appealed. Nor did he reduce the appeal of beer or spirits. Total revenues collected in wine tax after 1860 did not exceed those collected before, as had been the case when Sir Robert Peel cut duties on other products in his great budgets of the 1840s, which were in Gladstone's mind. And although the gross *per capita* consumption figures for wine rose more quickly than those of beer and spirits during the 1860s, during the following decade the position was reversed.

---

[8] See, for example, the thorough and detailed monograph by M.K. Jones, *Studies in the Medieval Wine Trade* (1971). For the seventeenth century, see G.F. Steckley, 'The Wine Economy of Tenerife in the Seventeenth Century: Anglo-Spanish Partnership in a Luxury Trade' in *The Economic History Review*, second series, Vol. XXXIII (1980).

[9] *Hansard*, 10 February 1860.

As one of the few social historians to turn to the nineteenth-century drink trade has put it succinctly: 'What occurred after 1860 was not a general change in taste from gin and beer to wine, but a general increase in the gross consumption of *all* intoxicants – from which wine benefited more than other drinks (only) during the 1860s'.[10] Hughes – and Victoria Wine – profited from this general increase. Yet he and they gave far more publicity to a wider range of wines than any firm had ever done before, and through the publicity initiated a process of extending wine consumption of which Gladstone would have approved. The presence of the word 'wine' in the name of the business was a talisman. Indeed, whatever happened to fluctuating national trends in wine consumption in the nineteenth and twentieth centuries, the consumption of Victoria Wine Company's wine always continued to increase. Today, almost a hundred years after Hughes's death, Victoria Wine stores, no longer localised in one part of the country, are one of the most familiar features of the urban scene. In Hughes's time almost all the stores were in the London area. Now, following a series of complicated take-overs and mergers, there are just over 800 of them dotted across the map of Britain, the furthest north in Ross and Cromarty, the furthest south in Penzance. There are 34 stores in Manchester alone, and 44 in Birmingham. In London, where the first Victoria Wine store was opened in 1865, there are now 90. Annual turnover is now around £300 million.

Every chapter in the story of the building up of this huge enterprise has its own special interest, and the last chapter, which deals with striking shifts in wine consumption since 1945, may have even more interest than the first. It is doubtful if Hughes himself would have been able to forecast the remarkable interest in wines of all kinds, including British wines and home wine-making, that is expressed in the late twentieth century not only in specialist stores and in supermarkets but in books and articles. No week passes without a new addition to the list. The story of the wine trade, therefore, is not simply one of successful – and changing – business enterprise, fascinating though this is in itself. The biggest changes since 1865 have been changes in society and culture, and these are traced along with the business history in this broad survey of 'Wine for Sale'.

Whatever the changes, however, there has been one constant. There

---

[10] B. Harrison, *Drink and the Victorians* (1971), p. 250. Statistics relating to drinking habits pose many difficulties. See also Harrison's 'Drink and Sobriety in England, 1815–1872' in the *International Review of Social History* (1967).

have always been individuals in Britain at every time throughout the long period since 1865 who have sung the praises of wine, just as they had done through the centuries before. For example, 'I should here acknowledge', wrote Alfred Duff Cooper, first Viscount Norwich, in his *Memoirs* published in 1949, 'the consolation I have never failed to find in the fermented juice of the grape ... Wine has been to me a firm friend, a wise counsellor ... Wine has lit up for me the pages of literature and revealed in life romance lurking in the commonplace. Wine has made me bold but not foolish; has induced me to say silly things, but not to do them.' Not surprisingly, then, it was to Duff Cooper that Hilaire Belloc dedicated his ode 'In Praise of Wine' which begins with the couplet:

'Wine, true begetter of all arts that be;
Wine, privilege of the completely free.'[11]

Such is the language not of the historian, but of the anthologist – the language of the vintage and of the decanter, of wine the eternal.

Yet for the historian also there can be poetry in the story. Whatever the trends in production, consumption and prices – and these have to be plotted meticulously – there are single great dramatic moments in the modern history of 'Wine for Sale' which stand out from the rest, particularly moments of fiscal change. 'Down the ages', the historian Sir Charles Petrie once wrote, 'the taste for wine has varied ... either as a result of the legislative activities of statesmen or in consequence of political or military development'.[12] And he pointed out some of these landmarks, like the year 1860 and the earlier year 1703, when the Methuen Treaty with Portugal was signed, a treaty which permitted Portuguese wines to be imported at a duty of £7 per ton as against a duty on French wines of £55 a ton. By the end of the eighteenth century, the proportion of Portuguese wines consumed in Britain had increased from 40 per cent to 72 per cent.[13]

There were some traditionalist lovers of port who would have preferred water to claret when Gladstone reduced the duties on French wines – if London water had not been particularly obnoxious at the time – and 1863, a poor year for claret, was a particularly good year for port.

---

[11] See A. Duff Cooper, *Old Men Forget* (1953), p. 65. See also Alec Waugh's *In Praise of Wine* (1959), where the passage is quoted.
[12] Sir Charles Petrie, 'Politics and Wine' in the *Quarterly Review*, Vol. 93 (1953). For nineteenth-century fiscal changes, see also S.

Buxton, *Finance and Politics* (2 vols., 1888).
[13] André Simon, *The Wine Trade of England, Past and Present* (1906), pp. 48–9. See also W. Fletcher, *Port, An Introduction to its History and Delights* (1978).

In another Trollope passage, Mr Toogood in *The Last Chronicle of Barset* (1867) is described as 'pushing about the old port' and 'making some very stinging remarks as to the claret drinking propensities of the age'. 'Gladstone claret the most of it is, I fancy', he added.[14] Meanwhile, 'Cape wines' had been imported in increasing quantities after 1813 when preferential tariffs were introduced, and 678,000 gallons entered into bond in 1860.

Nearly a century later, after the privations of the Second World War, but still in an age of austerity, the year 1949 stands out in the history of 'Wine for Sale', for the then Chancellor of the Exchequer, Sir Stafford Cripps, chief symbol of austerity in the post-war Labour government, was as enterprising in reducing duties as his Liberal predecessor Gladstone had been. His contribution has been far less acknowledged. Yet he it was who, when faced with what *The Times* called 'Bacchus in Eclipse',[15] reduced duties on light wines imported in cask by the equivalent of 12s a gallon, thereby bringing down the price of the cheapest bottle of wine on sale from 12s to 8s.[16] The immediate result was as striking as any previous outcome of fiscal change: the amount of French wine released for consumption rose by 50 per cent in the two years that followed, so that the total duty paid actually increased.[17]

This time, there were more long-term social consequences, for Cripps, better known for his drinking of carrot juice than of wine, proved a better prophet than Gladstone. Long before entering the European Community, the world's largest market for wine, in 1972, Britain had become far more of a wine-drinking community. On the eve of entry, *The Times* noted that it was too early to predict what the effects of joining the Community on the retail prices of wine in Britain would be.[18] Nor did it dare to forecast consumption trends. Yet ten years later in 1981/2 total wine consumption in millions of gallons had more than doubled from 48.4 to 106.3. If this was not quite the full social revolution of which Gladstone had dreamed, it was an extraordinary transformation in what was perhaps the most difficult decade of the whole twentieth century as far as economics and politics were concerned.

Since then the transformation has gone through new phases. An

---

[14] Ernest Dormer, writing in *Wine and Food*, No. 2, 1934, noted how in a wine list of 1819, described as 'Catalogue of a Genuine, most Extensive and extremely valuable selection of Foreign Wines of Rich and Exquisite Flavour, Superior Age, Favourite Growths and of the best Vintages', 'the quantity of claret was small'.
[15] *The Times*, 22 January 1949.
[16] *Hansard*, 4 April 1949.
[17] *The Economist*, 20 December 1952, gives a good summary of the effects.
[18] *The Times*, 10 November 1971.

interesting decision by the European Court of Justice in July 1983 raised many old and new issues. 'Cheaper wine but dearer beer likely after Court Ruling' was the headline in *The Times*. The Court held that the British ratio of taxation on wine and beer – just over 4 to 1 – was discriminating. The British system of excise duty – a traditional and initially highly unpopular system with its roots in the seventeenth century[19] – had the effect, the Court declared, 'of subjecting wine to an additional tax burden so as to offer protection to domestic beer production.' And the further effect, the Court ruled, was 'to stamp wine with the hallmarks of a luxury product which, in view of the tax burden which it bears, can scarcely constitute in the eyes of the consumer a genuine alternative to the typical domestic beverage.'[20]

The comment hardly did justice to the progress that had been made since 1949 but, like the comments of 1860, it was less concerned with experience than with potential. The sequel, Nigel Lawson's first budget of 1984, reserved for my Epilogue, incorporated a substantial, if for *The Times* 'entirely predictable', reduction of eighteen pence per bottle of wine.[21] The change was described by the chairman of the Wine and Spirits Association as 'wise and statesmanlike', adjectives that Gladstone – and Cripps – would have envied. It might not sound much of a reduction to those households who put out as many wine bottles every morning as they did milk bottles, *The Times* went on, but it was the strongest possible vote of confidence in cheap wine, the price of which had risen in money terms far more than Gladstone or Cripps could ever have foreseen. It meant that 'the life span of that dying breed, the under £2 bottle of wine, has thereby been considerably extended'. For Auberon Waugh, it was a chance to offer members of *The Spectator* Wine Club a Lawson Celebration Summer Offer.[22]

The history of 'drink' is a fascinating subject which even the most scholarly students of the subject, heedless of any sense of celebration, have often tended to reduce to the history of a 'problem'.[23] My own book is far less restricted in its scope. It pivots not only on taxation but on

---

[19] Excise on wine, spirits, beer and other commodities, like soap and paper, was first introduced during the Civil War in 1643. It was retained after 1660 on beer and spirits, but wine was now subject to an additional customs duty. There were riots in 1733 when Walpole tried to substitute excise for customs duty.

[20] *The Times*, 13 July 1983.

[21] *Ibid.*, 24–30 March 1984. Nonetheless, there were many wine merchants who had given advice to 'beat the budget buyers'

[22] *The Spectator*, 21 April 1984.

[23] See, for example, the invaluable study by G.P. Williams and G.T. Brake, *Drink in Great Britain, 1900 to 1979* (1980). There is useful comparative information also in E. Gordon, *The Anti-Alcohol Movement in Europe (1913)*.

popular attitudes to wine, rightly described as a very heterogeneous product, as well as on the changing structure, procedures and scale of the wine trade; and it relates that trade, as it must, though necessarily not in detail, to trade in beer and spirits (and 'soft drinks' as well). It uses every kind of source, documentary, statistical and visual, to point the way to an understanding of neglected chapters in social, economic and political history. Yet it could not have been written except on the initiative of Victoria Wine; and materials relating to Victoria Wine, fragmentary, alas, though they are, are central to the whole story.

Unfortunately many of the materials which were kept in the headquarters and warehouses of the company in Osborn Street, near the London docks, were destroyed by enemy bombs during the Second World War in 1941, and others, more recent, are now buried in bigger archives. Just twenty years later, after the formation of Allied Breweries, among the biggest drinks groups in Europe, Victoria Wine became one element in a huge enterprise which from an organisational and institutional point of view brought wine, beer, soft drinks (and other products) still closer together than they ever had been before. Nonetheless, Victoria Wine has kept its own distinctive identity within the bigger structure, and it is one of the objects of the last chapters of my history to explain just how and why.

CHAPTER TWO

Wine and the Victorians 1852-1865

The decade that ended with Gladstone's reduction of the duties on wine in 1860 had been a more prosperous decade than the 'hungry forties' which preceded it. There was less, too, of a threat to the social order from discontented elements in society pressing for large-scale political or constitutional reform. The mood at the beginning of the decade had been well expressed at the Great Exhibition in the Crystal Palace – pride in achievement: delight in display: national enthusiasm across the dividing line of class. Yet there had been significant shifts of mood later in the decade – during the Crimean War, for example, which began in 1854 and which introduced a strident note into literature as well as politics. There were also economic peaks and troughs, including a bank crisis in 1857 which led to bankruptcies and to unemployment.[1] Whatever the social harmonies, there was no shortage of contrast. During the middle period of Queen Victoria's long reign – the most characteristically Victorian part of it, when the adjective 'Victorian' itself was new – the rich lived in one world and the poor in another.

G.M. Young in his *Victorian England*, has written of 'the great peace of the fifties', and there was certainly a sense of balance of the great national interests based on land, commerce, industry and labour.[2] But particular interests could be as clamorous as they had been a decade earlier – and better organised. The fact that political parties were weak – and that there was no voting by ballot until 1872 – gave extra importance first to pressure groups and second to the Press, 'the fourth estate'. The mid-Victorians liked to argue. Before the controversy over Darwin's *On the*

---

[1] See J.R.T. Hughes, *Fluctuations in Trade, Industry and Finance: A Study of British Economic Development, 1850–1860* (1960).

[2] See G.M. Young, *Victorian England,*

Portrait of an Age (1977 edn.), p. 96. Cf. p. 87 'Of all decades in our history, a wise man would choose the 1850s to be young in.'

Origin of the Species, published in 1859, the spotlight turned on many less intellectual topics, from beef to opium; and wine – as well as malt – was always among them.

Against this background, it is fascinating to study in detail the campaign to lower the duties on wine. 'The distribution of wine over the globe', a Professor of Botany at Berlin University had maintained in the 1840s, 'is of particular importance to mankind; the use of wine or beer as the ordinary drink produces so very different an effect on the people, that the influence of the culture of the vine on the nation is not to be overlooked.'[3] A 'temperate use of wine' was not only wholesome, but 'desirable'. British advocates of an increase in the volume of the wine trade always argued, 'It increases enjoyment, cements domestic habits, and precludes the injurious resort to the use of ardent drink. While it has these advantages, its use refines the taste and elevates the social feelings in the same degree as dram drinking.'[4]

Yet it was 'dram drinking' and beer drinking, not wine drinking, for which the British were renowned, a reputation which suggested to the observant, particularly the travellers, that the British had a more 'bibacious disposition' than the French. Moreover, it was a reputation which was backed by statistics. The British drank more than six times as much beer as the French and almost twice as much spirits, more than twelve times as much tea and only less than a quarter as much coffee. It was probably because of this particular drinking pattern that there emerged in Victorian Britain the most articulate and best organised movement not only for temperance but for complete 'abstinence from all intoxicants'.[5] The movement had its origins in 1828, before Queen Victoria came to the throne, when it was associated only with abstinence from 'ardent spirits', of which 'Mother Gin' remained the most popular, as in the eighteenth century. In 1853, however, during G.M. Young's 'great peace', the United Kingdom Alliance was founded to outlaw all intoxicating drinks. Its stark programme divided teetotallers, but it appealed to many just because it was so uncompromising, and its income shot up to what was then a record height by 1860.[6] Wine – and how to tax

---

[3] Quoted in W. Bosville James, *Wine Duties, Considered Financially and Socially* (1855) p. 131.

[4] Quoted in *Ibid.*, p. 159.

[5] 'Victorian consumption statistics are valuable.' Harrison argued in 'Drink and Sobriety', 'not so much for their own sake as for the reactions they provoked.'

[6] See the graph of incomes of leading temperance organisations from 1830 to 1900 in Harrison, *Drink and the Victorians*, p. 21. See also D.A. Hamer, *The Politics of Electoral Pressure* (1977), ch. IX–XIII. The classic nineteenth-century study is Dawson Burns, *Temperance History, A Consecutive Narrative of the Rise, Development and Extension of the Temperance Reform* (2 vols., 1889). See also his *Temperance in the Victorian Age* (1897).

it – was to be one of the subjects, along with the use of the coercive power of the state to force people to be sober, which divided the temperance movement.

The debate about wine duties in Britain began in 1852, when a Select Committee was appointed to study their effects. The argument then and later ranged widely over the current drinking preferences and habits of different social classes; the relations between them; the history of wine drinking and of taxes on wine; the future both of the economy and of society; the vested interests of existing wine growers and wine merchants (the longest established of whom went back to the seventeenth century); the possibility of producing wine in different places (although England was seldom considered such a place); the counter-appeal of 'soft drinks', including tea, coffee and water (the last, a highly suspect product); the 'beer barrel' interest; the iniquities of cheap spirits; the demands of medicine, for wine could be prescribed by doctors even to teetotallers; the use and misuse of statistics; and, above all, the gospel of free trade, at the very heart of the reformers' campaign.

The style of the argument was as culture-bound as its content. What could be more Victorian in tone than the evidence to the Committee of 1852 given by G.R. Porter, distinguished statistician, former Secretary to the Board of Trade, and author of the widely read volume *Progress of the Nation* which had appeared in several editions since 1837?

> The great mass of the people are not consumers of wine: because the duties are so high, it is placed beyond their reach. There is a large class of people who would gladly consume wine with their families, if it was put within their reach, who at present do not consume it, but have recourse to a very much worse thing to take; namely ardent spirit. I have little hesitation in giving it as my opinion, that to introduce the consumption of wine to the great mass of the people of this country would prove a great moral blessing.

The same note (which treated cheap wine very much like the penny post[7]) was struck with even greater force by W.W. Whitmore in a remarkable pamphlet of 1854:

> I believe nothing, after religious instruction and secular education, would have a greater effect in improving the character of the people, than placing within their reach a light and wholesome beverage – one

---

[7] For the case for penny postage, see D.N. Briggs, 'The Bristol Post Office in the Age of Rowland Hill,' (British Historical Association, 1983).

that would enliven, but not intoxicate – one that could be enjoyed more in the family than in the gin-palace or the ale house. Give, then, that which is wholesome to the body and safe to the moral condition of mankind.

And then came the real sting in the tail:

I protest against the charge of a debased and barbarous taste for alcohol in its concentrated form as inherent, when I believe it is purely accidental – the result of our own barbarous policy and fiscal ignorance.[8]

The most convenient way of penetrating such mid-Victorian argument about wine and recapturing the mood in which it was conducted is to turn back to a book published half-way through the decade – W. Bosville James's *Wine Duties Considered Financially and Socially*. James was a traditional wine merchant with 24 years' experience, and his book was a riposte to *Wine: its Taxation and Uses* by Sir James Emerson Tennent, Porter's successor as Secretary to the Board of Trade. Characteristically, it bore as the bold motto on its title page a saying of Euripides – 'the simple energy of truth needs no ambiguous interpretation'. Written during the Crimean War when, as the author recognised, 'it would seem not only superfluous but useless to urge upon the attentions of the public anything tending to a reduction in duties, no matter upon what article', it looked beyond the present to the more distant future. 'When refinement has induced a general use of articles formerly denominated luxuries', James insisted, 'they should no longer be restricted by onerous and almost prohibitory imposts'. The correct course, he argued, 'would be, by judicious and moderate duties, to encourage the freer use, and obtain a larger revenue from the consumption of the many than from the excessive indulgence of the few'.

The strength of James's argument was reinforced by his knowledge – and that of his informed readers – that it was written in reply to what seemed a somewhat evasive 'semi-official' publication by a well-known and 'responsible public servant', in which 'very partial averages of dates and statements' were 'set forth to support inferences otherwise untenable'.[9] 'Public servants' were not placed on pedestals during the 1850s, particularly when they were outspoken in public: Edwin Chadwick, the best-known of them, who was more interested in pure water than in good

---

[8] W.W. Whitmore, *Wine Duties* (1853).
[9] James, *op. cit.*, p. vi, pp. 1–2.

wine, was pushed into oblivion in 1854. There was a final reason why James pressed his attack on Tennent with vigour. He had given evidence to the 1852 Committee which, he believed, had been thwarted in its efforts to change the situation by public servants behind the scenes.

Six points in James's argument stand out. First, the English had at one time been a wine-drinking people, and the fact that they stopped drinking light French wines and turned to Portugal and Spain was a matter not of preference but of taxation: the lighter wines were 'expelled'. Nor was the apparent 'national taste' of the British for beer or 'strong liquor' either 'inherent nor stubborn': there had been too limited access to alternative drinks. Second, wine was not a luxury: it was considered as such only because of high taxation. Next to corn, there was 'no more prolific gift from Providence than the vine'. Nature endowed it. Third, even if wine had been treated as a luxury in the past, the luxuries of yesterday were always becoming the necessities of today. 'To maintain a high duty on foreign wines as luxuries' was 'to resist the natural result of refinement in the popular taste, to check the growth of temperance, to retard those habits of sobriety which improved moral feelings encourage, and to create and commit a great wrong on the mass of mankind'.

Fourth, though there was a convincing general case for free trade, the momentum had been lost. Corn had been freed in 1846. Why not wine? Was free trade to become 'only a name' after Sir Robert Peel's death? Was his 'free trade fabric' never to be extended? Taxes of the kind Britain had imposed on wine were 'curses equal to the barrenness of the earth and the inclemency of the heavens'.[10] Moreover, the greatest statesmen had recognised this long before Peel. William Pitt had reduced the wine duties in 1786. So, too, had Frederick John Robinson (later the Earl of Ripon) – by 50 per cent – in 1825, when 'every one was oppressed by excessive taxation'. And during the 1840s, Peel's free trade budgets had preceded the repeal of the corn laws in 1846. In the background there was Adam Smith.

Fifth, 'high duties promoted adulterations and frauds', as well as 'loss of revenue and injury to trade'. Much of the wine sold in Britain was as dangerously concocted as London water or London milk. 'Purity' would follow from reform.[11] Sixth, and most important, there was an untapped potential for the wine trade. As an Oporto merchant had admitted in 1852, 'if wines . . . of a low character, but pure wines, were introduced, a

---

[10] A quotation from Adam Smith, *The Wealth of Nations* (1776).
[11] See J. Burnett, *Plenty and Want* (1966)

and H.W. Dickinson, *The Water Supply of Greater London* (1954).

new market would be raised immediately, and new consumers would be provided for those wines, and ... an immense number of wines, altogether of a character unknown in the country at the present moment, would be then consumed'. National revenue from reduced wine taxes would not fall, but rise.

The Victorians were seldom content to rest such arguments on an entirely economic base, and James himself added a social gloss to this bare statistical statement. If, he went on, 'an increased consumption of wine rested upon the upper classes, who, led by the caprices of fashion, will one day over-indulge, and another day, reject, then the high duties will be retained on wine, if only to encourage, by their operation, the present tone of moderation and refinement in the enjoyments of the table.' Yet 'there are other classes, worthy of a like consideration – classes creating wealth, and by their industry, intelligence, education, and refinement, linked to the aristocracy, rising to equal importance, and far exceeding that class in numbers, intelligence, and influence. Those classes will not long be excluded from the use of wine, because legislation, by high duties, grossly violating free-trade principles, declare it a luxury.'

However powerful this six-headed argument – and the order of the six points was odd – James knew that it would be difficult for Parliament to accept it. Indeed, he quoted an authority on 'ancient and modern wines' who, writing of the Oporto Wine Company, remarked that 'when errors in legislation have been confirmed by long usage, the return to true principles becomes proportionately difficult; so many plausible arguments are adduced to prove the danger of innovation.'[12] There was, in fact, to be the most curious of all combinations of interest in 1860, when Gladstone eventually reduced the wine duties. Brewers and teetotallers were to unite against his measures in what the *Spectator* called 'one of the most suspicious alliances ever yet seen in political action.'[13]

The origins of the alliance can be traced back to 1855, a year when James's tract and the 'semi-official publication' that provoked it were only two of many published works to appear on the subject of wine and the duties on it. *Fraser's Magazine*, for example, had an article on 'Wine, Its Use and Taxation' which emphasised how important it was 'to hear and record all that will throw light on matters which may become, even remotely, objects of legislation.'[14] And beer was in the news also, as total consumption fell.

---

[12] A. Henderson, *History of Ancient and Modern Wines* (1824).

[13] *Spectator*, 3 March 1860.
[14] *Fraser's Magazine*, Vol. 41, June 1859.

Whatever their stance, the articles and books of the mid-1850s all looked back to the Select Committee of 1852 which, to James's chagrin, had never taken a vote and had never published a final report. The motion to set up such a Committee had been proposed by Thomas Chisholm Anstey in March 1852, and in his painstaking speech in the Commons – Anstey was lawyer as well as politician – the wide range of his remarks was very similar to that of Bosville James. He would show the House 'by reference to former times', Anstey declared, 'that when the duties (on wine) were high, the amount of revenue derived from them was low, and vice versa: and that under the present rate of those duties, consumption had declined, frauds had increased and revenue, instead of progressing with the population, had dwindled.'[15]

Anstey's cannot have been an easy speech to listen to, for it was packed with ancient statistics; and it is not difficult to understand why he was so often ridiculed in the pages of *Punch*. Yet it was doubtless the kind of speech which suggested that a Select Committee was necessary; and towards the end of it Anstey may even have inadvertently raised a rare laugh when he said that he hoped that the House would entertain his proposition in a proper spirit.

He added that most people in the country would laugh to read the anti-French sentiments expressed in the preamble to a late seventeenth-century Act of William and Mary stating that:

> it hath been found by long experience that the importing of French wines, vinegar, brandy, and other commodities of the growth, produce, or manufacture of France ... hath much exhausted the treasure of this nation, lessened the value of the native commodities and manufacturers thereof, and greatly impoverished the English artificers and handicrafts, and caused great detriment to this kingdom in general.[16]

That was not the way the mid-Victorians, whatever their political persuasion, radical or conservative, looked at trade, and Anstey knew it. Indeed, the main impetus to Gladstone's lowering of duties at the end of the decade was the effort, zealously implemented by Richard Cobden, greatest of all free traders, to increase trade with France; and he knew that he had the support of Lancashire and Yorkshire manufacturers,

---

[15] According to *Who's Who in Parliament, 1832–1886*, Anstey believed that 'the abolition of excise duties, the reduction of customs, and the repeal of all currency laws are the only methods of ensuring protection to all.'
[16] 6 William and Mary, c.34.

Vernon Keeble

Eric Fisher

Commander McGrath

Tom Bloomfield

Sir Derrick Holden-Brown

Brian McGrath

Wilfred Crawt

Eric Colwell

David Bedford

Dan Keough

Lister Fielding

The Dell, home of William Winch Hughes

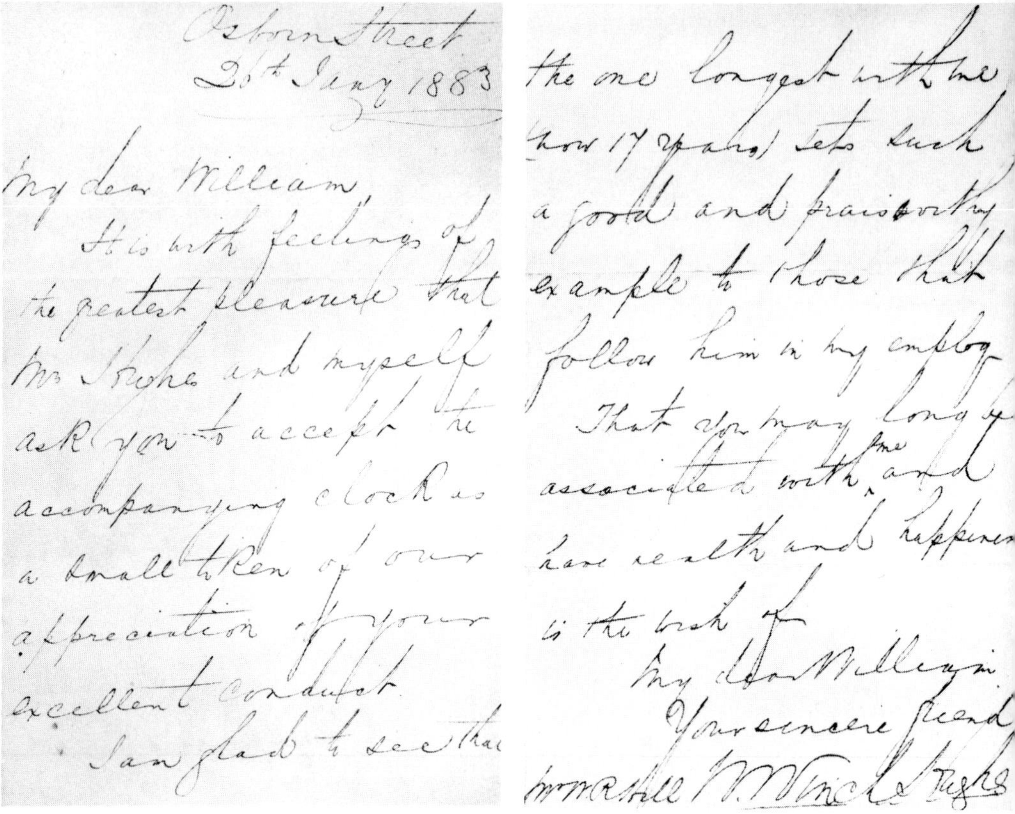

Osborn Street
25th Jany 1883

My dear William,

It is with feelings of the greatest pleasure that Mr Stokes and myself ask you to accept the accompanying clock as a small token of our appreciation of your excellent conduct.

I am glad to see that the one longest with me (now 17 years) sets such a good and praiseworthy example to those that follow him in my employ.

That you may long be associated with me, and have health and happiness is the wish of

my dear William,

Your sincere friend

Wm R Hill   W Winch Hughes

Letter from William Winch Hughes
to W. R. Hill, 26 January, 1883

Two views of the Shad Thames warehouse as it is to-day

Part of the General Offic[e]

The Manager's Office

Two views of the Victoria Wine Company's
London headquarters in the 1890s

some of them Nonconformist teetotallers, and of the Quaker radical, Cobden's close friend, John Bright.[17]

The only Government speaker to reply to Anstey in 1852 was Gladstone's political rival, Benjamin Disraeli, speaking in his capacity as Chancellor of the Exchequer in Derby's minority Conservative Government, many members of which still professed adherence to protectionist principles. Disraeli admitted that Anstey's long narrative was, as far as he could judge, accurate, but he added that his proposal presupposed what had not been the case – a decline in the wine trade between 1848 and 1852. It was better, Disraeli suggested – and it serves as a useful warning to historians – to forget the past and 'look at the times we live in.' The wine trade had accumulated too large stocks between 1850 and 1852, anticipating that foreigners visiting the Great Exhibition of 1851 would drink more wine than they did. Instead they 'drank beer, and particularly porter, in enormous quantities.' Britannia had ruled the trade as well as the waves. There had, however, been no decline in the revenue derived from wine, as Anstey had implied. Moreover, following the Exhibition, the volume of French wines taken out of bond in 1852 (447,559 gallons) had actually shown an increase of 104,811 gallons. So too had the volume of Spanish wines (2,469,000 gallons), an increase of 64,000 gallons. The only diminution had been in the taking out of Portuguese wine, now down to 2,524,720 gallons.

While sceptical, Disraeli did not oppose Anstey's proposal to set up a Committee. He believed that Parliament and the country already had enough information on the subject at their disposal, and added half seriously that a far more onerous burden than that of taxation was the increasing pressure on M.P.s to attend Select Committees. Yet he did not wish to stifle debate. Before import duties on wine could be diminished, he concluded, there were many other taxed articles which should be untaxed first.

Other Chancellors of the Exchequer have often spoken in similar vein. Yet the third speaker – one of only two others – in the brief debate on Anstey's motion was even more distinguished, at least at the time, than Disraeli, and he strongly supported the enquiry. Lord Palmerston had actually been Prime Minister until the end of 1851, and the burden of his short speech, not surprisingly, was foreign affairs. The Portuguese

---

[17] Bright has been described as 'a last-ditch free-trader'. See his *Scheme of Licensing Reform and Compensation* (1883).

Government, he observed, had not been paying adequate attention to the stipulations of the most recent British-Portuguese treaty of 1842, and if only for this reason the whole range of British-Portuguese trade, in which port wine figured prominently, should be reviewed. Henley, for the Government, sensibly agreed with this observation, and Anstey thus secured his Select Committee. In the light of Disraeli's remarks, however, he deleted the words 'causes of the decline' in its terms of reference. His Committee's agenda would now be as general as it possibly could – 'a consideration of the revenue derived from the import duties in wines.'[18]

In the aftermath of the debate, Thomas George Shaw, a wine merchant, wrote the third of three letters to *The Times*, subsequently extended to book length, sharply criticising Disraeli.[19] 'With alterations in the duty fifteen times since 1786, varying on French wines from 4s 10d to 19s 8d and on others from 3s 1d to 9s 1d,' Shaw wrote, 'no argument on the effect of each can be satisfactory, but it is scarcely too much to assert that nothing but the wonderful prosperity of the country could have prevented the almost total extinction of the use of wine.' Nonetheless, he added, it was probably no exaggeration that nine out of every ten wine merchants were opposed to a reduction of duty, believing that it would lower profits and prices, and 'open the trade to every one, making wine as commonly sold as tea, sugar or beer'. This might not be 'an agreeable anticipation,' he recognised, but it was not 'a reason that ought to influence a Chancellor of the Exchequer.'

Like others drawn into the argument, Shaw had a moral case to make:

There is no country in the world, where drunkenness and the crimes necessarily arising out of it, prevail to any such extent as among ourselves;[20] for indeed, the consumption of spirits is nearly a gallon yearly for every man, woman and child, which independent of large quantities illicitly made and smuggled, is four times the quantity, and five times the revenue from wine.

It would not be difficult to show the terrible evils and expenses which this curse of our country entails; but it is not by increasing the difficulty of procuring spirits that the evil can be remedied. The true

---

[18] *Hansard*, 30 March 1852.

[19] His first letters had appeared in *The Times* on 6 November 1850 and 30 January 1851.

[20] In fact, the evidence of the City Chief Commissioner of Police to a Select Committee of the House of Commons in 1853, quoted in James, *op. cit.*, p. 87, suggested that 'down-right drunkenness' had decreased, although the numbers of cases of 'simple inebriety' had not diminished.

method is to place within reach of all, a wholesome cheering beverage, which wine is, in its pure unadulterated state.[21]

Shaw's conclusion could claim authentic, if limited, Biblical justification from I Timothy v, verse 23, 'Drink no longer water, but use a little wine for thy stomach's sake and thine other infirmities.' And it was not only in the Church of England but in a number of other sects that the 'water drinkers', fanatical though some of them were, were always in a minority.[22]

The Minutes of Evidence of the Select Committee of 1852 are particularly interesting in that a number of witnesses turned in some detail from moral issues to the economic question of the potential market for wine. 'Do you think,' W.E. Tuke, a wine merchant, was asked, 'that there is any considerable or any growing taste for wines among the middle classes and the better class of artisans here?' 'I think there is' was his answer; and he referred to one of William Winch Hughes's predecessors – 'Barker', who had 'a large gin palace in Holborn [later identified as Henekey's] and another gin palace in Bishopsgate Street'. 'Barker has commenced the system of selling a gill glass of Port and Sherry for 4d', Tuke reported, and his main customers were 'small tradesmen and respectable artisans, men who will not drink ardent spirits, and who find beer too weak and washy for their stomachs; they want a pleasant exhilarating stimulant.' And if the price per glass were reduced from 4d to 2d, Tuke also reported Barker's opinion that 'he would sell not a pipe a week in glasses, but a pipe a day.' Bottle drinkers – and it had been estimated in 1831 that were were as many as 930,000 families who drank some wine at home – would increase their consumption at the same rate, while beer consumption would not fall. It would take some time, too, for spirits consumption to be affected 'particularly among the labouring classes.' Yet were it not for the high duty, wine 'instead of being regarded as a luxury, and sipped out of small glasses after dinner' would 'be used as a beverage, and drunk in tumblers, as beer now is'.

Tuke's evidence was free from all moralising of the kind that was to figure so prominently in James's book. Indeed, he remarked of 'the rich' that they were 'often as economical as others, and equally restrict

---

[21] See T.G. Shaw, *The Wine Trade and its History* (1856), p. 7.
[22] See N. Longmate, *The Water-Drinkers* (1968). Few novelists liked teetotallers. 'Lady

remember, (and this is, perhaps, the golden rule),' wrote Robert Louis Stevenson in *Virginibus Puerisque* (1880), no woman should marry a teetotaller.'

themselves in the use of this luxury.' Shaw, who had written the letters to *The Times* and was later to write more than one tract on the subject, was more discursive on these topics:

Q   Supposing another class of consumers were introduced to you, such as respectable tradesmen, mechanics getting good wages, shopkeepers and so on, do you think they would become consumers of the higher or lower class of wines?

A   Perhaps both, but mostly the general class of wine.

Q   Do you think there are many out of that class who would become consumers who were not consumers of spirits?

A   I would point to any place where wine is plentiful and cheap; there people do not consume spirits, but drink wine, and as far as we can trace the history of the habits of our ancestors, as described by Shakespeare, Walter Scott and others, we find constant allusion to wine, but never to spirits.

Shaw concluded, as Tuke had done, that if 'good common wine' could be bought at 1s or 1s 3d a bottle, 'thousands of clerks, lawyers and sedentary parties, authors and others, who are deprived of any generous medium beverage' would turn to it. Already at Wooding's Shades, London Bridge, there was 'a great concourse of people every day' visiting a wine vault: 'I see sometimes working people going in and out.' Henderson's in St Martin's Lane and Short's in the Strand were two other places where there was a general trade.

When James gave his evidence, he stressed that whatever others might say about short-run trends (and he did not mention Disraeli), the consumption of wine had not increased for the last fifty years despite the great increase in the population. He attributed this fact to an 'increase of temperance among the higher classes and the middle classes' and 'a greater liking for spirits and beer' among 'the lower classes'. On this occasion, however, James did not envisage a great increase in wine drinking on the part of the latter if the duties were reduced. They drank beer because they could 'drink it in large quantities, not only without injury', but in order to 'strengthen' them for their labour. If wine were to be cheaper, it would be among the middle classes that the new wine drinkers would be found.

A more pertinent witness on such points was Tuke, recalled to the Committee – almost a month after he had first appeared – to report on what Barker of Henekey's had subsequently told him. Barker's principal customers, he had gathered, were small tradesmen, bankers' clerks and 'a very large proportion of the sick poor, particularly in Bishopsgate Street'. Port was the main drink – at 10s 8d a gallon, 1s 4d an imperial pint, or 4d for an imperial gill glass:

Q Did he find that there was a growing taste for wines among the respectable artisans and inferior middle classes, or a declining taste?

A A decidedly growing taste, and he said that of this 4d a glass one half of it was duty, or rather more than 2d.

Another witness, Short, examined on the same day, said that in his wine house 'we have a great many cabmen and omnibus men, and that class of men who used to drink gin.' Now, 'five or six of them together,' they come to drink sherry which cost twice as much (4d) per glass. (A glass of porter cost 1½d a glass.) Short was the first witness to deal with what later became a crucial issue – the possible demand for light, as distinct from heavy, wines:

Q You would infer from their preferring sherry to gin, that they would prefer the light wines if they could have them?

A The French and Rhenish wines they would like, if they could get them; if we had them reduced here, there would be quite a change altogether; if we could get the low wines at 1s a gallon, and the best wines at 2s ...

Q You think the working people would even prefer the lighter wines to Port, supposing Sherry and Claret were of equal price?

A They would prefer them, no doubt. The French wines are not very light; they have a very good body; they are a full-bodied wine.

Q You are speaking of Médoc?

A Of French wine.

Q Do you find the season has anything to do with the demand?

A It is all the year round just alike ... Sherry, Port, and Claret, and Champagne all the year round.

It is important to note that in 1813 the preference given to Portugal in the Methuen Treaty had been abandoned and that duties on French and other European wines had been equalised and subsequently charged at a uniform rate of 5s 6d a gallon, a rate increased in 1840 to 5s 9d. Yet there had been no immediate move in 1830 towards French wines, and it was Spanish wines which benefited most from the change. Following the increase in duty in 1840, the high total consumption figure of 7,000,486 gallons in 1839 – incidentally a year of economic depression – was never reached again before 1852. Indeed, the 1842 figure was as low as 4,815,222 gallons.

Not surprisingly, details of taxation and of what contemporaries called 'political economy', a term now revived in the late twentieth century, were less interesting to most of the witnesses in 1852 than the range and quality of the wines available to the British public whatever their price. 'It is surprising,' wrote the author of the knowledgeable article in *Fraser's Magazine* in 1855, 'how few of the merchants who gave evidence (in 1852) knew anything of wines beyond the two or three in which they dealt.' Yet Sir J.E. Tennent, who was to be so sharply criticised by James, tried a few sinuous questions of his own on types of wine, including 'Have you ever tried Beni Carlos?' and 'Did you ever try Sicilian red wine?' The answer to the first was 'No, I never heard of it' and to the second a simple 'No'.

To complete the picture, with the sociology as well as the political economy thrown in, a further witness from the wine trade, W.C. Carbonell, did not believe that if the duties were reduced, the middle classes would consume light wines in place of port and sherry or, indeed, that they would drink one drop of wine more. Nor did he consider that the working classes either would drink more wine in such circumstances. Instead, he was convinced that a reduction in wine duties would diminish national revenues and quoted from a colleague the damning judgement, with which he said he was in complete agreement, that 'a greater delusion than that of believing the lower or middle classes will drink the common wines of Spain, Italy, Portugal, France or Germany, never entered the brain of man.'

That was the kind of superior wine merchant whom William Winch Hughes and Victoria Wine were to prove absurdly wrong. Yet on the other side of the Channel, where the substance of English debate was being noted if not analysed, there were Frenchmen who shared Carbonell's prejudices. Herbet, the French Consul General in London, wrote to the French Minister of Foreign Affairs in 1853 that one of the reasons why the consumption of French wines in England had not kept pace with population increase was a decrease in the incomes of the aristocracy following the repeal of the Corn Laws in 1846. He gave no evidence to support this reasoning, but added that high duties prevented all classes below the aristocracy from becoming familiar with French wines and that the aristocracy itself only knew champagne and the wines of the Gironde. Whilst he recognised that only a reduction of the British

duty on French wines to a figure below 1s a gallon would make it possible
for the middle classes to drink French wines, he saw no chance of such a
reduction in the near future. There was no popular interest in the
question, no prospect of a nation-wide agitation like the Anti-Corn Law
League.[23]

There was one other line of enquiry, not touched on by Herbet or
Carbonell, which was to be strictly relevant to the future of the Victoria
Wine business, for Victoria Wine was to deal, after all, not only in wine
but in beer and spirits also. What would be the effects of an increased
consumption of wine on the consumption of beer? Tuke, a very alert
witness, believed, unlike Gladstone, that there would be none or very
little, and he drew a very long-term comparison. 'In 1688 there was
threefold more beer consumed than there is now; and at the same period
90,000 pipes of wine were consumed in this country, and now (in
England and Scotland) we consume 60,000.' Another wine merchant,
Maxwell, had no doubt that beer-drinking would continue: 'his men', he
said, would steal his beer rather than the best wine in his cellar. And
Napoleon III across the Channel is reported to have said that
'Englishmen would prefer their own good beer to the wines of France and
Germany'.

Tuke had found his statistics, he said, in 'a book published by Mr
Mayhew, called *London Labour and London Poor*, originally published in the
Morning Chronicle'. Henry Mayhew's book was, in fact, one of the great
works of the period, which first appeared in book form in 1851, an
outstandingly vivid sociological investigation with a sturdy empirical
base which uncovered in exploratory fashion much of the detail of life in
mid-Victorian London. James's statistics were taken from a wider
variety of sources. He showed, however, how little French wine was
imported in the ten years after 1688 – only 540 gallons in 1697 – after a
seven-year prohibition, and 57,215 gallons in 1698. The figure for 1852
was ten times as much, 575,280 gallons, but this was considerably less
than the peak post-Napoleonic Wars figure of 1,083,538 gallons in 1825
and the figure for 1844 of 725,308 gallons. Paradoxically, the peak year
of all had been 1809, during the Napoleonic Wars – 2,899,755 gallons.
Total consumption of wines from all sources in England had reached its
post-Napoleonic Wars peak in 1825 (8,009,542 gallons), but this was

[23] Report of 11 February 1853, quoted in
A.L. Dunham, *The Anglo-French Treaty of
Commerce of 1860* (1930), pp. 281-2.

lower than the Napoleonic Wars figure for 1803 (8,226,444 gallons) and the figure for 1795 (8,238,438 gallons). Meanwhile, the population of England and Wales had increased from 9 million in 1801 to 18 million in 1852, so that *per capita* consumption of wines had sharply fallen.

Further details of the pattern of drinking in Britain in the three years after the Select Committee meetings were collected by James, who was just as interested in the decline in beer consumption over the three years as in the demand for wine – and in the movements in demand, too, for coffee and tea. (The effect of the increased use of coffee he found very discouraging, and he quoted the Chief Commissioner of Police on 'the demoralising effect of coffee shops on the rising generation'.) This was said to be the pattern:

		Jan 1853 returns	*Jan 1854 returns*	*Jan 1855 returns*
Wine	gallons	6,000,680	7,197,620	7,149,589
Beer	gallons	591,443,798	604,687,523	530,143,268
British spirits	gallons	25,200,879	25,021,317	25,883,584
Rum	gallons	2,199,997	2,022,786	3,103,331
Brandy	gallons	1,225,074	2,378,770	1,113,586
Coffee	lbs	35,043,573	37,191,770	37,470,570
Tea	lbs	54,724,613	58,860,147	61,970,347
Cocoa	lbs	3,385,632	4,126,687	4,563,782

TABLE 1 *British Drinking Patterns, 1853–1855*

In another revealing table, James compared this drinking pattern with that of France. His figures were based on average consumption:

		France	*United Kingdom*
Wine	gallons (annual average)	396,000,000	6,700,000
Beer	gallons (annual average)	90,310,000	585,720,000
Spirits	gallons (annual average)	16,000,000	31,000,000
Tea	lbs	470,000	61,000,000
Coffee	lbs	46,000,000	36,000,000

TABLE 2 *British and French Drinking Patterns, 1853–1855*

32

It was the hope of James that, leaving on one side the culture of the coffee shops, the British drinking pattern would eventually become more like that of France, and his hope was shared by the Association for the Reduction of the Wine Duties, which was formed in the City after the dissolution of the 1852 Committee. Gladstone, who became Chancellor of the Exchequer after Disraeli, showed considerable sympathy with the approach of the Association long before 1860. Wine for him was a 'great gift of Providence to man', and he felt that the British should acknowledge it. He was 'not one of those,' he proclaimed, 'who thought it impossible or visionary to expect a great extension of taste for, and consumption of, wine among the people of England'. He was anxious, therefore, he went on, both to increase the trade and to break down 'a set of virtual monopolies which aggravated the wine duties', especially monopolies in favour of particular districts. 'He knew no article burdened with a fiscal chain,' he remarked as early as 1853, 'with respect to which any stronger reasons for a change could be given'.[24]

Gladstone redeemed his promises to take action in February 1860, when he was once more installed as Chancellor of the Exchequer after the general election of 1859. His office, he had told an audience at Manchester, was never 'a very popular one', because the Chancellor had to spend a very large part of his time in saying 'No, No, No' to those who 'demanded public expenditure'. As far as he was concerned, however, he held that it was his duty to cut expenditure – and taxes – not to increase them. And in 1860 he pivoted his strategy on a new commercial treaty with France which was signed in January of that year one month before the Budget. Had there been no negotiations in Paris, the economic historian Sir John Clapham has written, there would probably have been no modification of the wine duties at that time.[25]

The makers of the Treaty, in its first form essentially 'a sketch', believed that increased trade rather than diplomacy was necessary 'for any permanent improvement in the political relations of France and England';[26] and in any negotiations about increased trade, wine, like coal, was bound to play an important part. Richard Cobden, as active a negotiator as he had been a free trade campaigner almost twenty years before, fully appreciated this. So also did Gladstone. And the export trade of 1860 was the largest on record. Yet to concentrate exclusively on

---

[24] Quoted in *Fraser's Magazine, loc. cit.*
[25] Sir John Clapham, *An Economic History of Modern Britain*, vol. 2, *Free Trade and Steel*
(1952), p. 245.
[26] J.A. Hobson, *Richard Cobden, The International Man* (1919), ch. x.

the Treaty in examining Gladstone's attitudes to the wine duties is to over-simplify Gladstone's own interest. Characteristically he spent much of the period between the signing of the Treaty and his Budget speech in reading – among an unbelievable mass of other books and articles, including Samuel Smiles's *Self Help* – pamphlets on the subject of the wine duties. He studied the most recent set of wine statistics and received a number of deputations including the Licensed Victuallers. He also saw one prominent total abstainer and was prescribed 'antinomial wine' himself – along with mustard plasters – by his doctor when a cough and cold delayed his Budget appearance.[27]

In a speech of 10 February, 'aided' in his own words 'by a stock of egg and wine', he stated firmly that 'apart from any treaty with France', fiscal considerations would compel the country 'in the course of a few years to reform the wine duties.'[28] And it was surely not purely general fiscal considerations that led Lord Houghton (Richard Monckton Milnes) to produce the couplet about Gladstone:

Trace we the workings of that wondrous brain,
Warmed by one bottle of our dry Champagne.[29]

Britain 'engages', Gladstone told the House in February 1860, to reduce the duty on wine from a rate reaching 5s 10d down to 3s per gallon and to reduce the duty on brandy from 15s per gallon to the level of the colonial duty – namely 8s 2d. The wine duty would be further reduced – and regulated – in April 1861, he continued, on a scale based on the proof strength of the wine, according to the Sykes hydrometer, with a maximum of 2s per gallon (on wines with less than 15 degrees). Gladstone was doubtless afraid that without such a scale of duties spirits might be smuggled in as wines. He was aware of the fact too, however, that 'alcoholometry' was becoming a science and that days were long since past when Her Majesty's Commissioners of Customs were said to assess the strength of wines by taking mouthfuls, spitting into a candle flame and observing the volume of the resulting conflagration. Sykes himself was a customs officer.

Gladstone's new rates applied to wine brought into the country in

---

[27] See H.C.G. Matthew, *The Gladstone Diaries*, Vol. v (1978), pp. 495ff. See also Gladstone Papers, British Museum, Add. MS 44749, f. 38, fs. 44135, 44393, 44530 and 44791 and F.W. Hirst, *Gladstone as Financier and Economist* (1931), Ch. XII.

[28] *Hansard*, Vol. 41, 10 February 1860. Duties on spirits had been made uniform in 1858.

[29] Quoted in P. Forbes, *Champagne, The Wine, The Land and the People* (1967), p. 169.

casks or barrels: the rate on all wine in bottles was 2s a gallon. Bottling itself was becoming a major British industry with standard bottles beginning to take the place of individualised (and now highly collectable) bottles, sometimes with seals bearing the names of owners and with dates of purchase.[30] Gladstone was more aware of such developments than has often been recognised. What most concerned him in 1860, however, was his fiscal responsibilities. He was careful to state, for example, that the Government reserved the power to increase the duty on wine if excise duty on spirits was increased for fiscal reasons or if there were other budgetary reasons. Later in 1860, however, when the spirits duty was increased in a supplementary budget to cover the costs of an expedition to China, wine duties were not raised.

Gladstone's sense of responsibility in February 1860 – and his oratory – did not save him from criticism, not least in the House of Lords, where Earl Grey, speaking on behalf of Lord John Russell, was prepared to spend precious time justifying a duty on brandy not of 8s 2d but 10s. And there were critics in the House of Commons, like Charles Du Cane, the Conservative M.P. for North Essex, who were more comprehensive in their complaints. 'For the sake of a mere speculative theory (increased demand for wine among the middle and working classes)', Du Cane maintained, 'we are to be asked to supersede our native beverage by taking off duties upon wine which was and must for some time continue to be emphatically a luxury of the rich.'[31] *The Times* observed also how 'country squires, professional men of all classes who cannot distinguish vintages and do not know a Latour 1847, or Lafitte 1844, from a St Emilion 1859 . . . require a very finished effort of oratory to accommodate themselves to the necessity of paying ninepence in the pound for a charge which at first view does not strike them as being worth the money'.[32]

In general, the magic of Gladstone's oratory worked, and he ended his speech with more admirers than critics. 'A debt of gratitude is owed to him,' the *Dublin University Magazine* suggested in an article which, given its source, must have given him great pleasure. He had enabled us to obtain 'delightful beverages cheaply'. Beer, it went on, might be a 'suitable drink for those who do much physical hard work or who take a great deal of exercise', but it was 'by no means fit for those whose

---

[30] Bottling of beer was a later development: it was first seriously discussed during the 1880s. Bottle-making machinery was in use in some firms by the end of that decade. See *The Lancashire Glass Bottle Trade* (St Helens, 1905).

[31] *Hansard*, 20 February 1860. There were few objections to an increased duty on spirits.

[32] *The Times*, 6 February 1860.

digestive powers are weak, who work chiefly with the brain, or who are of sedentary habits'. And among this latter group there was a high proportion of travellers who knew what conditions were like in wine-drinking countries. Thanks to Gladstone and the wine merchants, who had responded to the challenge of his reforms, 'a revolution in taste as regards wine, and one of a most beneficial kind' was 'gradually taking place'.[33]

In a long passage in his 1860 speech Gladstone had dwelt eloquently on the significance of what he had done, as he himself saw it. There was a hundredfold variation in the price of wines. His new system of duties would help the sales of wines of all prices. 'Between common and coarse wine and the fine wines there are ten thousand intermediate shades, and there is an immense capacity for producing wines fitted for the English market and for the taste of the middle and lower middle classes in the country, which capacity is at present entirely stifled by the operation of the wine duty.' As far as French wines were concerned, Britons had shown in the past that they liked them, and they would now show that they liked them again. 'It is idle to talk of the taste for port and sherry and the highly brandied wines as fixed and unchangeable.' A change in the law through a change in taxation would increase the demand for all kinds of wine, but the demand for light wines, in particular, would be affected. Finally, there was a touch of Gladstonian sentiment. 'We have got a law which makes it impossible for the poor man when he is sick to obtain the comfort and support derived from good wine, unless he is fortunate enough to live in the immediate neighbourhood of some rich and charitable friend.' Now all this would be changed.

The wine duty was duly lowered to 3s per gallon in March 1860, and the new scale according to strength was introduced on 1 January 1861. On 3 April 1862 the scale was further revised and lowered. The effect was that sales of French wine on their clearance from bond greatly increased. In 1860 the clearances of French wines from bond amounted to 1,125,599 gallons. The figure for 1862 was 2,227,662 gallons. Yet not all types of French wine benefited equally. To the irritation of some French wine producers, light clarets and sauternes were favoured against burgundies and the cheaper and stronger wines of the Midi. Not

---

[33] 'Cheap Wines' in the *Dublin University Magazine*, Vol. 80 (1872). An earlier article in the same journal (1855) had complained that there was a presumption that 'wine shall be reserved for the more favoured classes'. 'That a dusty labourer or exhausted cotton spinner should sit down to his bottle of wine' would seem 'unnatural'.

surprisingly, some of them pressed (in vain) for a uniform rate, irrespective of what the hydrometer recorded.

Clearances from bond were not registered completely in consumption figures, for, faced with the challenge Gladstone had offered the country, the number of wine sellers increased faster than the number of wine drinkers. This was because he also introduced concurrently with his new tax schedules his even more far-reaching reforms relating to distribution, reforms which had nothing directly to do with the Treaty. First, he proposed and had carried bills granting free scope to keepers of refreshment houses 'of good character' to sell wine on their premises on payment of excise licences, irrespective of magisterial jurisdiction – on the sensible grounds that 'the old system of separating eating and drinking is the most unwise one that we could possibly pursue if we want to promote sober habits'. Second, he successfully introduced a bill which enabled all shopkeepers on payment of a licence fee to retail wine to be drunk off the premises. An off-licence fee for merchants dealing exclusively in wines and spirits, the 'old trade', was fixed at ten guineas, but general shopkeepers – as Shaw had predicted – were now to be allowed to sell wine retail, not to be consumed on the premises, on payment of a fee of only fifty shillings. In this manner Gladstone was seeking, as far as he possibly could, to free trade in wine at home as well as to free trade in wine from abroad. And he was successful. The number of wine and spirit merchants increased from 7,810 in 1861 to 7,889 in 1871, but there was a far bigger expansion in licences:

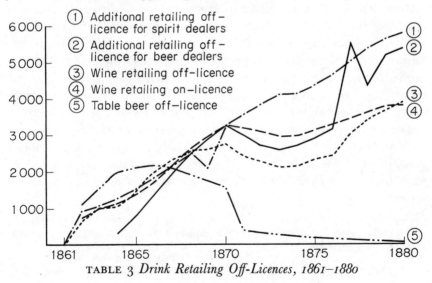

① Additional retailing off-licence for spirit dealers
② Additional retailing off-licence for beer dealers
③ Wine retailing off-licence
④ Wine retailing on-licence
⑤ Table beer off-licence

TABLE 3 *Drink Retailing Off-Licences, 1861–1880*

37

There was one last important reform in the 1860s. In 1866 the distinction of rates of tax on wine imported in bottles and wine imported in casks was removed. That was one year after Victoria Wine was founded; and in its foundation year Dr Robert Druitt, Member of the Royal College of Physicians, published his *Report on the Cheap Wines from France, Italy, Austria, Greece and Hungary*, dedicated (with permission) to Gladstone, who was eulogised by the author as the wise statesman who 'after two centuries of prohibitory duty put pure wine within reach of the English people'. Druitt believed that 'health and morality would be largely promoted by the more liberal use of wine' and extolled the virtues of a number of wines not then being drunk in England. He called himself an 'experimenter', noting that whilst one set of prophets were foretelling the day when 'all the English should give up their beer and cabmen call for claret instead of "half-and-half"' and whilst another set were foreboding a deluge of some red sour poisonous stuff that should set our teeth on edge,' the best thing to do was to go out and taste for one's self. 'I bought cheap wine from time to time for my own table, at such a variety of shops as should enable me to form a notion of what the public could really get at a moderate price, that is, at or under half-a-crown a bottle.'[34]

Druitt was ready for the entry of Victoria Wine, as devised by William Winch Hughes, and most likely bought some of his wine there. Before we formally introduce Hughes, however, there is room for one final piece of mid-Victorian writing which stands apart – or almost apart – from the controversy about the levels of duties on wine. In a Christmassy article in *Household Words* in 1853, Charles Dickens introduced (as Trollope also was to do – but with a sharper satirical edge) 'Our Wine Merchant', happy in his plate-glass windowed Emporium, replete with 'slender bottles of hock, big-bellied champagnes, imperial quarts of sherry, and dainty pints of liqueurs'. The early Dickens novels had lingered over grogs, punches and mulled brews.[35] Now he was less boisterous. Dickens's wine merchant was a man of dignity and standing, a pillar of society, who circulated to his clients a pamphlet 'got up in green and gold, labelled with the Royal Arms, and those of the City of London, with *Dieu et mon Droit* as the upper motto and *Domine dirige nos* as the lower'.[36]

---

[34] R. Druitt, *Report on the Cheap Wines of France, Italy, Austria, Greece and Hungary* (1865), p. v.

[35] 'It wasn't the wine,' Mr Snodgrass explained after the cricket dinner in *Pickwick Papers*, 'it was the salmon'.

[36] C. Dickens, 'Our Wine Merchant' in *Household Words*, 24 December 1853.

In the introduction to the pamphlet for his clients Dickens's wine merchant commented that 'while hundreds of familiar books [though not yet Mrs Beeton][37] have been written about domestic cookery and how to lay a table ... no book has yet been written to give young housekeepers an idea of how Wine is to be purchased, how to be managed when sent home, what Wines are necessary to accompany a dinner (and without good wine a dinner is worthless) and how to be served'. 'We respectfully present this little book to you,' the merchant concluded, 'in the earnest hope that there will be found in it some hints that may repay the trouble of perusing it.'

Dickens was pointing here to one way of trying to increase the demand for wine in an age of social change – one very familiar in the twentieth century – and he went on to summarise the chapters in his wine merchant's book. Chapter I was called 'Of a Wine Cellar' (and the merchant's own cellars were 'at all times on view to any respectable person who would wish to see a large stock of Wines well arranged ... Ladies can view them without inconvenience'). Chapter II had the title 'A Word of Advice as to Wines', which Dickens claimed began with the words 'Good Wine is to man what manure is to trees. Pure wine makes good blood ... A cellar without good wine, a house without women, and a purse without money are the three deadly plagues'. Chapter III turned to 'Port Wine': 'a glass of port wine and a biscuit, taken regularly at mid-day, is a capital thing for growing boys and girls delicate in health'. Chapter IV, 'Of Sherry', included the tit-bit 'the bitter in sherry [and it was often inserted in the sherry of the 1860s] is the *haut gout* of the wine', while Chapter VI, 'Of Champagne', 'every drop a diamond', included an *avant garde* recipe for champagne salad. Chapter VIII, 'Of Burgundy', 'the wine of princes', placed Romanée Conti, price 60s, first: 'Hear it, ye grocers and fruiterers', Dickens added. The comments made about claret were less memorable, although in a later number of *Household Words* an article on the subject of claret included the phrase 'the qualities claimed for good claret by their partizans rank with the merits of only children and the miracles of Russian Saints'.[38] After dealing with hock, Dickens's wine merchant ended his pamphlet with 'gin toddy'. He sold his gin in two gallons, twelve bottles, 'pure and unadulterated', 'commendably objecting to the frightful abuse of the spirit among the

---

[37] Isabella Mary Beeton's *Household Management* appeared in 1859. The volume *Every Day Cookery* followed in 1861. The latter had sections on cups and home-made wines including lemon flip.
[38] *Household Words*, 5 January 1856. Cf. George Meredith on port in *The Egoist* (1879).

lower orders who [and he gave no reason] never drink it pure'. 'One bottle of our gin will be equal in strength to one and a half bottles of the retail shops, and infinitely more pure.'

In 1865, when Hughes opened his Mark Lane store on very different principles from these, William Ray Smee published the second edition of his pamphlet *French Wines at One Penny Per Bottle Customs Duty*. He wanted to push Gladstone still harder, hopeful that 'he who has already gone so far in the right direction will, as soon as convinced, without doubt go a little further'.[39] 'The French government show great liberality with respect to British ale, which is imported into France at less than one third of a penny per bottle. Why should not their wines – on social, political and moral grounds – come in at one penny a bottle.' 'The English will receive as much as they give.'[40]

There was buoyant expectancy here, and it was shared by sponsors of Spanish Manzanilla, the praises of which were sung in 1861 in Richard Ford's *Gatherings From Spain*.[41] Yet the expectancy was not shared by the new periodical *The Wine Trade Review*, first published in 1863 two years before *The Grocer*. *The Review* for 1865 opened with the sombre words that 'heavy rates for money, a vast deal of over-trading, continual stagnation of business, and a very excessive stock, all combined to make 1864 a year of note'.[42] By the end of the year, it went on, 'perfect stagnation' had come to be regarded as 'a general state of things'. It was in these apparently unpropitious circumstances that Victoria Wine was born.

---

[39] W.R. Smee, *French Wines at One Penny Per Bottle Customs Duty* (1865), p. 13.

[40] *Ibid.*, p. 16.

[41] Peak sherry shipments were reached in the 1870s, though much of 'the still white wine made in the vicinity of Jerez' was sold as sherry.

[42] *The Wine Trade Review*, 21 January 1865. An earlier *Wine Trade Circular* had been published between January and May 1852.

CHAPTER THREE

The Origins of a Business 1845-1886

Whatever the omens in 1865, between 1865 and 1886 William Winch Hughes, the founder of Victoria Wine, built up his pioneering business so successfully that when he died in 1886, still only in his fiftieth year, the *Grays and Tilbury Gazette* could begin its obituary with the words, 'The best generally go first'.[1] Another obituary called his career 'a striking example of what untiring energy and unswerving honesty of purpose may achieve'.[2]

Hughes had made his will in 1857, one year after he married, when he was already described as 'a wine merchant, residing at 1 Wilton Terrace, Park Road, Dalston', and when he died he left behind him £45,733 10s 4d, and no children. There was a brief note in *The Times* on his death, but no obituary, and the longest account of his life and work was given in the *Grays and Tilbury Gazette*.[3] There was also an account of him in *The Wine Trade Review*.[4]

Hughes, like his wife Emma, who was his sole executrix and legatee, was a Londoner, born in the parish of St Clement Danes on 30 December 1834, two years before Queen Victoria came to the throne. His parents were Londoners too, and his uncle, with whom he lived as a boy, was a master lighterman. Their house was near the river—Shad Thames in Southwark. There were merchants in the Hughes family, but they dealt in coal, the commodity the French most wanted from Britain in 1860, not in wine, the commodity they most hoped to sell to Britain; and on William's marriage certificate the occupation of his father, who must

---

[1] *Grays and Tilbury Gazette*, 28 August 1886.
[2] *Ridley and Company's Monthly Wine and Spirit Trade Circular*, 11 September 1886.
[3] *The Times*, 24 August 1886; *Grays and*
Tilbury Gazette, 28 August 1886.
[4] *The Wine Trade Review*, 15 September 1886.

have died when he was young, was given as horse dealer.

There is a Dickensian ring to all this, as there was about the circumstances of Hughes's death, sixteen years after that of Dickens. On the evening of Tuesday 10 August 1886, Hughes attended the opening of a new Conservative Working Men's Club in the New Road, Grays, and at eleven o'clock he was about to walk home to his house, The Dell, when he was offered a ride back by a friend, Charles Smith, a corn merchant, who was driving his cart in that direction. Smith did not notice two large blocks of granite placed at each corner of Hughes's property to protect the banks, drove into them, and turned his cart over. Hughes was thrown into the road under the trap, but managed to crawl out and was taken back to his house by his own coachman, who lived nearby and had heard the accident. He seemed to have broken no bones and lay on a sofa for the night. The doctor was not summoned until the next day, and discovered that Hughes had crushed his chest and ribs. Hughes was apparently on the way to recovery, however, when he had a relapse and died at home a week later. At the inquest – with a jury – Smith testified that they had both been sober, and that Hughes was convinced himself that he had not been badly injured.[5]

The long report in the *Grays and Tilbury Gazette* noted how much work Hughes had devoted to The Dell, which was in a rough condition when he bought it in the mid-1870s; how every year he had given a treat to the poor there, the people who would miss him most; how active he had been in local Conservative politics as Vice-President of the Grays Conservative Association, and as a member of the Grays School Board and the Local Board[6]; and how crowded the streets were on the day of his funeral. 'Shutters were up and blinds down the whole length of the way the procession had to take and, in fact, throughout the town.' There were six mourning coaches and a hundred wreaths, and at the graveside the hymn 'Days and moments quicker flying' was sung.[7] *The Wine Trade Review* was more selective in its obituary than the local newspapers. It, too, noted Hughes's generosity to the poor of Grays, but stressed most

---

[5] Ironically on the following evening, August 11th, the total abstainers of Grays and district held their summer gala. 8,000 people were present. At the opening of the Conservative Club, Major Roach M.P. equally ironically had said that no great event had happened since the general election except 'the sending up to other spheres of some half-dozen gentlemen of the Liberal Party'.

[6] Hughes had been elected to the Local Board in June 1886, when he had polled 305 votes and come fifth with the man at the top of the poll securing 325. The man at the bottom of the poll secured 20 votes (*Grays and Tilbury Gazette*, 26 June 1886).

[7] The *Essex Herald*, 28 and 30 August 1886, gave some of these details.

strongly the element of self help in Hughes's own career. 'By his own exertions the deceased had built up the business of the Victoria Wine Company until he owned no fewer than 98 shops.' As for *The Times*, it added the address of the headquarters of the Victoria Wine Company – '8–10 Osborn Street, E.'

Before Hughes set up the Victoria Wine Company, he had served a kind of apprenticeship in the traditional wine trade, details of which can be pieced together laboriously from scattered references in London directories – and from his own marriage lines in 1856, when he was still a minor. There were many wine firms listed in the Post Office directories, a few of whom, as a curious and nostalgic late-Victorian book *The Romance of the London Directory* noted, still kept traditional tradesmen's signs, 'either flattened against the wall, or carved upon the now crumbling stonework.'[8] There were some very new firms too, although *The Wine Trade Review* reported in 1864 that notwithstanding the increase in their numbers, 'favourite brands still reign pre-eminent amongst purchasers.'[9] 'We did not expect that our *Wine Trade Review* would be patronised by wine retailers ... long established,' the editor noted, but 'these anticipations have been utterly and agreeably contravened.'[10]

At the time of his marriage, Hughes was working as a clerk in a firm of wine merchants, probably E.A. Southard's, set up at 20 Mark Lane in 1851, and later in the same year his name appeared for the first time in a London directory, when he was described as a wine merchant of 15 John Street, Minories. Two years after that, he figured among 800 other listed wine merchants in the Post Office Directory as a partner in the firm of Weller and Hughes, wine merchants of 10 Catherine Court, Tower Hill, E., a firm which moved in 1859 to 27 Crutched Friars; and by 1861 he appeared at last on his own as a wine and spirit merchant and broker at 52 Great Tower Street. Nor was that Hughes's last move before the founding of Victoria Wine. By 1862, he had moved down the street to number 63. The first reference to Victoria Wine as such in the Directory was in 1867, when the Great Tower Street address was given and when Alfred Cotsworth, a shadowy character, was mentioned as manager. The address 16 Mark Lane first appeared in the Directory a year later. *The Wine Trade Review* had noted in November 1866, however, that the

---

[8] C.W. Bardsley, *The Romance of the London Directory* (n.d.), p. 17.

[9] *The Wine Trade Review*, 16 January 1864. An advertisement offered specimen copies both of *The Grocer* and *The Wine Trade Review* post free.

[10] *Ibid.*, 16 July 1864.

Victoria Wine Company had imported 1,860 gallons of wine and in the following month no less than 9,917 gallons.

By 1869, nine Victoria Wine branches were already listed – 16 Mark Lane; 68 Mare Street, Hackney, N.E.; 23 Felix Terrace, Liverpool Road, N.; 691 Old Kent Road, S.E.; 111 Church Street, Bethnal Green, N.E.; 97 Bishopgate Without, E.C.; 118 Westminster Bridge Road, S.E.; 40 King William Street, E.C.; 28 Upper Street, Islington, N.; and 5 and 6 Hereford Place, Commercial Road, E. (In that year there were 24 entries in the Post Office Directory beginning with Victoria, only one in three of them a business firm, among them the Victoria Mining Company, the Victoria Soup Company and Victoria Station and Pimlico Railway Company.) Three years later Cotsworth was no longer referred to as Manager, and there were further premises at 120 Lambeth Walk, London S.E.; 15 Leather Lane, E.C.; 125 Rye Lane, Peckham, S.E.; 115 Hampstead Road, N.W.; 188 Walworth Road, S.E.; 500 Kingsland Road, E.; 53 Chalk Farm Road, N.W.; 19 and 20 London Street, E.C.; 60 Camden Road, N.W.; 19 Tachbrook Street, Pimlico, S. W.; 49 The Grove, Stratford, E.; 299 Goswell Road, E.C.; and 375 New Cross Road, S.E.

This was a mixture of neighbourhoods, with the East End still prominent,[11] but already by 1870 there was a branch of Victoria Wine far away in Bristol at 17 Southampton Parade, Whiteladies Road, which moved the following year to the High Street. Brighton (trading in a different name, Hughes and Saunders) and Birmingham soon followed. The best account of the early years of the Company was Hughes's own – in evidence he gave to the Select Committee on Wine Duties in 1879, a Committee which took up many of the issues raised in 1852. He described himself then as proprietor of 63 shops in the wine trade 'in London, and also in Bristol, and Brighton and Croydon, and other places, but mostly in London and the surrounding suburban parts', and in reply to one of the last questions put to him, he estimated that his annual sale of wine was 800 pipes and butts. He sold tea, coffee, beer and mineral waters also. He had turned his attention to areas outside London for some time, he explained, and even though the Committee knew of the extent of his business, it must have been quite a dramatic moment when after being asked during his evidence whether or not he had been increasing his

---

[11] There were many other nearby wine merchants. In Bishopsgate Without, for example, the London and County Wine Company was operating from No. 15/16 and No. 80/1 and John Geddes from No. 187. There were also two sets of coffee rooms and eight public houses.

trade, he replied that he had opened three shops that very week. (He added later that he had not opened many – only six indeed – in 1878, a year of bad trade.)

When asked how many shops he owned in the metropolis, he replied, as any born-and-bred Londoner would have done when confronted with London's huge growth during the 1860s and early 1870s, 'I hardly know what you call the metropolis and where it extends to now. We have a place at Wimbledon, for instance; we have places at Surbiton; we have places at Brentford, Richmond, Gravesend, Norwood, Acton, Ealing, two at Croydon, Blackheath, Hounslow, Lee, Penge and Tottenham.'

Hughes's evidence about what he sold was even more interesting than his evidence about the location of his shops. He had started by selling wine by the glass as well as by the bottle, for as little as 1d a glass, but the only three shops, all of them leased, where he now did this – and he now did it entirely for advertisement – were Bethnal Green, Commercial Road and Islington. The 'glass trade' had fallen 'about 1874'. Before that date, wine was a 'great novelty' and the trade was 'fabulous'. Soon, however, the old preference for beer and spirits had reasserted itself. Yet he had continued to do much to 'popularise' wine as the years had gone by, Hughes went on, and a large part of his continuing trade in it was not in full bottles, but in quarterns or even in half quarterns. Customers might bring their own bottles – or even jugs – and the wine was drawn from the cask. If he supplied bottles, the customer had to pay for them. The wine in question was 3d a quarter pint, $5\frac{1}{2}$d a half pint, 11d a pint, 1s 9d a quart, and 7s a gallon.

The cheap wine in question was not French but Spanish and Portuguese – Tarragona, a heavy red, 'often called port'; white wine from Malaga; sherry and port. There was no demand for Hungarian or Australian wine, and although he sold some 'British wine' – orange and ginger, to mix with quinine – it was only in small quantities.[12] Some of the wine he sold he had bought in Spain and Portugal: some he had bought through agents in London. In December 1871, he had paid duty on 4,932 gallons of wine.[13] There was a very large retail trade for cheap clarets, Hughes told the Committee. They had been sold for 10d a bottle in the 1860s and now cost 11d, but on the whole light wines were not in great demand. It was 'the strong alcoholised drink' which 'would keep'

---

[12] Stone's Ginger Wine has been described as being 'as classic and cheery a feature of Victorian Christmas as the Christmas tree'. (J.H.C. Abbott, *British Wines* (1975), p. 21).

[13] *Wine and Spirit Markets*, December 1871. In December 1872 the comparable figure was 5,070 gallons.

was most popular, and he fortified much of the wine he sold when it was in bond to raise it to 38 degrees. Hughes added that he had a very active trade in spirits also. Indeed, half his business was in spirits, not wine, and the consumption of spirits was increasing faster than that of wine. In 1875 he had sold 10,000 gallons of brandy, in 1876 10,200 gallons, in 1877 10,997 gallons, and in 1878 11,575 gallons.

Not surprisingly, given the objects and composition of the Select Committee, much of Hughes's questioning concerned the effects on consumption of the pattern of wine duties. Hughes, obviously not a Gladstonian, did not believe that current duties operated against the consumption of wine or that the half-a-crown duty on the very heavy wines operated 'disadvantageously to the development' of his trade: 'I do not know that it is generally satisfactory to the members of the trade, but it is satisfactory to myself'. When asked specifically whether reduced duties on cheap clarets would increase consumption, he answered yes, but not much: 'I do not think people look at the differences of 2d or 3d in the price of wine'. He did not see a huge additional market for French wine. 'Do you think that if the duties were lowered a great many more persons would enter the trade?', he was also asked, to which he replied yes, and when he was further asked by the Chairman, 'You would not look upon that with favour I presume?', he replied in characteristic Hughes fashion, 'I should not mind it; I like competition.'

Two other features of Hughes's evidence are particularly interesting – first his reflections on the influence of the trade cycle ('good' and 'bad' times) on the value of his trade; and second, the role of advertising. The late 1860s were years of boom, which lasted until 1873, and which were described by Disraeli as a 'convulsion of prosperity', and it was then (after the stagnation of 1864) that Hughes's business took shape. The depression, he said himself in 1879, had kept his business comparatively stationary between 1877 and 1879 after a very rapid rate of growth; though he was opening new branches, he did not see any signs of immediate recovery. Yet he was 'not at all dissatisfied': he had 'no cause to complain'.[14] And he had begun his business in 1865 – before the great boom began. Two years later, he had given wine away in order to advertise it. 'I had a stall at the [Smithfield Club] Cattle Show, at the Agricultural Hall, and I gave wine away at the rate of about 10,000

---

[14] In his obituary in Ridley's *Monthly Wine and Spirit Trade Circular* this statement of Hughes was picked out. Hughes's business had remained on 'an upward course' despite the depression 'which surrounded our own and almost every other trade.'

glasses a day in order to show the public that they could get genuine wines cheap.' 'I suppose you found a very good consumption,' the Chairman asked somewhat unnecessarily. 'As much as I could do,' Hughes replied, 'so much so, they would not let me go there any more.' 'Was that because you produced drunkenness?', the Chairman went on. 'No not at all,' explained Hughes, 'but it stopped the traffic.'

At the time, the *Morning Advertiser*, describing the Show, had referred to the Islington Arcade, where Hughes gave away – or sold – his wine as the 'most amusing, interesting and most crowded part of it' and Hughes's own stand as 'patronised more than any other'. The secret, it went on, was 'the quantity disposed of, upon the principle of small profits and quick returns'.[15] That was a formula valid in the long-term, not only for Victoria Wine, but for all 'mass retailing'. Yet the immediately valid secret was publicity. By stopping the traffic at the show Hughes increased it in his stores. Indeed, *The Wine Trade Review* headed a not very friendly paragraph on the subject, 'Smithfield Club Cattle Show: or the Puff Direct'.[16] It quoted from a newspaper which called Hughes's business 'a trading association called into existence by Gladstone's tariff treaty in regard to wines' and which, while it did not mention free wines (it referred instead to claret at 10d and port and sherry at 1s a bottle) did emphasise that all Hughes's wines were 'pure and wholesome' and had been put to the 'severe ordeal of chemical test by no less an authority than Dr Herepath'.

The Wine Trade Review disliked Herepath more than Hughes, accusing him of producing not a scientific report but yet another 'tradesman's puff'. With heavy irony it 'congratulated the manager of the Victoria Wine Company on his ability'. 'Chemistry', it went on, 'affords very little useful information as to the purity of wines. Of course, Dr Herepath knows this, and we do not suppose that he would willingly exchange the 48s port in his own cellar for the 12s port which according to his table resembles it so closely ... After our analysis of the *Lancet* and its "Analytical Commission on Wine", the less said the better on analyses of wine.'

Hughes would not have worried about such criticism. Rather he must have been happy to have reached the news pages of *The Wine Trade Review* which, as we have seen, was to honour him with an obituary in 1886. Yet possibly with Dr Herepath (and Dr Druitt before him) in

---

[15] *Morning Advertiser*, 11 December 1867.

[16] *The Wine Trade Review*, 15 December 1867.

mind, he told the 1879 Commission twelve years later that many of his customers had been told to drink wine as a medicine. His main customers were 'very poor people' and 'people of the middle class', and many of them were the kind of people who would go to a grocer. He did not reply directly to a question from Charles Palmer as to whether they were people who would otherwise drink beer or were beer-drinking as well as wine-drinking people.

The appeal Hughes made – or wanted to make – was summed up in an advertisement of 1873:

> Firstly, the Company guarantees that the wines it sells are unadulterated.
> Secondly, all long credits are abolished, and cash payments required.
> Thirdly, the Company imports its wines, clears them at the docks itself, and thus does away with intermediate profits.
> Fourthly, the Company uses every appliance for the careful bottling and keeping in condition of the wine it sells.
> Fifthly, it delivers free, in London, quantities of not less than a dozen; and
> Sixthly, it takes back from the customer any wines or spirits not approved of, returning the money provided the bottles be wrapped.

This was one of no less than 24 separate advertisements placed in the classified columns of *The Illustrated London News* on one day in 1873, the last of them stating that 'export orders received particular attention'. 'The Company will be happy to send prices free on board export ships for quantities of not less than six dozen. Most of their wines are always ready for immediate shipment.'[17]

The Illustrated London News was scarcely a paper of the poor. Nor were export orders the kind of orders Gladstone had in mind. Yet to judge the power of Hughes's enterprise it is interesting to compare such advertisements with his early local advertisements in newspapers like the *Hackney Express and Shoreditch Observer*, which included detailed price lists – for spirits not wines (the wine list could be secured on request) – and a special note on 'the very best black tea' at 2s 6d per pound.[18] There could be a touch of philosophy, however, even in such papers: until the advent of Victoria Wine, the advertisement reads, 'the consumption of wines was

---

[17] *The Illustrated London News*, 13 December 1873. Hughes's first advertisement in this weekly was printed as early as 15 July 1865.

[18] *Borough of Hackney Express and Shoreditch Advertiser*, 31 March 1877.

then in a great measure restricted to the least numerous but reputedly most wealthy classes'. Now Victoria Wine, 'by a combination of knowledge and experience in the trade', was offering 'wines at prices hitherto unheard of in England, thereby placing an expensive luxury within the reach of all classes'.[19] There was an appeal, too, to the communications grapevine as well as to the grape. 'The proprietors of the Victoria Wine Company beg to thank customers for their many kind recommendations, the unceasing sale proving that quality can be combined with lowness of price, and prejudice overcome in time by fairness in dealing.'

The first advertisements outside London – in the very first year of the business – appeared on the same Tuesday, 12 December 1865, in the *Chichester Express*, the *Guildford Journal*, the *Croydon Journal*, the *Eastbourne Express* and the *Dorking Journal*, where other wine advertisements had appeared earlier in the year from the European and Colonial Wine Company, 122 Pall Mall, and The Times Wine Company, like Victoria Wine in Great Tower Street. (There was also an Imperial Wine Company.) The Victoria Wine advertisements – in sections – referred specifically to eleven wines, five ports, five sherries and one composite offer of claret and sauternes. 'The above are guaranteed to be genuine foreign wines,' the advertisements ended, 'the cheapest ever yet sold in this country, and fit for any gentleman's table.'[20]

However much Hughes emphasised that his wines were within range of the poor, the idea of the 'gentleman's table' still figured in his and most other wine advertising. Yet in his 1879 evidence Hughes brought in other ideas also – each with a strongly Victorian flavour. He never opened his shops on Sundays, he stated, for example – as a matter of principle, for he wished his employees to have a holiday – but much of his Saturday trade was for customers wishing to drink at home over the weekend. And here he turned to the hallowed Sunday lunch or dinner. 'Many a man will have a decanter of wine on his table on Sunday who would never have had it before, because he can now have it cheap and good. Instead of drinking beer, he would drink a glass of wine, and he could afford to give a glass of wine to his friends. They look upon it as a more genteel thing than drinking a glass of beer.'

One year after Hughes gave his evidence to the 1879 Committee,

---

[19] *Ibid*, 7 April 1877.
[20] *The West Sussex Journal*, 12 December 1865.

Pictorial World, a paper in which he advertised – and he advertised in *Punch* also – printed an interesting account of a visit to the Victoria Wine Company's premises. 'The East End of London,' it began, very much in the vein of the 1870s and 1880s, 'is to many persons almost as much a *terra incognita* as Central Africa.'[21] The author had travelled by omnibus along Whitechapel Road to the headquarters of the Company, which by then 'on account of increasing business' had moved to Osborn Street, E., where he met Hughes himself. The warehouse there had sixteen floors and a frontage of 160 feet. The offices were on the ground floor as was a retail department for the sale of wines. In the vatting, storing and bottling department were two of the largest casks said ever to have left Spain and Portugal, one containing 800 gallons of sherry, the other 750 gallons of port.

Hughes himself conducted his visitor from basement to garret, lingering longest in the bottling section, where beer as well as wine was bottled:

> The bottles are placed in a frame, which, revolving, carries them through a tank containing a strong alkaline solution. This removes all labels and dirt from the outside, and softens any incrustation inside. They are then placed on brushes, which revolve at great speed, and thus the inside is thoroughly cleaned. They are then placed on a machine which, being turned, ejects a stream of water into the interior, and, after undergoing an examination by gaslight, are sent to an upper floor, where they are again examined, so that not the slightest particle of dirty or deleterious sediment can remain.

It is fascinating that the bottles were given more attention by the author of the article than their contents, although he referred briefly to the beers of 'Bass, Guinness, Barclay and other well-known firms'. And when he came to the different warehouse floors, he noted one for bottling spirits, too, along with one for storing sparkling wines such as champagnes, hocks, and moselles, and one packed with 'rack after rack of wines of a superior quality ... independent of the four vaults which extend under the street'. There was a sample room also which 'looked like a very large chemist's shop'.

'Care in the selection of wines' came low on the author's list of preoccupations. Indeed, he pointed out at greater length that the

---

[21] *Pictorial World,* 18 December 1880. The label *terra incognita,* 'unknown land', was to be used by Charles Booth in his *Life and Labour of the People in London* (1889).

Victoria Wine Company also sold tea, coffee, sugar – and sardines – besides mineral waters and eau-de-Cologne.[22] Moreover, he believed that they were 'arranging to sell other "packet" goods at their various branches'. The latter were all managed by ladies who were 'selected with great discretion for their business capabilities and lady-like manners'. During the previous week, no less than 17,000 customers had been served in the 83 shops. As many as 438,226 bottles of wines and spirits had been sent out from Osborn Street to the shops during the same period, and 432,464 bottles of beer. In London itself, the Company held more licences than any other wine and spirit merchant, and £3,500 – it seemed then like an astronomical figure – was being paid per annum to the Inland Revenue.

The account of the visit ended with warm references to 'the perfect friendly feeling that seemed to exist between Mr Hughes and his employees – all working away together like a happy hive of bees'. 'Here, at least', for the author, 'the vexed question of "Capital v. Labour" [already a vexed question at that time] has been satisfactorily solved'. Hughes was deeply concerned for his workers' welfare. He had provided, for example, a library and reading room for them, and they could eat their meals there as well as read. 'Here beer and coffee' were 'provided, besides the daily and weekly papers, as well as chess and dominoes.'

If that was the spirit of the enterprise, there is unfortunately no way of analysing its economics. Presumably Hughes leased most of the premises for his branches, and some of them were not held for long. Of those which existed in 1871, several of them were described as 'uninhabited', that is they were shops only, but at one, at least, 68 Mare Street, Hackney, the manageress Susannah Shaw, a widow aged 50, was living on the premises with her son. At 500 Kingsland Road, Susan Wheeler, a widow aged 26, born in Germany, was in residence, and there was a manageress-widow in residence also at 97 Bishopsgate Street. By 1886, some of the addresses suggested well chosen locations in established shopping areas – like 113 Holloway Road or 279 and 454 Fulham Road.

The question of whether or not the shops should sell packaged goods other than wine, spirits and beer was the kind of question all successful mass retailers were facing at this time. Jesse Boot, the Chemist, for example, who did not develop his chain of branches until the mid-1880s – by 1893 he had 93 branches – had a grocery section at his first

---

[22] For tea, see D. Forrest, *Tea for the British, The Social and Economic History of a Famous Trade* (1973).

Nottingham store, and for a time sold ironmongery as well as patent medicines.[23] If the answer for some retailers lay in specialisation by product, it was neither an obvious nor a universal answer.

Victoria Wine price lists for the period survive, although not in continuous series. The first of them, indeed, was issued just before the name 'Victoria Wine' was introduced. It is a long *Bi-Monthly Circular* of 21 January 1865 of a conventional character which includes a letter describing the London wine sales and the state of the rum and brandy market. There was an interesting footnote, however: 'Please be particularly careful in addressing letters W.W. Hughes as there is another Mr Hughes in the same building'. One reason why, apart from publicity, Hughes to his everlasting fortune chose the name 'Victoria Wine' in that year was because there was some confusion between his name and that of the other Hughes, C.W.[24] A further *Bi-Monthly Circular* (1866) still did not refer to Victoria Wine as such, although by then *The Wine Trade Review* had noted the change of name ('a new idea in the wine trade') and had wished 'good health' to all Hughes's customers.[25] In the first Victoria Wine *Illustrated London News* advertisements of 1865, port and sherry were advertised at 12s per dozen and claret and sauternes (with very little classification) at 10s per dozen, and this minimum price was being maintained in 1870, when better ports, including vintage port, were being sold at up to 32s per dozen. Champagnes were 28s per dozen, and still hocks and moselles, like marsala, 17s per dozen. In 1873, when the 'country branches' included Norwich, genuine 'foreign ports and sherries' were advertised at 1s 2d 'reputed quart bottle' and 'on draught, imperial measure'. 'Good pale cognac brandy' was selling at 2s 2d, fine London gin at 2s, old Demerara rum at 2s, 'Scotch Malt Whisky' at 2s 2d, and Irish Whiskey at 2s 2d per bottle.

The range continued to widen. By 1877, for example, there were three prices for marsala and six prices for sherry, the most expensive a 'pure Amontillado, exceedingly dry, soft and delicate' at 44s per dozen. There were four champagnes too, the second best at 32s per dozen 'excellent for dinner or supper parties', the best 'rather rich in flavour' at 44s per dozen. In that year an advertisement in *Punch* offered Christmas cases, costing one guinea. They included two reputed quart bottles of port and sherry, one of gin, rum, whisky and brandy, and one pound of tea, and they were delivered carriage free to any railway station in England.[26] A

[23] S. Chapman, *Jesse Boot* (1974), p. 72.
[24] *The Wine Trade Review*, 18 February 1869.
[25] *Ibid.*, 14 February 1866.
[26] *Punch*, 8 December 1877.

year later, two new sherries were added to the list – a fino at 36s per dozen and an amontillado pasado at 44s per dozen, the same price as a 'beautiful pale amoroso sherry, possessing a splendid, soft, rich, nutty flavour'. Finally, in 1879, the year Hughes gave his evidence to the Select Committee, there was 'pure plantation coffee' at 1s 8d and 'prepared cocoa', 'strongly recommended to invalids as being palatable, nutritious and easy of digestion', at 1s.

A full list exists for 1880 (when there was no longer any reference to a Norwich branch, but when there were 29 country branches, most of them in the London area). There were now fourteen ports and sixteen sherries, all carefully numbered, two marsalas, eight clarets, six sauternes, three Beaujolais, six burgundies (three red and three white), five champagnes 'and for those who preferred a cheaper wine, 'Saumur Champagne' at 25s per dozen), or in 'extra quality' 30s, three still and three sparkling hocks, and three still and three sparkling Moselles. The cheapest port and sherry now cost 14s per dozen. There was also a list of 'sundry wines', among them two Tarragonas, one Rota Tinta, two Roussillons, one Hambro Sherry and one Bucellas, 'not cheap, a pale wine made from the German grape transplanted into Portugal'.

The spirits list included three sweetened and three unsweetened gins, eight brandies, six rums and six whiskies, along with spirits of wine, 'pure white, and flavourless' in a 'white capsule', and Hollands Number two, bottled in Rotterdam in square bottles and costing 2s 9d per bottle. The cheapest bottle of English gin cost 2s 1d and the most expensive bottle of brandy, sixteen years old, 6s 1d. Guinness Dublin stout and Bass Pale Ale cost 4s per dozen, London Cooper 'of the finest quality' 2s 6d per dozen and 'family dinner ale' 3s 0d. These were the kind of prices that prevailed until Hughes's death, although there were sometimes exotic new items on the list, like 'Bovine Wine' introduced in 1881 (at 36s per dozen). It was said to contain 'essences of beef and other valuable ingredients' as well as port *and* sherry, and was recommended as 'nourishing and invigorating'.[27]

On his customers' tastes in wine, Hughes believed in 1879 that they liked not only strong fortified wines, but sweet wines too, 'the old story of the sweet tooth as opposed to the trained palate'.[28] Referring to the evidence of an earlier witness, Mr Houldsworth, about a decrease in national sherry consumption, Hughes attributed it to the fact that the

---

[27] *Evening News*, 26 July 1881.
[28] Laffer, *op. cit.*, p. 119.

sherry had become too dry. 'The public are very good judges as a rule, but their taste has been so played with (through campaigns to promote dry sherry) that sherry has gone down. ... I have always found that the old-fashioned style of sherries suit the public best, and I can show by my statistics that people who do sell dry wine do not sell a quarter of what I sell, for I sell only rich wine.' He was doubtless contrasting his sherries with sherries like Tio Pepé which began to be drunk in the 1870s and which if not drunk chilled – and quickly – could easily 'wither between lunch and dinner'.[29] There is no reference to Harvey's 'cream' sherry until 1882.[30]

Rich wine for people who were not (necessarily) rich was the William Winch Hughes recipe for success. And in the process Hughes became moderately rich himself. By 1871, before he moved to The Dell, he had two servants. At The Dell he was far better provided for. We know nothing about his own drinking habits or of his dealings with his competitors. Yet we can reconstruct the more general pattern of the wine trade – and of national drinking habits – between 1865, the first year of the Victoria Wine Company, and 1886, the year of Hughes's death. It was still a time when the only wine merchant's advertisement in Murray's famous *Handbooks*, foreign and domestic, included the statement that the merchants who were advertising their wines availed themselves of the opportunity 'to return their sincere thanks to the Nobility and Gentry for the patronage hitherto conferred on them and hope to be honoured with a continuance of their favours'.[31] The same advertisement offered 'dry and spacious warehouses' for the storage of their clients' 'works of art and all descriptions of property during the Owner's absence'.[32]

Such 'Owners' often seemed to be selling property rather than storing it in 1886 itself when the economic situation seemed even more depressed than it had been in 1879 or in 1864. The general verdict was expressed in the statement in a wine trade periodical: 'the great staple industries hang fire, and experience teaches us that they must move before we can'.[33] Hughes, however, would not necessarily have agreed. It was not the

---

[29] See G. Saintsbury, *Notes on a Cellar Book* (1920 edn.). It is not known whether the tastes of those of Hughes's customers who bought champagne tended towards 'dry' champagne, the preference both of Gladstone and the Prince of Wales (though not of the French *bourgeoisie*).

[30] See G. Harrison, *Bristol Cream* (1955). A lady visitor is said to have been offered two sherries to taste. 'If that is milk ("Bristol milk?"),' she said, 'this is cream.'

[31] *Handbook for Travellers in Sussex* (1884), Handbook Advertiser, p. 2.

[32] *Ibid.*

[33] *The Wine Trade Review*, 15 January 1887.

'Owners' who interested him most. Nor would he necessarily have agreed with a further generalisation that 'the revenue derived from alcoholic drinks has always been looked upon as a reliable barometer of the prosperity of the nation'. He would have been forced to agree, however, that 'stocks of good wine of all descriptions' were 'light' and that the European vintage had not been 'so satisfactory as could have been wished'.[34] The port vintage was 'poor' and the claret of 'irregular quality'.[35] If Hughes could have chosen his year to die, it would not have been 1886.

---

[34] *Wine, Spirit and Beer*, 29 January 1887.
[35] A. Simon, *Vintagewise* (1946), pp. 41, 76.

CHAPTER FOUR

The Supply and Demand for Wine 1865-1914

The statements made by Hughes to the 1879 Select Committee are buried away in over three hundred pages of *Minutes and Evidence* which, taken together, give a fuller picture of the wine trade at the beginning of the last period of Queen Victoria's reign than any other source. It was a trade which one witness said was 'almost in its infancy', a limited trade which members and witnesses of the Committee alike felt was bound to increase. The young John Harvey of Bristol might be revelling during the autumn of 1879 in the delights of Phélan Segur, 'one of the prettiest spots in St Estèphe,' and celebrating his wedding anniversary with 'a lovely bottle of Rauzan '47',[1] yet the import of foreign wines into Britain was lower in that year than in any other year of the decade, as was expenditure on them, having reached a peak of 18,671,000 gallons in 1876; and even at the beginning of the year messages from Bordeaux had spoken of a 'dead calm as regards business' and reports from Jerez had described 'how the new year does not open very cheerfully'.[2]

The year 1879 itself was something of a general turning point in Victorian history too. In particular, there was an exceptionally bad harvest which played havoc with cereal growing agriculture. Already foreign corn was coming into the country in increasing quantities: thereafter, it was all too clear that English corn could not compete in price. As G.M. Young has written, 'great wars have been less destructive of wealth than the calamity which stretched from 1879, the wettest, to 1894, the driest, year in memory'.[3] And it was in 1879 that the poet Tennyson described how:

---

[1] G. Harrison, *op. cit.*, p. 105. Clarets were classified in 1855 in time for the Paris World Fair.

[2] *The Wine Trade Review*, 15 January 1879.
[3] Young, *op. cit.* (1936), p. 145.

The cuckoo of a joyless June
Is calling through the dark.

Nor was it only landlords and farmers who were increasingly uneasy. After the great boom of the late 1860s and early 1870s, there were almost as many worries about industry as about agriculture. What Clapham called 'a tang of doubt' was in the air.[4] Businessmen, like farmers, were facing increasing foreign competition, and this was leading also to the increasing tension between 'Labour' and 'Capital', each given capital letters, which was a major topic in newspapers and periodicals. The harmony of interests which had characterised the mid-Victorian years was manifestly breaking down. Yet there was an exception. As the *Brewer's Journal* put it at the time, '1879 gave brewers no reason to complain ... When the fact is considered that the large brewing companies go on paying 10, 14 and 18 per cent, it will be perceived that the business is a remarkably good one ... However much people may be disposed to economise in other directions, it is evident that they will not be without the national beverage'.[5]

It was against this background that in March 1879 W. Cornwallis Cartwright, Liberal M.P. for Oxfordshire, successfully moved in the House of Commons that a Select Committee be appointed 'to inquire into the system under which Customs Duties are now levied in this country on Wine, and its results, fiscal and commercial'. The timing was well chosen. There were fears of a 'war of tariffs' in Europe; and already in France, as in Germany and Spain, there was a strong protectionist movement. In 1879 itself Bismarck reversed German free-trade policies and raised customs duties; in Spain attempts were being made to limit imports of British coal, and in Portugal the British Consul in Oporto was active in discussions with the port industry in reviewing the schedule of duties. The gospel of free trade had lost its evangelising power – to such an extent that in more than one textbook of late nineteenth-century economic history the brief index reference to free trade reads 'see tariff'.

In such circumstances, the details of the wine trade were thought of as only a part, if a significant part, of a bigger network of changing international trade, and the composition of Cartwright's committee reflected a wide range of preoccupations. Yet the members included people with very special interests in, and knowledge of, brewing and

---

[4] Clapham, *op. cit.*, p. 110.
[5] Quoted in R.G. Wilson, *Greene and King, A Business and Family History* (1983), p. 123.

wine importing, like Pickering Phipps, a Northampton brewer, and T.C. Cobbold, who had been an unpaid commercial attaché at Lisbon and Oporto. It was difficult, of course, to separate wine and coal in the business talk, not least in relation to France, where the Cobden Treaty, once thought of as the great covenant of free trade, was in peril. It had been denounced in Paris as early as 1872, two years after the fall of the Second Empire of Napoleon III and the French defeat by the Germans, and in 1882 it was finally to be abandoned. There were alarms in Italy too, where it was estimated that no less than 80 per cent of the population relied on wine for a living.

In Britain, there was a Conservative Government in power in 1879, as there had been in 1852, and it had been led from 1874 by Disraeli, a politician with a protectionist past, who was more interested in adulteration than in taxation and who saw through the great Sale of Food and Drugs Act of 1875, the first comprehensive piece of legislation on the subject. (A later amending act of 1878 dealt with spirits.) Disraeli had benefited at the general election from the opposition of the brewers to his predecessor Gladstone's licensing legislation of 1872. Indeed, his critics said that he had been brought into power on a tide of beer. Yet wine was a different matter. His Government laid down firmly in 1876 that whatever other countries might do with their duties on wine, this had no bearing at all on what Britain did or should do. But by 1879 there were signs that in the light of what was happening across the Channel the Government now felt that there should be a re-examination of wine duties within the framework of fiscal policy. The duty of 2s 6d a gallon on wine was higher than that in any other European country, and it was often pointed out that even in Russia the duty was only 2s. By 1879 the Press, led by *The Times*, was demanding *inter alia* 'a comprehensive new enquiry into the pattern of wine duties' which, it was pointed out, loomed larger than ever before in broad bilateral discussions of imports, exports and customs policies.[6] The whole free-trade argument was at stake when in 1878 the Foreign Secretary was trying to make it clear in correspondence with the Spanish government that 'duties should be levied for purposes of revenue only'.

If Spain – on the road to protectionism – figured most prominently in the brief debate in the Commons which led to the setting up of the 1879 Committee, France could never be left out.[7] And the situation there was

---

[6] *The Times*, 15 March 1879.
[7] *Hansard*, 18 March 1879.

a discouraging one. Whatever the misfortunes of English farmers during the late 1870s and 1880s – and the most enterprising of them could find ways out of 'depression' by turning to milk marketing or to market gardening – they were nothing compared with the misfortunes of French wine-growers who could turn to nothing else. The latter were confronted not only with the weather but with the dreaded disease that afflicted vines, phylloxera, identified in wild vines in the Mississippi valley in 1854 by an American entomologist, Asa Fitch. After crossing the Atlantic, it had first been reported in France in 1863 in the Department of Gard, an important producing centre of *vins ordinaires*,[8] and had subsequently spread rapidly throughout France after 1875. The little beetles which carried it reached Bordeaux in 1869 – after an extraordinary run of fine vintages – Beaujolais in 1870, Burgundy in 1878, Champagne in 1890, and the Meuse and Moselle districts six years later. Earlier in the century, there had been another serious fungoid disease affecting vines, oïdium (first identified in Margate in 1845), but it did not last for so many years or create quite so much havoc. It seemed, indeed, to prophets of doom, that as it spread phylloxera spelt the end of the world of wine.

Because of phylloxera, there was a terrifying statistical contrast in France between impressive figures relating to the area planted with vines and gloomy figures relating to the output of grapes. In England the corn acreage shrank dramatically: in France the vineyards remained dark in the shadows however brightly the sun shone. Between 1877 and 1900 the production of wine in France reached 50 million hectolitres only once, and in many years scarcely touched the 30 million mark. Total exports had reached a peak of 3,981,000 hectolitres in 1873 – the peak year for wine exports to Britain also – but between 1880 and 1890 they never reached the 3 million mark again, and between 1890 and 1900 they never even reached the 2 million mark. The worst year of all was to be 1893. Meanwhile, imports of wine into France – always resisted as a matter of national pride[9] – which had amounted to only 183,000 hectolitres in 1860, the year of the Cobden Treaty, went on to pass the 12 million mark in 1887 and 1888.

Of course, wine in France was politics, and even had there been no phylloxera there would have been protectionism in France following the

---

[8] F. Convert, 'La viticulture et la vinification après 1870, en crise phylloxerique' in the *Revue de Viticulture* (1900). See also R. Dion, *Histoire de la vigne et du vin de France* (1959) and A.E. Bateman, 'Wine Production in France' in the *Transactions of the National Association for the Promotion of Social Science* (1884).

[9] Wine had been imported into France in 1852 as a result of the spread of oïdium.

defeat of the country at the hands of the Germans in 1870 and the fall of Napoleon III's Second Empire. Under the new Republican leadership there was a sharp reaction against the free-trade policies of Napoleon III's ministers and agents. As one English observer put it in 1885, 'Napoleon III, with the assistance of Mr Cobden, forced free trade upon France. The dose was homoeopathic in quality, but, even so, the manner in which it was administered made it seem larger than it was, and gave it an ill flavour'.[10]

In this gloomy setting, the initial optimism generated by the Cobden Treaty on both sides of the Channel had long been dissipated. Following the Treaty, exports of French wine to England had risen between 1860 and 1864 from 132,000 to 157,000 hectolitres, but the sense of unprecedented potential had already been lost by the year of Hughes's death, 1886. It was estimated (in France and to the chagrin of the Spaniards), however, that France's share of a larger British market had risen from 9.5 per cent on the eve of the Treaty to 40.4 per cent,[11] yet there was no longer the urge to expand the market in a period of declining production. In 1875 Bordeaux had reported that British consumption of clarets had increased tenfold in fifteen years, yet even before the arrival of phylloxera French wine-growers in the *vins ordinaires* (and burgundy) districts grumbled that they had not benefited as substantially as those in the claret and champagne areas. In 1877, for example, Montpellier was reporting no appreciable increase in the shipment of local and regional wines to England.[12] Twenty years later, it was at the centre of the revolt against free trade.

The evidence presented to the 1879 Select Committee touched far more frequently on the general international trading situation than the evidence offered in 1852. Within a narrower context, however, it clearly illuminated the different ways in which British wine merchants, including Hughes, had responded to the Treaty of 1860 and its aftermath and how they conceived of the future of wine-drinking in Britain. Most

[10] F.G. Walpole, 'The Wine Duties' in the *Fortnightly*, Vol. 44 (1885).

[11] A. Arnauné, *Le commerce extérieur et les tarifs de douane* (1911), p. 255. According to Arnauné's estimates, the share of Portuguese wines had fallen from 21.0 per cent to 17.8 per cent and of Spanish wines from 39.6 per cent to 28.4 per cent. An Appendix to the Minutes and Evidence of the Select Committee of 1879, prepared by the Statistical Department of the Custom Office, gave the figures as follows:

TABLE 4 *British Imports of Wine, 1859, 1878*

	1859 (gallons)	1878 (gallons)
From France	1,010,888	6,028,596
From Spain	3,629,325	5,714,948
From Portugal	1,797,854	2,920,285
From Other Countries	1,767,446	1,778,709
Totals	8,195,513	16,452,538

[12] See Dunham, *op. cit.*, p. 287.

wine merchants had thought of the Treaty as an opportunity, but there had remained a difference of outlook between traditional wine merchants, concerned with small known clientèles (and increasingly with good vintages) and more adventurous – though often equally knowledgeable – merchants looking to the possibilities of a wider and unknown market.

Given such differences, some historians of the wine trade, notably André Simon, have suggested that there were far too many wine merchants in Britain after 1860, newcomers who had to build up stocks before they could hope to do business and who lacked the means necessary 'to embark successfully in the wine trade'. More seriously, Simon claimed, most of them lacked the knowledge also. In this one-sided account, competition within the wine trade inevitably became 'keener and less fair' in Britain after 1860 as 'the practice of small profits and cash payments' was introduced and rapidly gained ground. And while, the account concedes, the Gladstone changes 'benefited at first the wine trade by placing wine within the reach of a greater number of people',[13] this was only 'a passing benefit, soon to be followed by a serious calamity', a calamity not on the demand side but on the supply side. During the 1870s, when wine was abundant and excellent, all was well. During the 1880s, however, as phylloxera devastated the French vineyards, 'ignorant and unscrupulous dealers' put people off drinking wine by 'persevering' in times of supply difficulties with low prices and 'cheap' wines. 'The phylloxera had destroyed vineyards, but low prices, which spelt bad quality, had destroyed the confidence of a large number of former wine-drinkers, and this last evil has been even more disastrous than the first.'[14]

In fact, history was more complicated than this, for all was not well in the 1870s and there is only impressionistic evidence to suggest that any former wine drinkers were being put off by what was happening. If they were tempted to drink less wine, it was probably because of a fall in their incomes during a period of agricultural depression rather than because of what was happening to wine prices – there was a general price fall[15] – but there is little hard evidence of this either. The complexities of the

---

[13] For a more colourful and sympathetic account of this phenomenon, see the *Edinburgh Review* ('Wine and the Wine Trade', Vol. 126, 1867). Before 1860 'a man fagged with hard work would not have dared to go into one of these grand establishments, as he may now go into the grocer's shop next door, and get a bottle of cheap light wine to take home for his dinner.'

[14] A Simon, *op. cit.*, p. 58.

[15] See W.T. Layton and G. Crowther, *An Introduction to the Study of Prices* (1938).

British situation were certainly apparent enough at the time to the first witness appearing before the Select Committee of 1879, Henry Parry Gilbey, the senior partner in the 23-year-old firm of W. and A. Gilbey, which had been ensconced since 1867 in the magnificent eighteenth-century Pantheon building in Oxford Street (now a Marks and Spencer store) and which in 1893 became a private company. The Gilbey family had made an immediately successful switch after 1860 from selling Cape of Good Hope wines, in which they had put their trust before the end of colonial preference, to mass marketing. They treated wine as an article of commerce. And subsequently, with Reading, Torquay and Wolverhampton leading the way, they expanded their business – not through branches, but through a network of 2000 Gilbey agents selling their products, the prices of which they reduced as far as possible, in Gladstone's new off-licence stores. Towards the end of his life Gladstone wrote to the Gilbey partners that he had 'always regarded the proceedings of your firm with a particular interest. You have been, as far as I am able to form an opinion, in an eminent sense, and in an eminent degree with which no one can compete, the openers of the wine trade.'[16]

They were operating on a far bigger scale than Victoria Wine. In December 1866, for example, when Hughes imported 9,917 gallons of wine[17], the comparable Gilbey figure was 437,687 gallons, and in the following month the respective figures were 1,334 and 45,711 gallons. Gilbeys' first advertisement, after the details of the Treaty had been announced, had been headed 'Wine at the Reduced Duty', and it pointed to the many connections which the firm already had with 'hospitals, military messes and public institutions'[18]; and sales increased by a fifth in the following year. By 1879, coincidentally the year when H.P. Gilbey's younger brother Alfred, a staunch Gladstonian, died,[19] their network of exclusive agents was wider by far, and they had a more thorough knowledge of the demand for wine throughout Britain than any of their competitors. 'You have agencies, have you not, in almost every town?' Cartwright asked Gilbey, to which the reply came – 'In every town of a certain population that will admit of the amount of the

[16] Quoted in N. Faith, *Victorian Vineyards, Chateau Loudenne and the Gilbeys* (1983), p. 21. Walter Gilbey was granted his peerage by a Liberal government.

[17] See above, p. 44.

[18] See A. Waugh, *Merchants of Wine, Being a Centenary Account of the Fortunes of the House of Gilbey (1957)*, Chs II and III, and A. Gold,

Four-in-Hand: A History of W & A Gilbey Ltd (1957). N. Faith, *op. cit.*, includes some useful and interesting chapters on the Gilbey family and the growth of the business.

[19] *The Wine Trade Review*, 15 December 1879. For H.P. Gilbey's obituary, see *ibid*, 13 December 1892.

heavy licences now paid.' A large number of them were grocers; some were chemists, and there were twenty or thirty of them in Manchester alone. Their main concern was turnover, and 'cheapness', in consequence, was 'an essential part' of Gilbey's business. Yet they were in no way threatening the traditional wine trade: instead, they were seeking, their spokesman said, to popularise wines – 'to bring wines at a low price within the reach of the public'.[20] H.P. Gilbey felt that they had reached 'quite another strata [sic] of consumers' from traditional merchants, while not yet succeeding (where Victoria Wine was already succeeding) 'in what is called the east end of cities and towns'.[21]

If duties were to be lowered again, Gilbey told the Committee, 'the result would be a keener competition with smaller profits, and an extended sale'. Yet, he went on to prophesy, there would be no sharp decline in the consumption of beer or spirits: indeed, 'where beer and spirits increase, wine increases . . . they do not in any way collide . . . They have a separate set of consumers'. Statistics bore out such a conclusion, although when wine sales went down, as they did in 1879, beer and spirits sales could – and did – go down too. Only the consumption of table waters, it has been suggested (in the absence of reliable statistics) rose in 1879 to a peak for the decade. Nonetheless, there could be – and were – switches of taste. For example, while agreeing with Gilbey that there was ample room for extended consumption both of wine and spirits, if people could afford to pay for them, another witness before the 1879 Committee, Sir Louis Hallet, discerned a recent tendency for people who had turned to wine for health reasons to 'give up wine and to take up spirits'.

Blended whiskies, lighter than the heavier malts, were to transform the taste for spirits, particularly from the 1890s onwards, and already by 1879 the Distillers' Company, originally a combination not of blenders but of six Lowland grain patent-stillers, was two years old. Increasingly thereafter the English followed the Scots in turning away from brandy and rum. 'Whisky and soda' was to become a favourite drink, and it was a sign of the times that in the last years of the century at least one notable port was flavoured with Scotch whisky instead of with brandy. In 1892 there were 130 working distillers in Scotland: in 1898 161.[22] And the 'Big

---

[20] They provided information too and in 1869 published *Wines of the Principal Wine Producing Countries*. They also mobilised their agents in the 1870s in an Off Licence Holders Protection Association.

[21] See also the profile of A.N. Gilbey in *ibid.* 4 January 1924, which gives a profile of the

business and its history.

[22] See the report of the Select Committee of 1890–1 on British and Foreign Spirits, Sessional Number, 210; D. Daiches, *Scotch Whisky* (1969), p. 62, and *DCL and Scotch Whisky* (1966).

Five' were already in active existence. Haig was the oldest, and Dewar was the first to produce 'a whisky baron'. James Buchanan arrived in London in 1879 as agent of Mackinley and Company, and seeing the possibilities of the boom five years later set up a business of his own. Of the other two, Walker set up a London office in 1880, and James Logan Mackie started his White Horse business in Glasgow three years later.

The demand for whisky did not affect the demand either for champagne or for beer. Indeed, although the former was not much mentioned in the Minutes of the Committee, it had been given more effective publicity than ever before in 1867 in George Leybourne's music hall hit song 'Champagne Charlie'. The praises of 'Moët and Chandon' in the song encouraged other champagne firms, notably Clicquot, to produce their songs too.[23] Nor did the fact that in 1862 champagne had been singled out for a higher rate of duty than other wines seem to reduce the demand for it. Sales had trebled in the 1860s, and during the 1870s, with a new taste developing for drier champagnes, there was a further boom. The 1874 Pommery was deliberately sold as an extra dry wine, and the vintage of the following year was the most prolific of the century.[24]

Meanwhile, of course, beer drinkers went their way cheerfully, whatever the price of champagne or any kind of wine: for most of them then and later the choice was not between beer and wine or beer and spirits but beer and no beer. There was a Stock Exchange boom in brewery shares during the late 1880s following a great Guinness issue of £6 million in 1886. It was oversubscribed many times, and with Barings as the bankers, it provided, according to the *Brewers' Journal* 'a theme of universal interest and discussion.' In that same year alone 28 firms, with a capital of £9.5 million, changed from partnership status to limited liability, among them Ind Coope, Whitbread and Courage. Two years later a separate Stock Exchange list of brewery companies was made: there were then more than 200 of them, many of substantial properties, the product of amalgamations, some highly speculative.[25] Significantly

---

[23] 'Are you over-run in London with "Champagne Charlie is My Name"?', Edward Fitzgerald, author of *Omar Khayyam*, wrote to a friend in November 1869, 'A brutal thing: nearly worthless the Tune … [but] I can see, to my sorrow, that it has some go – which Mendelssohn had not.' Quoted in W.A. Wright (ed.), *More Letters of Edward Fitzgerald* (1901), p. 88.

[24] For the change in taste, see G. Saintsbury, *Notes on a Cellar-Book* (1920).

[25] For the background, see H.A. Shannon, 'The Coming of General Limited Liability' and 'The Limited Companies of 1866–1883' reprinted in E.M. Carus Wilson (ed.), *Essays in Economic History* (1954) and P.L. Payne, 'The Emergence of the Large-Scale Company in Great Britain, 1870–1914' in the *Economic History Review*, Vol. xx (1967). In 1840 there were almost 50,000 brewers in the United Kingdom. By 1880 there were less than half that number, and by 1900 the number had fallen to just over 3,000.

The Brewery Manual of British and Foreign Brewery Companies began publication in 1890, a year when output of beer in standard barrels had increased to 32 million from 20 million thirty years before.

Expansion in the wine trade, by comparison, had been slow and undramatic. Nor was there any wine as cheap as beer – at $2\frac{1}{2}$d per pint. To the question, 'What is the cheapest wine that is now consumed in this country in any large quantity?' Gilbey's answer – and it would not have been the 1895 answer – was claret at 1s a bottle. 'We tail down as we get to the high qualities.'[26] Burgundy fell far behind. Yet Gilbey did not believe that even in the 1880s 'the lower class' would take at once to lighter wines instead of or even in addition to beer: 'education would take longer with the lower classes than with the upper'. His was a sophisticated analysis, which dealt more realistically with the social aspects of the subject than Simon was to do.

Another wine merchant, T. Lyte Willis, told the Select Committee that his firm was dealing largely with publicans who bought mainly port and sherry, although the proportion of clarets sold by them was increasing too. Like Gilbey – and Hughes – he did not consider that increased consumption of wine would drive out beers or spirits, the latter drunk in large quantities 'in the East End and low neighbourhoods where wine was almost unknown to the consumers'. For Willis – and it was an illuminating observation – any greater consumption of wine generated by a lowering of duty would primarily affect not 'the lower class' but 'a class that now drink nothing at all, practically speaking', the 'so-called teetotallers'. This was a shrewd judgement. Total abstainers remained a prominent pressure group in late-Victorian England, most of them demanding prohibition, but Willis was wise to predict that however strong their influence Britain would 'perhaps get up to a consuming point something approaching other countries'. There were limits to the appeal to the British middle classes, particularly in the big cities,[27] of total abstinence, which had perhaps been strongest in the 1850s, and even more limits to the appeal of statute-based prohibition.

While Lyte Willis had little to say about traditional drinkers, he was sensitive to new social trends. 'Are there many gin palaces in which I could go and get a glass of wine?' asked Whitewell, one of the members of the Committee. 'Yes, hundreds of them,' replied Willis; and later in his evidence he referred to the increasing use of wine in cafés and restaurants as an accompaniment to food. The whole of this subject has been neglected, like the general history of cafés, restaurants and hotels,

---

[26] *Minutes of Evidence taken before the Select Committee on Wine Duties* (1879).

[27] See B. Harrison, 'The Power of Drink' in *The Listener*, 13 February 1969.

although there has been increasing interest in the 'leisure complex' (forbidding term) which was to expand dramatically during the last decades of the nineteenth century.

A quite different slant was provided for the Committee by R.H. Houldsworth, a partner in Gonzales, Byass and Company, the largest shippers of sherry into Britain. Their peak year for imports, as for the sherry trade as a whole (68,467 butts), had been 1873, when they shipped over 10,000 butts, and they were particularly sensitive to the demands of Spanish winegrowers that they ought to be put on the same footing as France in a period of economic depression: the alcohol test, they felt, worked against them. And Houldsworth supported their case. He believed, indeed, that if wine duties were reduced to 1s per gallon, irrespective of strength, there would be an immediate reduction in the Spanish tariff on British imports. A decline in wine imports from Spain since 1873 was due partly to the substitution of clarets for sherries and partly to 'the depression of trade, which prevails not only in this country but in all countries of the world': 'I know of noblemen who used to give sherry at 42s and 48s a dozen at luncheon, who now give sherry at 24s.'

Sherry, in fact, was a drink in decline during the late 1870s and 1880s – despite the introduction of branded bottling[28] – although port, the most conservative of drinks, almost held its own, and 1878 was an exceptionally fine vintage year. (George Saintsbury named the Dow 1878 as 'one of the best wines of the century'.)[29] In terms of quantity, the import figure for 1879, a bad year, was low, but it was to be exceeded in 1900, a year when the quantity of most other wines imported was to show a fall. The trade was never to be without its problems, some of them political, both in Portugal and in England, and it was bitterly opposed in 1880 to new fiscal proposals relating to wine brought forward by Gladstone who returned to power in that year. It found itself in opposition on this issue not only to Gladstone, who once again sought to reduce duties on lighter wines – and, indeed, on 'the whole scale' – but to the recently founded Wine and Spirit Association, and it was in open alliance with the English maltsters.[30]

'Since the wine duties were altered in 1860', Gladstone declared,

---

[28] The first firm in Jerez to bottle was J. de Fuentes Parrilla, founded in 1871.

[29] See G. Saintsbury, *Notes on a Cellar-Book* (1920 edn.). He also said of the 1874s that 'as long as they lasted nothing quite touched them'.

[30] See E. Cockburn, *Port Wine and Oporto*

(1949). p. 34. There were other difficulties as the century went by. In 1895, for example, following an exceptional apple harvest in England, the demand for empty casks to contain cider caused the price of empty port wine pipes to advance to a record price of 18s. See also A. Simon, *Port* (1934).

'great progress has been made in facilitating the consumption of wine, of cheap wine, and of sound wine throughout the country.' 'The character of the trade has been as I think fundamentally changed; and ... the quantity of adulterated wine has been very greatly diminished.'[31] In consequence, Gladstone went on to propose, that if the French agreed during further discussions on the renewal of the 1860 Treaty, he would reduce the lowest duty on wine by a half from one shilling to 6d per gallon. He admitted that there would be a cost to the Exchequer, and proposed in addition to convert the old malt tax into a beer duty. The French did not agree, but the malt tax went.[32] Its abolition was described later by Gladstone as 'the most important single financial charge which I have ever been concerned in recommending to this House'.[33] Leaving on one side its fiscal implications – an increase in licence duties for publicans and hoteliers and an extra penny on the income tax – Gladstone did not endear himself to the 'beer interest' when he expressed doubts as to 'whether we are justified in priding ourselves as much as we sometimes do upon the general quality of British beer'.[34] Yet he won other familiar accolades. According to John Morley, his biographer, everybody except the maltsters and the port shippers said that 'none but a *cordon bleu* would have made such a sauce with so few materials'.[35]

A few members of the Wine and Spirit Association had radically different interests from the traditional merchants of Oporto. One of the most interesting of them was Peter Bond Burgoyne, who was called to give evidence immediately before Hughes. Burgoyne had dealt mainly in Australian wines over a period of eight years and owned vineyards in South Australia, where wine was disposed of locally at 2s per gallon wholesale in its first year. He also had interests in South Africa and had a bottling plant in the East End. The sale of Australian wines in Britain, Burgoyne went on, had not increased as much as he expected. 'Do you expect to see a large consumption of Australian wines amongst the lower classes in this country', he was asked, 'or chiefly amongst those who are called the higher and middle classes?' 'I should say among the higher and

---

[31] Hansard, *Parliamentary Debates*, 10 June 1880.

[32] M. Buxton, *op. cit.*, p. 276. It had remained at the same figure per bushel (2s. 8½d) from 1840 to 1880 except when it was raised to 4s. during the Crimean War.

[33] Hansard, *Parliamentary Debates*, 4 April 1881.

[34] *Ibid.*, 10 June 1880. He had once stated in 1864, however, that beer was 'the staple drink of the people in England ... this excellent and truly national beverage' and he had paid tribute to the brewers of Burton in 1865.

[35] J. Morley, *The Life of Gladstone* (1980 edn.), vol. II, 184–5. Morley says little of the difficulties in 1880 and does not mention that the Spanish government refused to ratify a new arrangement about schedules of strength and related duties.

middle classes', was his reply, followed by the terse afterthought, 'I do not think that the lower classes drink wine.'

Burgoyne must have been a popular witness in that he offered the members of the Select Committee not statistics but some wine to taste. He obviously knew little about precise numbers, and his vistas were long-term. He was acquainted with one grocer in South Australia, he exclaimed, who had not sold one drop of his wine. 'Then you wish the English to drink what they will not drink at home?' he was asked by Whitewell, to which he replied 'Not at all; they are drinking as much as they can, but the supply exceeds their requirements.' For another witness, James Blyth, who had married a Gilbey daughter, Australian production was capable of 'immense development'.[36] The first recorded shipment to Britain of 1,389 gallons had been taken into bond in 1854, but only once between then and 1879 had the annual figure risen above 50,000 gallons: in 1879 itself – at 17,089 gallons – it was lower than in any year since 1868.[37]

At a time when the French vineyards were in trouble, hopes of new sources of wine were as significant as the angry complaints that in the Spanish Cortes a Bill had been introduced to prohibit the use of English coke and coal in Government establishments. They were significant too in the absence of evidence relating to the United States which was to redress its original responsibility for introducing the disease of phylloxera and save the European vineyards (while continuing, through cheap corn, to destroy the English wheatfields) by offering Europe phylloxera-free grapes. In general, there was a 'great preponderance of evidence' before the 1879 Committee that a further reduction of duties on wines would materially increase their consumption, for as the final Report of the Committee put it, 'the existing mode and scale of duties, though they stimulated a larger consumption of wine than had existed previously, have not yet been calculated to promote that consumption which there would be reason to anticipate under a less onerous rate of duty'. Whether or not that conclusion was convincing was not to be put to the test. The duties were not to be reduced in any radical fashion after the Committee had ceased to meet.

One question posed in the sessions has a particularly topical ring. It was put to Gilbey by B. Samuelson:

---

[36] Blyth became a baronet in 1895 and a peer in 1907.

[37] See H.E. Laffer, *The Wine Industry of Australia* (1949). In 1950 the Burgoyne business was to be taken over by the Emu Company, founded in the 1880s.

Q: Do you think generally that the trade abroad, say in Spain or Portugal, are aware how much more moderately alcohol is taxed in beer than in wine?

A: I do not think it is known generally; I do not think it is known even in England, and I think it would be a fund of information to consumers in this country if they knew it, and a powerful information for good.

It was on the basis of such information, the 1879 Committee concluded, that the country should after all choose, for, as its Final Report put it, 'the consumption of wine is very far below what the country is capable of absorbing if the reduction of duties were such as to bring it within the reach of the masses'. And the Report went on boldly to suggest – far more boldly than anyone had dared to suggest in 1852 – that even if there were to be a reduction of total revenue as a result of lowering wine duties, this might be 'more than counterbalanced by the advantage to the general commercial interests of the kingdom from an increased trade with the wine-growing countries'.

Gladstone's budget of 1880 was in line with the Select Committee Report, but there was a move in the opposite direction in 1888, following a fall in revenue, when again under a Conservative government – this time Lord Salisbury's – a new set of duties was imposed on wine imported in bottles.[38] If the wine came into the country in imperial half-pint half bottles or less, the duty was to be 1s 3d per dozen; if in imperial pints or between half pints and pints at 2s 6d per dozen; and if in imperial quarts at 5s per dozen. The duty was higher on bigger bottles, up to £1 on bottles exceeding two imperial pints, and by a further Act of the same year, a duty was imposed on bottled sparkling wines of 2s 6d per gallon in addition to the duty in respect of alcoholic strength, an extra duty which was reduced to 2s per gallon in 1892. One M.P. referred specifically to problems with France, while two spoke affectionately of Italian wines. 'There was less objection to the tax on champagne', it was suggested, but what about Robert Browning's 'good Chianti and old Barolo'?

In 1890, it was decided that wine 'made effervescent' and bottled in warehouses – a product for which there was increasing demand – should be treated like sparkling wine brought into the country in bottles. Thereafter, there was no further major change in the customs until 1899, when the duty on wines not exceeding 30° proof (an increase of 4°) was set

---

[38] Hansard, *Parliamentary Debates*, 26 March 1888. The revenue from beer in 1887, Jubilee Year, was the highest ever. Wine revenue fell, however, by £28,000. Gladstone's critics pointed out that revenue from wine had fallen from £1,842,137 in 1859 to £1,222,173 in 1882.

at 1s 3d, not 1s, and the duty on wines exceeding 30° was set at 3s instead of 2s 6d. As in 1876, for every degree above 42° an extra 3d was charged. The duty on sparkling wines imported in bottles remained unchanged at 2s 6d per gallon, and on still wine imported in bottles it was fixed at 1s per gallon. The main opposition on this occasion came from M.P.s who wanted special treatment for Australian and 'colonial' wines,[39] while the Chancellor of the Exchequer stated explicitly that the policy initiated by Cobden and Gladstone had in his view failed: 'foreign countries had raised their tariffs to such points as they thought advantageous to themselves with very little, if any, regard to the amount of duty we charged upon their wine'. He did not anticipate any fall in wine consumption from the increase in duty: 'consumption depends far more on the habits and tastes of the people.'[40]

Far more interesting, indeed, than the pattern of duties, which remained highly distinctive when compared with that of other countries, was the equally distinctive British pattern of drinking, although the pattern of duties doubtless influenced it. The most important general point was that between 1860 and 1914 Britain did not become a nation of wine drinkers. Beer and spirits prevailed. The hopes of the early 1860s, when total wine consumption had almost doubled in five years, were all dashed. Until 1883 the average annual home consumption of wine was maintained at over 16 million gallons, but from 1884 to 1889, following a bad vintage, it had dropped to under 14 million gallons. There was an increase again from 1890 to 1900, although the 16 million gallons mark was never reached again, and this was followed by a sharp decline between 1903 and 1914. By then *per capita* consumption was lower than it had been in 1859 on the eve of the Cobden Treaty. Meanwhile total beer and spirits consumption reached a peak in the years 1900–1904, although the *per capita* peak in both cases came much earlier – in the years from 1875 to 1879.

The detailed quinquennial pattern for the United Kingdom is shown in Table 5 opposite, with the *per capita* figures presented in brackets:[41]

What stood out by the early twentieth century, when there was a lively debate on temperance following the Report of a Royal Commission on the Liquor Law in 1899, and the publication – a best seller with 60,000 copies – of the Licensing Act of 1902, was that of the total 'drink bill' of

[39] Mallet, *op. cit.*, p. 141.
[40] Hansard, *Parliamentary Debates*, 13 April 1899.
[41] See H.L. Wilson, *Alcohol and the Nation* (1940), p. 335, and A.R. Webb, 'The Consumption of Alcoholic Liquors in the United Kingdom', in the *Journal of the Royal Statistical Society*, Vol. 76 (1912–14).

	Average Population (Thousands)	Spirits (Thousands of Gallons)		Wine (Thousands of gallons)	Beer (Millions of gallons)
		Home	Imported		
1860–64	29,184	20,022(.68)	5,556(.19)	9,799(.34)	718(24.6)
1865–69	30,308	21,679(.71)	7,888(.26)	13,742(.45)	874(28.8)
1870–74	31,873	26,889(.84)	9,474(.30)	16,613(.52)	993(31.1)
1875–79	33,572	29,770(.89)	10,829(.32)	16,864(.50)	1115(33.2)
1880–84	35,188	28,490(.81)	8,305(.24)	14,784(.42)	1026(29.2)
1885–89	36,598	26,336(.72)	8,198(.22)	13,604(.37)	1040(28.4)
1890–94	38,154	30,253(.79)	8,181(.21)	14,420(.38)	1136(29.8)
1895–99	39,992	32,980(.82)	8,261(.21)	15,848(.40)	1248(31.4)
1900–04	41,889	35,237(.84)	8,322(.20)	14,421(.34)	1267(30.2)
1905–09	43,745	30,881(.71)	6,663(.15)	11,829(.27)	1197(27.3)
1910–14	45,498	25,309(.55)	5,478(.12)	11,424(.25)	1229(27.0)

TABLE 5 *Consumption Patterns, 1860–1914*

£195 million, expenditure on beer acounted for 60 per cent and on spirits for 30 per cent.[42] Wine came a bad third. Prices remained more or less constant – the average price of beer, 2½d per pint, and of wine, 3d per pint, remained the same until 1914[43] – and although there were changes in taxation (and in licensing), the main changes in drinking habits had less to do with fiscal policy than with more general economic and social factors – family size, the level of employment and of incomes, education, and the range of goods (not only cigarettes)[44] and services available. In 1905 the Chancellor of the Exchequer, Austen Chamberlain, spoke of money 'formerly being spent on drink now being spent on railway

[42] A.E. Dingle, 'Drink and Working-Class Living Standards in Britain, 1870–1914' in the *Economic History Review*, Vol. 25 (1972), which also gives a critical account of the statistics and of the relationship of drinking to income.

[43] A.R. Prest, *Consumers' Expenditure in the UK* (1954), pp. 76–80.

[44] For a remarkable Tolstoyan discourse on the relative appeal of tobacco and alcohol, see L. Tolstoy, 'The Ethics of Wine-Drinking and Tobacco Smoking', in the *Contemporary Review*, Vol. 59 (1891), in which he argued that 'people drink and smoke not merely for want of something better to do while away their time, or to raise the spirits, not because of the pleasure they receive, but simply and solely in order to drown the warning voice of conscience'.

excursions, music hall entertainments etc.', and the following year his Liberal successor, Asquith, took up the same theme. 'The decline in the consumption of wine,' he pointed out, is 'more marked' even than that of spirits and beer.[45]

Taxation mattered most, perhaps, in 1909, when, following the rejection by the House of Lords of the Liberal Licensing Bill of 1908, duties on spirits were sharply increased by Lloyd George (an extra 3s 9d per gallon), causing a rise in price and a temporary reduction in consumption.[46] The Liberal majority in the House of Commons included a substantial temperance party.[47] There was a fall in the consumption of beer then also. Yet there was a small increase in wine consumption by over 100,000 gallons.[48] The statistics are notoriously tricky and in places unreliable.[49] It is clear, however, that while there was as much talk of the drink problem in 1914 as there had been in 1879, there had been a fall between the 1870s and 1914 in expenditure on drink of all kinds as a percentage of total consumer expenditure (see Table 6 opposite).

There had also been a fall in the total 'drink bill' from £195 million in 1900 to £182 million in 1913, with a slightly increased proportion of it spent on beer, and a fall in the profits of many brewery companies.[50] Convictions of drunkenness had fallen too from 207,000 in England and Wales in 1905 to 152,000 in 1910. Meanwhile, the weight of cigarette tobacco consumed increased fourfold from over 11 million pounds in 1900 to 45 million in 1913.

The influence of class and region on the statistics are difficult to separate out. Leone Levi estimated in the 1880s that the 'working class' consumed 75 per cent of all beer and spirits, but only 10 per cent of wine.[51] And certainly the Scots drank more whisky per head than the English, although it is impossible to tell whether they drank more or less wine. On the eve of the slight improvement in wine consumption in 1909, the wine merchants' guide of 1908 noted that while Gladstone's fiscal

---

[45] Mallet, *op. cit.*, p. 241, p. 256.

[46] The duty on spirits had been revised in 1890, when 6d was added, though a further 6d added in 1894 was dropped a year later. In 1900 it was added again.

[47] See G.P. Williams and G.T. Brake, *Drink in Great Britain, 1900–1979* (1980), pp. 26ff. There were 156 total abstainers as against 88 in the previous House, and 75 out of 129 M.P.s with financial interests in the liquor trade had lost their seats at the general election.

[48] See G.B. Wilson, letter to *The Times*, 31 March 1910, the first of a number of letters by him on the same subject. He was Secretary of the United Kingdom Alliance.

[49] See G.B. Wilson, *Alcohol and the Nation* (1940).

[50] See J. Vaizey, *The Brewing Industry, 1886–1951* (1960), pp. 15–17. The Brewers' Society was formed in 1904.

[51] L. Levi, *Wages and Earnings of the Working Class* (1885), p. 69.

Sketches at the Victoria Wine Company's premises, Osborn Street East, 1880

Exterior View of Premises

Interior view of the premises

Bottle beer department

Bottle Beer Department

Wine & Spirit Floor

Wine and spirit floor

Cased wine and
spirit floor

Spirit floor

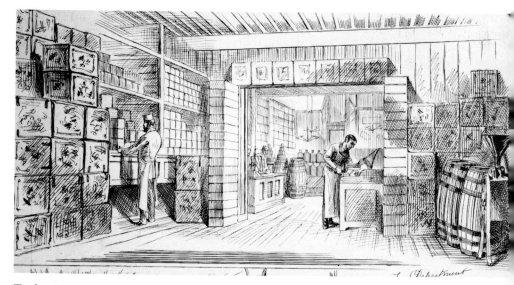

Tea department

Claret floor

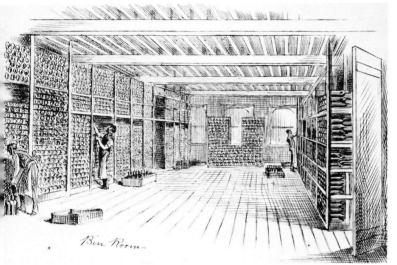

Bin room

Bottle washing

Ground floor

Examining bottles

A branch of the Victoria Wine
Company in Kensington, 1903

Part of W. Glendenning and Co's
cellars, 8 Hood Street, Newcastle
upon Tyne, 1920

WINES SPIRITS TYLER & Co LTD. BEERS MINERALS

Tyler and Company's branch
at 3, Chertsey Road, Woking in 1923

Interior of a Tyler's shop in the 1930s

Tyler's Cranleigh premises in the 1930s

A record consignment of 1,024 cases of
Warnink's Advocaat at the start of its journey
from Amsterdam to London, 1924

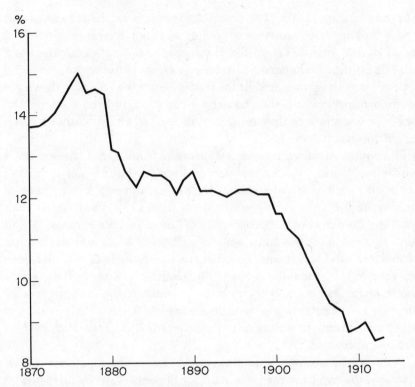

Sources: J.B. Jefferys and D. Walters, 'National Income and Expenditure of the United Kingdom 1870–1952' in *Income and Wealth*, Ser. v, p. 27; Prest, *op. cit.* pp. 75, 85.

TABLE 6 *U.K. Expenditure on Drink as a percentage of total Consumer Expenditure on Goods and Services at Current Prices*

changes might have brought 'the rich man's luxury within the poor man's reach', it had not brought it any nearer his mouth. 'Neither then nor since has light claret become the beverage of those who earn by manual labour.'[52] In middle-class circles wine was used commonly enough for Sheila Kaye-Smith in 'Rambles round an Edwardian dinner table' to recall someone telling her as a child that 'a peculiarity of the Americans was that they did not drink wine'. [53] Yet in 1909 *The Wine Trade Review* discerned no signs of real progress in wine-drinking habits

---

[52] *Ridley's Wine and Spirit Trade Circular* (1908).

[53] L. Russell (ed.), *The Saturday Book* (1948), p. 76.

over the years since 1860. 'The time is not very remote,' it suggested – and it was looking backwards to a golden age, not forwards – 'when a knowledge of wine was regarded as part of the ordinary education of a lad, but all that is changed.' 'Modern methods of living, moreover,' it went on, 'are altogether against the trade. People who dwell in flats have no opportunity, even if they had the inclination, to keep a cellar, and they buy wine just as they need it and, we are afraid, without much regard to quality.'

The comment raised more questions than it answered, among them 'which lad?' and 'how many people lived in flats?'. Yet a further comment ended with a question by the author himself. 'A large share of the responsibility for the present state of things,' he maintained, 'rests upon the shoulders of the proprietors of hotels and restaurants. We all know that the luxurious apartments of such establishments must be paid for in some way' and it was 'no exaggeration to say that wine has been expected to keep the hotels going.' The chairman of one of the greatest hotel companies had recently stated that, compared with the figures for ten years ago, the receipts for the sale of wine had fallen off to the extent of 50 per cent. 'It might well be asked', wrote *The Wine Trade Review*, 'And who are to blame?'

'Wining and dining' was a favourite Edwardian pastime which separated the rich from the poor in an age of picturesque social contrasts when a guest at a dinner party for 24 could cheerfully count 362 plates and dishes in use, plus 72 wine glasses. Victoria Wine was outside this extravagant complex. But it continued to expand because it was operating successfully in a very different market from that described in *The Wine Trade Review*. It was a market with marked seasonal ups and downs – Christmas was still the peak period – which had to take account of the fact that most working-class drinking (particularly heavy drinking) and a considerable amount of middle-class drinking took place outside the home in the pub or the hotel. Indeed, if licensing laws had been less stringent, particularly as far as legal hours of drinking were concerned, the amount of home drinking would have been even less.

The tightening up of the laws had begun with the Aberdare Act in 1872, following an earlier and more extreme attempt in 1871 which united 'the trade' against the Government. In 1869 the Beer Act had placed beer houses under the control of the magistrates, and now they were expected to enforce shorter hours and to increase penalties for drunkenness. Thereafter the number of beer houses fell, although the amount of money spent on big, imposing public houses greatly increased:

they were in their glittering heyday in the 1890s. As Mark Girouard has put it, after 1899 the carnival was over, and the fall in investment in the building of new pub premises and the lavish decoration of old ones can be directly related to the fall in consumer expenditure in relation to income.[54] Even in their heyday, however, they concentrated mainly on beer, with whisky, gin, and port and lemon falling far behind; there was little wine for sale. Moreover, their clientèles were restricted. 'The West Enders (and I am speaking here of my own class)', wrote the Secretary of White's Club in 1896, 'are not attracted to the public house'.[55] The remark was exaggerated, but it is fair to add that women were not attracted in large numbers either.

Before turning to the record of the fortunes of Victoria Wine during these late-Victorian and Edwardian years, it is interesting to re-examine within the limited pattern of wine consumption what was happening to the taste for particular wines at home as well as inside pubs, hotels and restaurants. The switch to 'pure, light and exhilarating' clarets during the 1860s and early 1870s was not associated, following improved classification during the late 1850s, with any extensive increase in knowledge of the range and quality of different vintages, although connoisseurs took delight in the 1864s, the 1874s and the 1875s. Burgundies were little drunk, although, again, connoisseurs appreciated the 1875s, with André Simon judging the Romanée Conti of that year the finest burgundy he ever drank.[56] Moreover, as eloquent spokesmen of the claims of French wines always pointed out, 'the taste of Englishmen, and even more of Englishwomen' had been 'so long corrupted by a long course of port and sherry, that the pure unbrandied wines now introduced at a price suitably low to place them within the reach of almost every one' were 'not at first relished'. Claret seemed 'sour'. The 'new wines' were 'ignorantly looked upon as merely substitutes of an inferior kind for port and sherry', and consequently the more they differed in taste from these, the less they were esteemed.[57]

It was still noted, of course, that it had not always been so – at least in Scotland – for, as the poet Thomas Campbell recalled, in the days of his grandfather, before Scotland 'had been reduced to degeneracy and corn spirits by wine duties and the Union', gardens, fields and paddocks had

---

[54] M. Girouard, *Victorian Pubs* (1975), p. 217.

[55] Quoted in *Ibid.*, p. 3.

[56] A. Simon, *Vintage Wine* (1946), p. 107.

[57] 'Cheap wines' in the *Dublin University Magazine*, Vol. 80 (1872). Cf. a leader in *The Times*, 8 September 1865, 'People have never had an opportunity of taking their choice. French wines have never been offered to them on fair terms. Powerful class interests have stood between the public and the wine growers.'

been fenced in with claret staves. The first port, north or south of the border, it was claimed too, had had 'a clarety-burgundy character, very much like some of the pure vintages drunk by Portuguese at the present day.'[58] And if there had been a demand for such wines in the past, there could be a demand for them in the future.

Port in Britain, as it was presented in the late-Victorian era, was a highly fortified drink, 'fortified' often by products other than brandy, while, as Dr Dorman had told the Select Committee on Wine Duties in 1852, 'no natural sherry came to this country'. 'The demand is for wine to suit an artificial taste.' 'Are you aware of the existence of an impression in the trade,' another witness had been asked, 'that there is something in the air of the Thames fatal to the quality of the wines (Greek and Italian) not now imported into our ports and which prevents their importation?', to which he replied that while there was such an impression, 'these wines will go round the world, and do go round Cape Horn and the Cape of Good Hope, and get consumed in Java and other places, but they do not stand up to the Thames, it is said'.[59]

The worst concoction of all on sale was 'Hamburg' sherry, one million and a half bottles of which 'found their way into the stomachs of infatuated Britons' in 1865: 'What an amount of indigestion, liver complaints and headaches do these figures bring before the imagination,' wrote the *Pall Mall Gazette*. 'The Germans are wise. Their beer they drink themselves: their sherries they send to help depopulating the British Empire.'[60] That the comment was not unjustified is suggested by an advertisement placed in *The Times* a year later:

> Partner wanted – A practical distiller, having been experimenting for the last seventeen years, can now produce a fair port and sherry, by fermentation, without a drop of grape juice, and wishes a party with £2000 to £3000 to establish a house in Hamburg for the manufacture of wines. Has already a good connection in business. Apply to ...[61]

German wines figure remarkably little in the British articles and books on wine published in the 1860s and 1870s, one of the liveliest of which was

---

[58] Quoted in 'Wine and the Wine Trade' in *Edinburgh Review, loc. cit.*

[59] For a mid-Victorian eulogy of Greek wines, see F. Bremer, *Greece and the Greeks* (1863).

[60] *Pall Mall Gazette*, 9 August 1866. See also a letter to *The Times*, 19 September 1869,

headed 'The Wines We Drink – Sherry'.

[61] Quoted in 'Wine and the Wine Trade' in the *Edinburgh Review, loc. cit.* Later in the century, *The Lancet* printed the report of an 'Analytical Commission on Sherry', 29 October 1898.

T.G. Shaw's *Wine, The Vine and the Cellar* (1863), although there was to be a boom in hock in late-Victorian and Edwardian England.[62] Champagne, however, was always mentioned in any treatise, even if it was noted that 'not a hundredth part of the wine that ever goes forward with showy labels and with well-known labels ever comes from the Champagne district at all'.[63] The problem about champagne was bound to be that in an age when 'cheapness' – (and greater social access to wines) – were the main themes of debate, it was known by anyone who was knowledgeable that champagne had to be expensive. 'No delusion can be more absolute than that of cheap champagne', it was written in 1864. 'The price alone must always be one test of that wine, for the genuine article cannot be produced except at considerable cost.'[64] The message was taken for granted at the end of the century: indeed, after Roederer had devised his *cuvée exceptionnelle* for Tsar Alexander II of Russia in 1876 the sense of champagne as a luxury drink was further enhanced. Bottled in crystal, it was not available commercially, but most other varieties were and sales reached an all-time record in 1897 – $9\frac{1}{2}$ million bottles. Three years later champagne was said to be 'easily holding its ground as pre-eminently the popular wine for festive gatherings of all kinds',[65] although there were some signs of a change of taste towards the end of the brief Edwardian period as champagne sales continued to fall and the consumption of foreign liqueurs went up more than 10 per cent in two years.

At the other end of the social scale, Tarragona was picked out by *The Wine Trade Review* in 1900 as the wine with growing importance, 'to be ascribed to the extension of the habit of drinking wine on the part of the lower middle classes':[66] indeed, clearances of 'Spanish red' had risen by almost a third in two years. There was 'nothing pleasant' to say of sherry, the writer added, but by then there had been an increase in the consumption of sparkling hock and in the quality of wine imported direct from Germany. Meanwhile, on the other side of the trade – and the Wine and Spirit Association was soon to represent both – the consumption of home-made spirits was 'growing at a tremendous rate'.

[62] See also J.L. Denman, *The Vine and its Fruit, more especially in relation to the Production of Wine* (1864).
[63] Quoted in *ibid*.
[64] *Saunders' News Letter*, 16 December 1864.
[65] *The Wine Trade Review*, 15 January 1900. Cf. Simon, *Vintagewise*, p. 132: 'Whether a vintage wine at a guinea or twenty-five shillings per bottle, at any of the West End luxury hotels or restaurants, or a non-vintage Champagne, at from six to ten shillings a bottle, in Soho, the dancing bubbles in the glass helped all alike.'
[66] *The Wine Trade Review*, 15 January 1900.

By then, too, France clearly headed the league table of countries from which wines were imported, although 'owing to the habit of cigarette smoking and other curses the taste for fine clarets' appeared 'to have entirely vanished'.[67] The figure for 1913 showed five-yearly increases in imports both of French and Spanish wines, although there was a fall in the former as compared with 1911 and 1912, a further increase in the imports of sparkling hock, of Moselle and of Italian wines, and 'a steady advance in the position of port'.[68] Indeed, on the very eve of the First World War imports of port once more surpassed imports of wine from France:

	Imports of Port (Gallons)	Imports of French Wines (Gallons)
1911	3,201,592	3,460,000
1912	3,306,582	3,490,102
1913	3,623,061	3,062,399

TABLE 7 *Wine Imports, 1911–1913*

It must have seemed to old-fashioned Liberals – and there were still some of them left, like John Morley, Gladstone's biographer – that Gladstone was turning in his grave. They had other and graver reasons for their apprehension, however, for as the war clouds gathered over a heavily armed Europe, the kind of Europe which Gladstone had always feared might emerge, the wine trade was on the eve of a deeper disturbance that it had undergone for centuries. Then, and yet again between 1939 and 1945, war on an unprecedented scale – with unforeseen results – was to transform both economy and society.[69]

---

[67] *Ibid.*, 13 January 1909.
[68] *Ibid.*, 15 January 1914.

[69] See A. Marwick, *Britain in the Century of Total War* (1968).

CHAPTER FIVE

'The Conduct of a Great Enterprise'

1886-1921

In 1897, the year of Queen Victoria's Diamond Jubilee, when the only wars in which Britain had recently been engaged were 'little wars' on distant imperial frontiers, Victoria Wine produced a 'short account of a well-known business', written by Joseph Hatton, who described its progress in enthusiastic terms as 'quite American', while pointing out, correctly, that it had no American counterpart. Victoria Wine had shown, he declared, that a wine business need not be housed in a 'grim, mouldy, spider-webbed excavation'. Instead (and here there was more than a touch of rhetoric), it could mount 'storey upon storey to the sky'. Its owners organised their trade on 'floors' and believed in 'light and pure air and fresh ventilation'. There was nearly one acre and a half of floor space. 'In the four great storehouses of the firm [three at Osborn Street, with a fourth in John Street] . . . the most delicate of light wines, as well as the rarest Ports and Burgundies' were dealt with 'in a manner that appears to have secured the confidence not only of the public at large but of private buyers'. Indeed, its organisation expressed what was best in the general development of British business.

'Strolling over the establishment the other day,' Hatton went on, 'it was interesting to listen to the enthusiastic reminiscences of one of the managers of the business, who is still young enough to recall its beginnings and compare them with its present magnitude. . . . It may today be regarded as a remarkable instance of commercial evolution, from a traditionally circumscribed class of trade into a company that embraces every branch of the business of the wine merchant, and covers with equal efficiency the specialities of Wines, Spirits, Champagnes, Liqueurs, Beer and Cyder. This multiplication of departments [and they included carpentry and case-making as well as bottling] is a peculiarity of the progress of the age. It minimises labour, concentrates the operation of capital, and cheapens both the necessities and luxuries of life to the consumer.'

Hatton referred back not to the 1880 article in the *Pictorial World*[1], but to a series of articles on 'The Conduct of Great Businesses' in *Scribner's Magazine*, published in the United States. Yet there was something quintessentially British about Victoria Wine, he suggested: it reflected 'that power of organisation and discipline of forces that may be said to have made England the pioneer of international commerce and the mistress of an industrial Empire that is the glory of modern civilisation'. As the concern had grown, Hatton argued, it had exerted 'an elevating influence upon the employed, down to the humblest servant, for each man and boy may be said to have the highest office in the concern open to him. Most of the chiefs have risen from the ranks of the merest subordinates, and in some instances the heads of firms themselves have begun their careers on the lowest rung of the ladder.' Moreover, a high proportion of the staff had been with the firm for many years. 'I meet in every department a foreman who has seen not less than from fourteen to twenty years' service.'

There were at that time 330 weekly wage-earners on Victoria Wine's pay roll, and they were all extremely well treated. The manager at Osborn Street was more anxious, indeed, 'to talk about the duties of masters to men ... than the puncheons, butts and pipes of wine'. It was 'as good as finding a permanent home' to be employed by Victoria Wine. And during the dinner hour the reading room, which Hughes had provided, looked like a quiet little club. ('In fiction the taste of the readers is in favour of the standard authors, the neurotic novel has a small show, and books of travel, history, and science are in popular favour.')

Not many women were employed in the stores and cellars in Osborn Street and John Street, but without exception the 87 branches, both in town and country, were managed by ladies, 'a great compliment to the sex'. The Company found in its lady managers 'an honest, industrious, and reliable staff, thus affording an example of the successful employment of women in managerial positions where good business instincts and correct administration are indispensable'.

We have no surviving lists of managers – or of manageresses – although we do know that the manageresses wore black dresses and black aprons of the kind which Queen Victoria, still in mourning, would have

---

[1] See above, p. 50.

considered appropriate, and that they were not allowed to wear jewellery. We know also that Victoria Wine was itself controlled by a woman, for when William Winch Hughes died in 1886, it was not a subordinate but his widow, Emma Susan Durrant Hughes, who succeeded him. The family tradition was maintained.

Emma was the daughter of a ship's carpenter and the same age as her husband, and for a time she may have run a private school. She was also well used to managing a large household. In 1871, seventeen years before William's death, she had two servants to help her with the management of her house, then in Walthamstow, and when the Hugheses moved to The Dell the numbers were doubled. For seven years after William's death she managed the Victoria Wine business on her own. Indeed, she seems to have continued to manage it for some time on her own after she had re-married in 1893. Her second husband, William Russell, was a widower aged 62, and his address on his marriage lines was given as The Knoll, Darlington. He was an ironmonger and had known Hughes, and he had also been an Alderman on the local Council.[2] They were married at St Marylebone Parish Church, the same church where Mrs Hughes had married William, and after his new marriage, Russell moved from north to south and – the names are Betjamenesque – from The Knoll to The Dell, though they kept both houses. Emma was to survive her second husband also, although she was ill for the last two years of her life. Russell died early in 1901, leaving an estate worth £40,231 3s 5d: Emma lived on until 19 September 1911, leaving an estate valued at £156,679 11s 3d. There were then 96 Victoria Wine branches.

The three key figures in the business, who were responsible to Mrs Russell in the early years of the century, were William Law, John Henry Bishop and Frank Wood. It was Wood who was Mrs Russell's right hand man, and it was he who took Hatton round Osborn Street and John Street, warehouses which he managed. Law was a teetotaller, but an excellent wine taster. He was also a cripple, and after arriving at the office by brougham was wheeled into the building. Bishop worked on the financial side of the business – with Arthur Pease as cashier – and is said to have known little about wine. Every business has its folklore, and one surviving anecdote relates to both men. One day, Law asked Bishop if he

---

[2] There was no local obituary, but Russell seems to have endowed a William Russell Scholarship at Darlington Grammar School for boys who had entered the school from public elementary schools in Darlington. He was in business from 1848 to 1901 – at 22–24 Blackwell Gate – as plumber, brassfounder, brazier and tinplate dealer as well as ironmonger.

would taste some port and say what he thought of it. Having done so, he replied that it tasted like Tarragona. Law then gave him another port to taste which he judged very good but said that he could not recognise. Law then told him that the port which he liked but did not recognise was Tarragona and that the port which he thought was Tarragona was port. The story is recalled by Lewis Johnson, whose father, G.H. Johnson, joined the Company shortly before the death of Mrs Russell and who described to his son visits he made to The Dell to have tea with her when he was a boy. G.H. Johnson was later a Director of the Victoria Wine Company.

Lewis Johnson can also remember Frank Wood, who was manager of the warehouse, and has stories, also, of a fire in Osborn Street in 1908. Fire was one of the great hazards of early business, but on this occasion the fire brigade managed to put it out without too much difficulty, and the incident ended with a football match between the staff and the firemen – with a fireman's helmet as the ball. Folklore has it that after the fire a new whisky was introduced called Luckie Burn. In fact, it had appeared on Victoria Wine lists years before.

Whisky as a popular Edwardian drink figured prominently in the Victoria Wine price lists. One of the fullest of these goes back before that date to the year 1897, the year of Queen Victoria's Diamond Jubilee and of Hatton's visit, when Mrs Russell was in command and 8–10 Osborn Street was still the Head Office. By then, of the 87 Victoria Wine branches, 48 were in London and 40 outside, most of them, however, in the London suburbs. Of these, 14 were still Victoria Wine branches in 1980, the oldest 51 The Broadway, Wimbledon. The property had been let to Hughes by the ground lessee in 1879 at £70 per annum, and the lease was to be renewed by Emma Russell, said to be trading as *femme sole* in 1900.

By then, the Osborn Street Head Office had been further extended – and was later to be renumbered. Hatton noted how customers, about whom he had little to say, except that in a week there were 23,000 of them, were buying their wines and spirits in smaller quantities than formerly, and that this accounted in part for the success of Victoria Wine, which sold three million bottles of wines, spirits and beer in 1895. The customers 'live in flats, have less accommodation for storage, fewer servants, and have come to recognise the immense advantage of an institution, such as the Victoria Wine Company with its branches ... where the finest wines and spirits, of known brands or otherwise can be procured at once, and in any quantity from a bottle upwards. In the country also, householders who in the old days were accustomed to lay down wines and store spirits and beers in large quantities make the wine merchant's establishment their cellar.' What *The Wine Trade Review* saw as a problem Wood saw as an opportunity.

The Jubilee list, which was to be reprinted in the twentieth century,[3] was headed with two wines which would not have entered many such cellars – two so-called Spanish ports, one at 12s a dozen, the other at 15s – and it ended with sixteen Australian wines and four wines from California. Hatton, who was struck by the 'up to datism' of the stocks, picked out these items, especially the Australian wines, 'driven forward against untold difficulties'. Among them there were exotic names like 'Ophir' (26s per dozen bottles) and 'Muscat of Alexandria' (30s per dozen bottles). There were also 'Kangaroo Port' and 'Coomaroo Amber'. The Californian wines were more simply described – two 'reds' at 18s per dozen bottles, one white 'Chablis type' at 20s per dozen, and a Muscat at 30s per dozen. Victoria Wine's sale of Californian 'Big Tree' branded wines was something of a novelty, although British immigrant wine makers in the Sonoma Valley are said to 'have practically taken over the local wine business' during the 1880s.[4]

Clearly the tastes of Victoria Wine customers had not greatly changed. Hughes had told the 1879 Committee that they liked not only strong fortified wines in particular, but sweet wines too.[5] Among the 22 sherries in the 1896 list there were two very old brown sherries and several other heavy and sweet ones. There were also five other Spanish wines below 30° in proof, however, on which there had now been a reduction of duty. The most expensive sherry, an amontillado 'of the very finest quality procurable', cost 70s per dozen, while the cheapest light Spanish wine was a 'natural mantilla' at 16s per dozen. There were 27 ports, the cheapest at 18s per dozen, the most expensive at 70s per dozen. Among the ten clarets, three were described as Médocs (the cheapest at 64s per dozen), one as St Julien and one as Pauillac. There were now seven burgundies also – including two Beaunes, one Macon, one Savigny, one Volnay and two Chablis. In no case were the years of vintage given. There were seven 'House' champagnes (the cheapest at 32s per dozen), and no less than 23 branded champagnes, this time with vintage years given, the most expensive an 1889 Veuve Clicquot at 100s per dozen. The sparkle was there too in four hocks, four Moselles, one

---

[3] See below, p. 145.
[4] See 'Wines, Vines and Cooperation' in the *Pacific Wine and Spirit Review*, 31 December 1900, and W.F. Heintz, 'The British as Wine Pioneers' in *Wines and Vines*, May 1981.
[5] See above, p. 53.

Burgundy, two Saumurs and a number of often unspecified reds and whites. The taste for sparkle as well as for sweetness was to be strong in Edwardian times.

Spirits were prominent on the 1896 list. They included ten numbered brandies – the last at 85s per dozen 'quite a liqueur' – and five named brandies – Martell's (one, two, and three stars), the cheapest at 54s per dozen, the most expensive at 64s, Courvoisier's, Augier Frères', Gautier Frères' and Pellisson Père's. There was also a Spanish brandy – and among the whiskies a Welsh whisky which had won First Award at the Chicago World Exhibition of 1893. (It was to reappear in *The Times* ninety years later.)[6] There were now 14 branded blended whiskies but no single malts, and there were still seven rums, including one white. The nine liqueurs included green and yellow Chartreuse, Curaçao, Benedictine and Kümmel, and there were no fewer than six British liqueurs, including an old one, 'Shrub', at 2s 7d per bottle, and British Maraschino and Curaçao at 5s 2d.

The 'extras' still included tea, the cheapest 'a good useful tea' at 1s 4d per lb and the dearest a tea 'possessing remarkable strength and flavour' at 2s 10d per lb; and there were now several mineral waters (including Seltzer to go with the hock).There was no tonic to go with the gin, but Rose's Lime Juice had made its appearance on the list at 11d per bottle. The cordial cost 2d more. There was a concentrated squash, 'Zetril', at 1s per small bottle, which was said to be greatly preferable to lemon juice for mixing with spirits, 'as its flavour is much more acceptable'. There was a long list of bottled beers and ales, including Tottenham Lager Beer and Oakhill Invalid Stout, 'first brewed in 1767'.

This was the kind of wine list that seems to have persisted until 1914. Yet the width of its range – and, indeed, the apparent cheapness of many of the choice items in it – can be misleading. Within the range there was a heavy concentration on a limited number of lines – with port and spirits still prominent among them – while low prices must always be related both to taxation and to the pattern of incomes and of prices of other goods. Converting them into modern decimal currency, urban workers' weekly incomes averaged £1.45 in 1900, when the price of a bottle of whisky was 16p, but on upper incomes, income tax was still very low – a maximum of 3.75p in the pound. An average nine-course dinner for two at the Carlton Hotel cost £2.97½p in 1900, a packet of cigarettes 2½p for twenty, sugar 1p per lb, and butter 3½p per lb.When Seebohm Rowntree

---

[6] See below, p. 184.

collected statistics of poverty in York at the end of the nineteeth century he estimated that one-sixth of working class income on average was spent on 'drink': Charles Booth had given the London figure as a quarter.[7]

Although prices of beer, spirits and wine remained unchanged or little changed between then and 1914, many other prices rose and real wages fell. The kind of business handled by Victoria Wine does not seem to have changed much against this background, and, like other working-class and middle-class trade, it had an important seasonal element to it. Typical Christmas trade at East End branches like Poplar was mainly in the cheaper wines and spirits, so that a typical order – for 20s – would be a quart of Tarragona – that cost as little as 1s – a bottle of Stone's ginger wine at 1s per bottle (you could also buy Stone's orange, elder, raisin, and red or black currant) and one bottle of Invalid Port. By contrast, a store like Baker Street in the West End had a conspicuously superior trade, and there some of the biggest orders might come not at Christmas but during the London season. The contrasts of society, already picturesque, were heightened rather than reduced during the years from 1900 to 1914, and the only major change in Victoria Wine was in its direction.

There was an additional item on the Victoria Wine list, however, introduced in 1911, the year of Mrs Russell's death and the Coronation Year of George V. One day in 1911, Everardus Houweling, a Dutchman, is said to have walked into Osborn Street and offered Victoria Wine the sole agency of a 'luxurious, yet at the same time, nourishing' liqueur, hitherto unknown in England, made from yolk of eggs and brandy, flavoured with sugar and vanilla. Victoria Wine decided to give the drink a trial, and as a result became sole agent for Warninck's Advocaat. It was to become the best-selling liqueur in the British Isles.[8]

By Mrs Russell's will, the stock at the Victoria Wine warehouses in Osborn Street, Whitechapel and at her retail shops – and also the leases of the shops – were to be left to John Henry Wright Bishop, William Law, William Rolfe Hill and Frank Wood, although Bishop's name was struck out when he left the business, Arthur Pease's was added, and William Law's was removed on his death. If three or any of the men whose names were listed accepted this bequest, they were also to be given the opportunity of taking over on underlease or lease the warehouse and premises of Victoria Wine at Berners Street, Commercial Road. The

---

[7] B.S. Rowntree, *Poverty* (1901), p. 143; C. Booth, *Life and Labour of the People of London* (1902–4), p. 70.

[8] See 'Advocaat: A Few Notes about a Notable Liqueur' in *The Wine and Spirit Trade Record*, 11 October 1924.

of £1,000 was left also to be divided between the Victoria Wine manageresses, and all male employees were to be paid an extra month's wages. The residue of the estate was to go to Frank Wood, subject to the purchase of certain items for his wife Helen Alice Wood, née Teasdel, – and, after her mother's death, Emma's ward – and various annuities for servants.

Wood, a key figure in the history of Victoria Wine, had worked with the firm from the mid-1870s, when he was in his early twenties. In a sense, he had even married into the family, for he met Helen at The Dell when she was living there as a young ward, and he was on familiar terms both with Hughes and his wife. He had become sole manager of Victoria Wine – under Mrs Russell – in 1905 – and now in 1911 he carried on a kind of family tradition when, as a result of Mrs Russell's will, he became sole proprietor. He immediately bought out William Rolfe Hill and Arthur Pease – it is said for about £20,000 each – and acquired complete control of the firm. Although both Hill and Pease stayed on as employees, Hill managing the manageresses and Pease dealing with cash, still the basis of all the business, Wood was the man to whom they were accountable. Clearly he had the instincts of a businessman, but, equally important, given the nature of the business, he was a fine – and experienced – judge of wines, particularly of champagne. On one occasion, a story runs, he took six bottles of unlabelled champagne and identified each one. To test him, his colleagues then mixed two bottles and found that he could tell not only which were the mixed bottles but what were the contents of the mix. There are many such anecdotes in the wine trade, but this one rings as true as any.

Wood survived Mrs Russell by ten years, and after a life-time in the business, died in the village of Holmbury St Mary in Surrey in March 1921. His wife Helen lived on until August 1946. Their one son was called Frank *Russell* Wood, who died in 1974, and their one daughter, also named Helen Teasdel, who married Joseph King, is the one surviving link with the very early history of Victoria Wine.

Before he died, Wood made one important shift in business policy and one other important institutional change. The biggest shift in policy – and one followed by the most successful of the other chain store founders – was to buy urban properties, rather than lease them, and to look not just for convenient premises but for properties in good locations with a long-term future. And this was the policy he followed when in 1912 he bought at an auction 51 The Broadway, Wimbledon, which Emma Russell had leased for 21 years at £90 per annum in 1900, and for which he paid £2,150. The location was described as 'one of the choicest and most flourishing districts of London'. Yet leases continued to be secured: one of the most interesting of them, 136 North End, Croydon, was acquired three years later from John James Sainsbury whose retail business was rapidly expanding.

Wood's institutional change, like his property changes, looked to the long-term future. In 1920 he turned Victoria Wine into a private limited company, 27 years after Gilbey's had taken this crucial step. The profits of the business then – only the second year for which we can identify the figure – were £93,494 (they had been £58,151 in 1919). Most nineteenth-century businesses, including Sainsbury's, had been founded on economic individualism. An energetic individual had pioneered a business as William Winch Hughes had done. Most twentieth-century business was to rest on a corporate base, although there could often be an awkward hiatus – sometimes something worse – between the family business and the private or public company while an heir, uninterested in the business or incapable of conducting it efficiently, got deeper and deeper into trouble. Since William Winch Hughes left no male heir, it was Frank Wood who not only presided over a successful transition, but who set the terms for future development in a corporate age.

Meanwhile, the history of other independent businesses which were eventually to form part of the Victoria Wine cluster were unfolding in parts of the country far from the Wood empire. Most of their records are unfortunately lost so that even the outline of their chronologies is difficult to establish. Yet a few advertisements survive, some giving the location of branches.

E.A. Mitchell, the first group to be merged with Victoria Wine – in 1943 – were of recent foundation: it was in Edwardian times that Ellen Anne Mitchell opened her first shop in Bristol. Also in Bristol, the firm of J.R. Phillips had eighteenth-century origins; and as early as 1808 James George took his accountant, J.R. Phillips, into partnership (with an initial stock of 4,578 gallons of brandy, 4,463 gallons of rum, and 53 hundredweight of new Kent hops). Phillips', whose lime juice was as famous as their rum, had become a limited liability company in 1889 (with a capital of £80,000), four years before Gilbey's. Yet it was a company with a difference. Augustus Phillips, nicknamed 'the Despot', had laid it down in the Articles of Association that 'all the other Directors (if any) for the time being of the Company shall be under his control and shall be bound to conform to his directions in regard to the Company's business'. He could not do without a Company Secretary, however, and the first Secretary, John Heming, remained in the post for 57 years until 1924.

Nearer to the cluster of Victoria Wine shops was Tyler and Company, incorporated in 1908, which had started business six years earlier with a shop in Woking. They had six shops in the area in 1921, when they also acquired a grocer's shop. The Company Minutes survive, and they describe Tyler's relationship with Friary Holroyd and Healey's Breweries through which, for example, in 1910 they had leased The Plough and The Cricketers' Inns and an off-licence at Knapp Hole.[9]

In the north, William Glendenning had opened a store at Newcastle 'for the sale of wines, spirits and teas' in 1867, two years after William Winch Hughes had started Victoria Wine. 'For Cash I shall buy, and for Cash I shall sell' was his motto, along with 'honest goods at an honest price'.[10] A 1902 price list of Glendenning's survives. It refers not only to retail items – by then monthly accounts were accepted – but to bottling, and includes three malt whiskies ('single or straight' Scotch) and nineteen mixed blends, the cheapest at 24s per dozen, the most expensive at 40s.

Also in the north of England, Beverley's, who were to provide the basis of Victoria Wine's post-Second World War Northern Division,[11] had started business in 1872 as a firm of wholesale tea and coffee dealers as well as wine and spirit merchants. With the name Black and Green they had been incorporated in 1899. This name was changed on more than one occasion – Sugar Bowl was the most evocative other name which was adopted – before Beverley's was registered as a company in 1924. The scope of the business changed even more than the name, however, for at one time it included the manufacture both of chocolate (which in Quaker hands eschewed the drink trade) and of margarine (which in William Lever's hands was associated not with alcohol but with soap).

Of all this (to him) distant world of wine-retailing Frank Wood was ignorant, although he would have understood the language of the advertisements of his contemporaries and the messages which accompanied them. In particular, perhaps, he would have warmed to the words of the Glendenning catalogue for 1902 – and by then Glendenning had a London branch at 67 Shaftesbury Avenue:

> We do not wish to see customers overstock themselves, but we can deliberately assert that a great deal more money is lost by understat-

---

[9] Tyler and Company, *Minutes*, January 1910.

[10] Printed Statement of July 1867.
[11] See below, p. 137.

ing one's requirements than by over-stocking. Wines and spirits do not spoil by keeping, but business lost is profit lost, and may mean the loss of a good customer through disappointment.

CHAPTER SIX

Wine in War and Peace 1914-1945

For four years of his controlling ownership of Victoria Wine, Frank Wood was operating in the most difficult conditions. The First World War destroyed the continuity of the European wine trade far more than the Napoleonic wars had done. It also brought with it taxation at an unprecedented level, particularly on beer and spirits. The effect was to reshape British drinking habits far more drastically than any nineteenth-century legislation.

Yet the year 1914 began with a 'tendency to optimism',[1] and although there was a decline in imports and clearances of wine in January, exports of British and Irish spirits were up and beer consumption was reported high. The value of brewery shares had fallen during the previous decade, when there was 'a feeling in the industry that the heady days of mid-Victorian expansion were over',[2] but it rose in 1913 in a year when, as *The Wine Trade Review* noted, 'the wine and spirits departments of their business' were 'of great importance.'[3] In the light of what was to happen later in the year, it is interesting that imports of German wine were up $4\frac{1}{2}$ per cent in February, as compared with the previous year, and that French imports were 9 per cent down.[4] Moreover, exports of British and Irish spirits to Germany rose in the same month to 75,288 gallons, as compared with only 12,492 gallons in February 1913. And there was extra good news for 'the trade' when the House of Commons, which still included an exceptionally large number of teetotallers, threw out a bill to prohibit the sale of liquor on Sundays by 198 votes to 179.

---

[1] *The Wine Trade Review*, 15 January 1914.
[2] R.G. Wilson, *op. cit.*, p. 130. There was a decline of almost 12 per cent in output in 1905 as compared with the golden year 1900.

[3] *The Wine Trade Review*, 15 January 1914. See also *ibid.*, 15 February 1914.
[4] *Loc. cit.*, 15 March 1914.

The prices of the leading brands of champagne all rose, but five months before the War the higher prices were said to be readily paid, 'retailers having no difficulty in making a good profit by the enhanced prices their customers are willing to pay, knowing they must pay or go without'.[5] There was something of a falling-off in consumption, however, in June and July. Meanwhile, a commercial treaty with Portugal protected the hallowed word 'port' both in the country of production and in the country of consumption.

On a glorious summer's day, 4 August, war was declared in a mood of popular enthusiasm which it is difficult to recapture. And although the leader in the August number of *The Wine Trade Review* began with the words 'may the war be speedily over', its writer had no intimation of either the duration – or the slaughter. He quoted the remarkable prediction of Sir Alfred Mond that in a relatively short time British trade would actually increase, but he had the sense to put Mond's words into somewhat incredulous italics, and he went on in quite different – and supremely practical – vein to describe the 'shock' felt by the wine trade when an order had been issued under the Defence of the Realm Act, immediately after war was declared prohibiting the export of wines, spirits and beers. A military seal had been placed on all stocks in bond, and a number of ships already loaded with wines and spirits had been unloaded of their precious cargoes. Yet the order had been withdrawn three days later, when wines, spirits and beers were classified as foodstuffs and the trade could breathe again; and in the spirit of Mond, it was emphasised that the order had been designed not to restrict international trade, but to enforce national sobriety. It was intended, it was argued, 'to keep the men of the various forces sober during mobilisation'.[6]

In looking across the Channel there seemed to be grounds for optimism too. 'As regards the French wine trade in general, the effects of the war will not be disastrous so far as can be seen at present. It is even possible that it may have a favourable influence ... since from the point of view of the merchant the 1914 vintage will have the additional prestige of the "war year".' In fact, the prospects of the vintage were good, stocks were high, and Nature, if not Man, seemed kind: 'insects and pests were present, but in fewer numbers than usual'. The *Review* quoted an appropriate prophecy from the Sologne, already current in 1793. 'When men fly like birds, ten great kings will go to war against each other. The

---

[5] *Loc. cit.*, 15 April 1914.
[6] *Loc. cit.*, 15 August 1914.

nations will be under arms. The women will bring in the harvest. They will begin the vintage, but the men will complete it.'[7]

There was little sign, therefore, during the 'strenuous days' of this first war-time month, of the economic, political and psychological dislocations which were to come, when it could be noted with curiosity rather than with alarm that horses were being requisitioned and 'labourers were enlisting'. It was anticipated, too, that the price of barley after the harvest would be up 50 to 60 per cent on the previous year and that all 'cargoes would have to run the gauntlet of war risks'. 'So suddenly has this great war cloud burst, so unforeseen was it,' the *Review* concluded cautiously, 'that no trade has yet had time to adjust itself to the new conditions, and although panic effects are settling down, the more permanent effects cannot yet be rightly appreciated.'[8]

At the very end of the month of August, however, an important new Intoxicating Liquor (Temporary Restriction) Act was passed which remained in force until one month after the end of the War: it authorised the Chief Officer of Police in any licensing district or the licensing Justices for any licensing district, acting upon the recommendation of the Chief Officer of Police, to impose such restriction on the hours of sale of alcohol as 'might seem desirable' for the maintenance of order or the suppression of drunkenness. In many parts of the country very different opening and closing times were subsequently stipulated from those to which people had been accustomed before the War – with far reaching social consequences. Thus, in London, the introduction in October 1914 of an eleven o'clock closing time was said to have led to 'a transformation of the night scenes of the metropolis'.[9]

Lloyd George wanted to go much further. 'We are fighting Germany, Austria and Drink,' he said in a speech of March 1915, 'and ... the greatest of these deadly foes is Drink.'[10] And he included under the heading 'Drink' drinking at home as well as drinking in pubs, bars or night clubs. The Central Control Board (Liquor Traffic) of June 1915 followed. More important than control, however, or voluntary abstinence – with King George V seeking to lead the way in April 1915 – was diminished alcoholic strength and an increase in the price of beer and spirits. Following the first war-time budget the price of beer went up from

---

[7] *Loc. cit.*, 15 August 1914.
[8] *Ibid.*
[9] Quoted in A. Marwick, *The Deluge* (1965), p. 64.
[10] Quoted in *ibid.*, p. 65. See also F.A.

King, *Beer has a History* (1947), p. 55, for a Lloyd George speech at Bangor, 'Drink is doing us more damage than all the German submarines put together.'

3d to 4d a pint: by 1916, in a land of localised shortages, it could cost 10d in some areas; and the Government was forced to introduce price control of beer in October 1917 at 4d and 5d a pint. Meanwhile, its strength had declined (the national acreage under hops was reduced by more than a half in 1916), as had the strength of spirits from 1915 (a maximum strength of 70 degrees proof). In 1918 a bottle of whisky, which had cost four shillings in 1914, cost double that amount.[11]

As supplies fell, customers for beer, spirits – and wine – faced unprecedented privations 'in the national interest'. Already, indeed, by the end of 1914 *The Wine Trade Review* was painting a very different picture of the state of the wine trade from that which it had painted during the previous summer:

> The financial, transport and service conditions in France are very difficult to deal with, and are naturally staying the forwarding of stocks. Practically all the most effective members of staffs are with the colours, the transport services are deployed almost entirely for military purposes; transport by road is difficult, slow and expensive; money for ordinary purposes of trade is comparatively little in circulation. All this is having a marked effect upon London business, and it is perhaps as well, under the circumstances, that while the orders that cover Christmas parcels are not materially less in numbers than last year, they are for much smaller quantities.[12]

The wine-growing area in France which had suffered most then – and was to suffer most throughout the War – was the Champagne district, bombarded for months by the Germans. Many people in Rheims were living in the wine cellars, yet the vintage had been admirable, and the wine stocks were undepleted. Less champagne had been cleared to Britain, however, and more Saumur, from a district far from the trenches ('Fancy the clearances of Saumur reaching half the total of champagne clearances in any month!' the *Review* declared).

Meanwhile, whatever the Government might say or do about beer or spirits, port consumption had reached a three-year peak. Clearances for home consumption in November 1914 had been 383,690 gallons: the comparable figure for the previous two years were 309,625 and 359,132 gallons. (And the Anglo-Portuguese Commercial Treaty of 1914 was

---

[11] See A. Shadwell, *Drink in 1914–1922, A Lesson in Control* (1923).
[12] *The Wine Trade Review*, 5 December 1918.

further strengthened in 1916, establishing for the first time a definition of what port wine was.[13])

All in all, at the end of November, the total bonded stocks both of wines and spirits were higher than they had been in 1913 – 4,912,000 gallons of wine as compared with 4,751,000 gallons, and 146,966,000 gallons of home-made spirits as compared with 143,922,000 gallons. For the time being, at least, in war as in peace, therefore, the reserves of spirits seemed big enough to sustain a sense of insular security. Yet consumption had gone up also from 616,239 gallons in November 1913 to 670,097 gallons in November 1914.[14] And soon higher spirits prices were to push drinkers further towards port.

In January 1915 a kind of balance sheet was drawn up by *The Wine Trade Review*, setting out 'specific adverse factors affecting the trade' and 'encouraging signs for the future'. Among the former were early closing rules, the stopping of the banqueting season and the reduction in the number of public festivities. Among the latter were 'increased entertaining in the home, which is much to the advantage of the wine merchant though prejudicial to the caterer'. The position deteriorated further in 1916, yet port consumption reached a higher figure than that for 1913; and the consumption of 'British wines', a mixed group, mainly of low quality, had risen steadily to surpass the 1913 figure in 1916, 1917 and 1918.

In 1917 there were new hazards for the wine trade as restrictions were placed both on imports and on duty payments for wines already in bond, with the result that landlords of public houses and owners of retail bars were forced to use up larger quantities of duty-paid wines, including those of the very best vintage; and in 1918, when the stocks of duty-paid wines were largely exhausted, there was a serious shortage. Throughout the war, however, *The Wine Trade Review* remained cheerful. 'The growing appreciation of the value of wines to the gallant armies of the Allies,' it noted in September 1918 on the eve of victory, 'is of first importance ... What follows cannot fail to materially improve the wine trade conditions when the happy days of peace return to us. We anticipate that as the British people like the best of things the greater attention which is being directed to wines will lead to the more general cultivation of a taste for wines and a judgement of their merits.'[15]

---

[13] Cockburn, *op. cit.*, p. 44.
[14] *Ibid.*
[15] *Ibid*, 15 September 1918.

If there was more than a touch of consoling rhetoric in this judgement, there was a note of realism in a further terse comment that 'the great thing needed is a larger shipment of wines to this country'. The consumer, however, was having to pay more for his wines as well as for his beer and spirits. A pint of port, which had cost 1.95s in 1914 cost 3.80s in 1918, and a pint of sparkling wine, which had cost 7.70s, cost 11.64s. It was of small consolation to connoisseurs that the price of a pint of British wine had increased relatively even more.

The higher prices did not deter wine drinkers, and when war controls were lifted in 1919 imports and consumption rose dramatically, as the following table shows:

Imports retained for Home Consumption: Total	1913	1914	1915	1916	1917	1918	1919
Quantity (000 gall)	11,367	10,630	10,175	9,910	7,099	11,317	19,174
Expenditure £m	9.14	8.48	7.82	8.09	7.01	17.64	39.22
Port Quantity (000 gall)	3,181	3,452	3,656	4,264	3,301	4,946	9,307
Expenditure £m	2.32	2.69	2.89	3.42	3.02	7.52	18.12
Price (s per pt)	1.83	1.95	1.98	2.00	2.29	3.80	4.69
Other Still Quantity (000 gall)	7,221	6,266	5,895	5,005	3,342	5,588	8,369
Expenditure £m	3.42	3.06	3.01	2.67	2.32	6.47	10.86
Price (s per pt)	1.22	1.22	1.28	1.33	1.74	2.90	3.25
Sparkling Quantity (000 gall)	1,165	912	624	641	456	783	1,498
Expenditure £m	3.40	2.73	1.92	2.00	1.67	3.45	10.24
Price (s per pt)	7.30	7.50	7.70	7.81	9.17	11.64	17.10
British Quantity (000 gall)	996	956	996	1,126	1,255	1,385	1,574
Expenditure £m	0.10	0.1C	0.10	0.11	0.16	0.32	0.44
Price (s per pt)	.25	.25	.25	.25	.33	.57	.73

TABLE 8 *Wine Prices and Consumption, 1913–1915*

95

Whatever the attitudes to drink of the Prime Minister or of *The Spectator*, which urged total prohibition, the Exchequer was the chief beneficiary of the war-time pattern of drinking. There was a total cessation of distilling of whisky in 1917 – an action which weakened independent whisky firms, and strengthened the case for amalgamation[16] – and by 1918 the consumption of spirits, British and imported, which had surpassed 34 million gallons in 1915, had fallen to less than 15 million gallons, while beer output had been several times reduced – to save shipping space for food and to release land from barley – and consumption (whatever the quality) had fallen from 34 million barrels in 1914 to less than 13 million barrels in 1918. Meanwhile, the consumption of foreign wines had fallen from just over 10 million gallons (.22 gallons per head) in 1915 to just over 6½ million gallons in 1918. The expenditure figures looked quite different, of course:

	Beer	*Spirits*	*Wine*
1913	115	49	9
1914	129	49	9
1915	116	54	8
1916	140	58	8
1917	117	76	7
1918	131	80	18
1919	233	117	40

TABLE 9 *Expenditure on Alcoholic Beverages 1913 to 1919* (£ million)

The Wine Trade Review, while in general optimistic, ventured to comment at some length in an article on 'Wine in War Time' on the old sharp contrast between France and Britain:

The French government attach such value to the use of wine that they allow any of their cruisers, mine-sweepers, or any other vessels calling at Oporto, to carry any wine cargo they can to France.
The British government, quite rightly, do all they can to prevent wine from the Spanish Peninsula from going through neutral countries into Germany (where it is much wanted), yet at the same

---

[16] D. Daiches, *Scotch Whisky* (1969), p. 105.

time they are preventing the British public from making all the use they wish to make of so valuable a commodity, by restrictions on importation, and on payment of duty on wine already in the country.

It should be borne in mind that something like seventy-five per cent of wine imported into this country is used by the industrial classes.[17]

The last sentence stands out more boldly within this context that any such statement might have done – and few were so made – before 1914. So too, however, did a few sentences in the *The Wine and Trade Review* commentary:

Food is the great want. Wine is food. It is of the utmost importance to get wine to the country, and when it is here, to place it at the disposal of the people. It is not the rich people of the country today who are drinking wine for their pleasure. They have almost ceased to do so. The wines are needed for the war workers of the country, and all the wines that are in the country and that may reach the country should be at once released from bond, for the good of the community.

There was no suggestion in these forthright sentences that wine was a luxury. And when, without giving figures, the writer then went on to point to the alarming increase during the War in the price of a glass of port as stocks had been used up, he insisted also that at least 80 per cent of the port consumed in the country was consumed by 'the industrial classes'. Most of the consumers would doubtless have subscribed to his argument that since wines were produced not from cereals, of which there was a world shortage, but from 'vines which are grown for the most part where other crops cannot be grown', the only factor which should restrict their import was the availability of shipping. On the home front there was optimism, too, in the brewing industry. For all the reduction of beer output, the pre-war losses of the breweries were turned into handsome profits as receipts rose more rapidly than costs. It was the big breweries which benefited most, however, and the way was thus prepared for the amalgamations of later years.[18]

When the war was over, the final business judgement was that the wine trade, like the brewing industry, had passed through 'the terrible and prolonged war period with greater ease than any in the trade anticipated'. The demand for wine had been consistently greater than the supply, and it was recognised that as shipping conditions improved

---

[17] *The Wine Trade Review*, 5 April 1918.
[18] See Vaizey, *op. cit.*, pp. 24–5.

the supply position in the future would be bound to ease. The only real problem would be if growers sent wines direct to Britain for direct sale as some of them had been doing during the war. 'It was in their best interests', *The Wine Trade Review* argued in December 1918, 'that all wines should be shipped by known firms and agents who alone by their knowledge and experience are able to judge the fitness of the wine for the particular market'.[19]

The inter-war years did not for long generate the same kind of optimism as had been common in 1918.[20] The post-war boom, characterised by heavy drinking, soon came to an end and by 1925 wine consumption, total and per head, was down on the 1920 figures, when imperial preference was at last granted to wines from the Colonies and Dominions. Beer consumption was down also:

	1920	*1925*
Wine: Gallons Per head	19,933,932 .42	15,653,703 .34
Beer: Standard Barrels Per head	24,756,783 18.8	21,952,443 17.3
Spirits (British): Proof gallons Per head	17,825,871 .39	12,287,035 .27
Spirits (Foreign): Proof gallons Per head	6,441,681 .14	2,213,547 .04

TABLE 10 *Consumption of Wine, Beer and Spirits, 1920 and 1925*

These falls took place before the depression of the late 1920s and early 1930s and were commented upon by the Royal Commission on Licensing of 1929 to 1931, chaired by Lord Amulree, which referred to 'a distinct advance in sobriety' with the change 'particularly noticeable among the younger people'.[21] The Commission had little to say about wine, but considered at length the conditions in hotels and restaurants where it was drunk. There were no obvious Gladstonian vistas. The most

[19] *Ibid*, 15 December 1918.
[20] It is difficult to disagree with Laffer's statement (*op. cit.*, p. 120) that 'after the 1914–18 experience of so many soldiers in France, it is rather remarkable that the habit of wine drinking did not become more general'. 'The explanation is probably to be found', he suggested, 'in the difference of price between wines consumed in France and in Britain, the great difference being a matter of import duties'.
[21] *Report of the Royal Commission on Licensing, 1929–31*. p. 8.

contentious issues the Commission faced related to clubs, which had increased in numbers from 6,554 in 1905 to 13,526 in 1930.

The year 1928, just before the American crash, while a year of 'satisfactory vintage', did not live up to business expectations. Following a new system of taxation based on revised grading of strength, consumption of wines declined by 3½ million gallons, of which 450,000 gallons were French wines. Italy had been the only country in Europe to increase its share of British consumption in 1927, largely because the Italians were able to escape the higher wine duties and to export to Britain a large quantity at the new critical strengths of 24 and 35 degrees. There had also been a heavy fall in Australian imports, traceable simply, in this case at least, to over-consignments in 1927. The only consolation, looking back in January 1929, was that there had been a million-gallon increase in exports of whisky.[22]

Given the power to look forward in that year, there would have been further gloom about the future, although wine consumption increased in 1930 to 18,219,700 gallons; and in 1939, after the worst years of the depression were over, it stood even higher at 18,304,531 gallons, and that at a time when beer consumption was significantly lower than in 1930 and when the consumption both of British and foreign and colonial spirits was down too. The 'beer trend' was much commented upon during the 1930s; so, too, was the trend towards further amalgamations of breweries. And despite a publicised movement to improve public houses, the consumption of beer in 1935 was as low as 12.8 standard gallons per head as compared with 27.5 in 1914. *The New Survey of London Life and Labour*, the last volume of which was published in 1935, stressed that 'the outstanding difference between London then and London in the days of Charles Booth was the decrease in the amount of drinking per head, as distinct from the amount spent on drink, and the decreased extent to which actual excess, and the economic and physical effects of excess, are found'. Concentrating on the 'problem' aspects of drinking, it concluded that 'the social status of drunkenness had steadily fallen in the eyes of the working-class population'. 'Where once frequent drunkenness was half admired as a sign of virility, it was now regarded as, on the whole, rather squalid and ridiculous.'[23]

Beer might still be thought of as *the* national drink, so that Mass-Observation's magnificent survey of industrial Bolton, 'Worktown',

---

[22] *The Wine Trade Review*, 4 January 1929.
[23] Quoted in Marwick, *op. cit.*, p. 305. See also C.L. Mowat, *Between the Wars, 1918–1940* (1955), p. 250.

published during the Second World War but based on pre-war data, could begin its chapter on 'Drink' with the sentence that 'For almost everyone in Worktown Drink equals Beer'. Nonetheless, there were more inns and beerhouses in Bolton in the middle years of the nineteenth century, when the city was far smaller, than there were in 1936, when the detailed evidence was collected; and the Mass-Observers maintained that 'the pub, like the church and the chapel, played a smaller part in the life of Bolton than it ever had done'.[24] Only the registered club had gained in influence.

Spirits consumption per head was dramatically down also in the 1930s. The consumption per head of British spirits was .18 gallons in 1935 as against .58 proof gallons in 1913 and of foreign and colonial spirits .03 proof gallons as against .10 gallons. Not even the cocktail habit, popular though it was as a theme of London gossip writers,[25] significantly changed the trend in spirits consumption. Whatever the fashions of London's West End, in Bolton four out of seven pubs did not sell spirits in 1936. Indeed, spirits as medicine remained more acceptable in the North than spirits as 'drink', although at holiday times a place like Blackpool, where Mass-Observers saw two women at the bar ordering whisky (and more women Advocaat), broke routine drinking habits.[26] Turning to wine, there was at least one inhabitant of Bolton whose family had 'sherries all round' before Sunday dinner, 'Sauterne during the meal', and for the 'old man' five 'goes' of port. 'Old man has whisky shortly afterwards', the Mass-Observer reported, 'goes up to bed at 10.30 taking the whisky decanter with him, speaks of having a "posset".'[27]

For all the signs of reduction of 'drinking', Bolton was still a place, doubtless a not uncharacteristic place, where wine as well as beer could find a real, if strictly limited, place in local urban society. And it certainly retained a place in smaller towns and in rural society, where wine remained an element in the social scene – and that not only at hunt balls.[28] A series of interesting articles in *The Field*, printed in 1931 and reprinted in 1937, included 'The Heritage of Burgundy' – there was probably more interest in Burgundy than there ever had been before – , 'A Briton's Wine, Port and its Old Associations', 'Testing a Fine Brandy', and a 'Claret Catechism'.[29] Port figured prominantly in a 1933 guide to

---

[24] Mass-Observation, *The Pub and The People* (1970 edn.), p. 26, p. 74.

[25] And of novelists then and later. See the beginning of Angus Wilson's *For Whom the Clock Tolls* (1953): 'Came back from poor Maisie's funeral tired and depressed, but felt much better after Harold had insisted on mixing me a cocktail.'

[26] *The Pub and The People*, p. 51.

[27] *Ibid*, p. 47.

[28] For a small town, Tewkesbury, see John Moore, *Portrait of Elmbury* (1946), Part III.

[29] *The Field*, 26 September 1931, 11 December 1937.

good manners, *The Pleasure of Your Company*, where hostesses were told wisely that 'whatever sort of drink you provide, let no glass long remain empty'. 'At dinner-parties on a more familiar scale a dry white wine, sparkling or otherwise, will take one right through to dessert, when port – and fine port too – becomes more or less indispensable.' Only Madeira was a possible alternative. The authors also told their waiters that 'the empty wine bottle from which an interesting wine has been decanted may be very properly and pleasurably put on the table so that those who are enjoying the contents can know something of its history, as presented on the label'. The book gave a list of vintage years, too, adding equally wisely that 'a wine will not necessarily be good because it belongs to a vintage year, nor bad because its year was in general a failure. Such a list merely indicates the probabilities'.[30]

Britain was never seriously drawn to prohibition at a time when the United States made it the basis of national policy, following the Hobson amendment to the Constitution which went into effect in 1920.[31] Nor did the actual experience of the American 'experiment' seem worthy of imitation.[32] It proved extremely difficult to implement the prohibition policy throughout the American continent, and its implications for the balance of wine and spirit drinking were not foreseen. Until the policy was changed in 1933, its main effects were to encourage illicit stilling, to keep the United States out of the market for European wines, and to prevent the export of American wines to Britain and other parts of Europe.

Meanwhile, the French had problems enough of their own. There were some superb vintage years for claret – during the 1920s, there were only two really bad years, 1922 and 1927, out of the ten,[33] – and the vintage in 1929, the year of the American crash, was said to be the best since 1900.[34] Yet the overall export statistics spoke for themselves (see Table 11 overleaf). Britain, which took 9.9 per cent of the exports in 1913, was still taking 8.9 per cent in 1938, but the volume was down from 3,625,000 gallons to 2,019,600 gallons.[35]

---

[30] June and Doris Langley Moore's textbook of hospitality, *The Pleasure of Your Company* (1936 edn.), p. 60, p. 62.
[31] See E.H. Cherrington, *The Evolution of Prohibition in the United States* (1920); D. Leigh Colvin, *Prohibition in the United States* (1926); C. Mertz, *The Dry Decade* (1931). For a recent assessment, see A. Sinclair, *Prohibition, The Era of Excess* (1962).
[32] Shadwell, *op. cit.*, was a strong believer in temperance, but he wrote in 1923 that 'when

drinking by legalised channels is made too difficult, recourse is had to illegal ones, and the practice tends to spread with disastrous effects'. (p. 150).
[33] See *inter alia* A. Simon, *Vintagewise* (1946), p. 95. In 1922 the St Emilion was good.
[34] The best vintage years for burgundies during the 1920s were 1923, 1926 and 1929 and for hocks 1921, 1925 and 1929.
[35] *Ibid.*, pp. 102–3.

	1913	*1938*
Clarets and Bordeaux Wines	12,903,000	6,978,400
Other French Wines	16,077,600	11,044,000
Total Exports	28,980,600	18,022,400

TABLE 11 *Exports of Still and Unfortified Wines from France (gallons), 1913 and 1938*

In such circumstances, the writer of a Second World War article in *The Field* on 'The Outlook for Empire Wines', recalling the experience of the 1930s, drew the old comparison between France and England (and Australia). 'Every Frenchman has knowledge of wine and feeling for it.' Englishmen and Australians did not. Despite the fall in beer consumption, which he did not mention, he drew a familiar conclusion. 'Let us face the facts. The people of these islands are largely beer-drinking and almost universally tea-drinking. ... Alike for gentle and simple, bread and wine in France are the prime necessities. With us wine is the concern only of a minority.'[36]

Amongst wines drunk in Britain between 1918 and 1939, only the share of sherry increased steadily. There was a slump in the shipment of vintage port during the 1930s following over-selling in the late 1920s, and port consumption, like that of champagne, seems to have been hard hit by the depression.[37] 'Many rich men not only gave up buying wine but offered the content of their cellars for sale by auction.' The champagne figures were particularly striking during the worst years of the depression:

1930	3,344,098
1931	2,491,748
1932	1,684,056

TABLE 12 *Imports into Britain of Bottles of Champagne, 1930–32*

---

[36] S.G., 'The Outlook for Empire Wines' in *The Field*, 13 September 1943. See also 'Wine Production in South Africa' in *ibid.*, 23 April 1932.

[37] The 1927 vintage proved to be 'one of the greatest', though it had been thought that the port would lack staying power. The 1931 was a good year.

During the same period, the increasing demand for sherry was steady, if unspectacular. Before the cocktail party, which in the opinion of John Harvey IV ruined 'the finer perceptions of the palate',[38] came the sherry party; and in the background – as powerful business forces – were the Sherry Shippers' Association in London and (after 1931) the Sindicato Oficiel de Criadores Exportadores de Vinos in Jerez.[39] Nonetheless, in 1939 *The Wine and Spirit Trade Review* – the word 'spirit, was introduced into its title in 1938, when the magazine acquired a new format – was printing an article with the title 'Dice loaded against great wines: Protection vital to the Sherry Trade'. Turning for an example to the Milk Marketing Board – at first sight an unlikely parallel – it demanded a legal definition of the word 'wine'. 'In 1939 let us wish for – and, what is more, let us work for – better protection for the Wine Trade through adequate legislation.'[40]

Other wishes – and fears – were to be realised in 1939, a year when Sir William Crawford predicted 'the greatest trade boom the world had ever known'.[41] *The Wine and Spirit Review* more modestly presented details of a 'valuable symposium of opinion' on 'what is the best thing that can happen to this trade in 1939'. 'To promote trade,' it was rightly insisted, 'we need some return of confidence in our living conditions.' Yet there was a lack of realism in one wine dealer's demand for 'much less war talk', not echoed by the rest. One dealer paid special attention to 'the public appreciation of Australian port-type and sherry-type wines and their dramatic leap into prominence', and another, representing the Australian Wine Board, urged 'expansion of business with increased consumption of wholesome, national wines, the only thing which will make Britain a wine-consuming nation'.

The latter recognised, however, that there was 'a dividing of the ways' and that sectional interests still obtruded themselves. 'The brewer will say that beer is the natural beverage of England, largely home grown at one time, and home produced ... And there is the spirit trade.' He referred more briefly to 'the several sections of the Wine Trade', and it was obvious from the comments on the symposium that this sectionalism was strong. Thus, one dealer was content to wish for a 'further increase in the consumption of Brandy as a beverage already apparent last year'. 'Were anyone hard-hearted enough to wish for a series of epidemic

---

[38] Harrison, *op. cit.*, p. 131.
[39] *Ibid.*, p. 26.
[40] *The Wine and Spirit Trade Review*,

13 January 1939.
[41] *Ibid.*, 14 July 1939.

illnesses,' he went on, 'the sale of brandy, the doctors' standby, would no doubt benefit', but his firm, after all, were brandy merchants, not armament manufacturers. Forgetting the war clouds altogether, another dealer stated simply that 'the best thing that could happen to the trade in 1939 is that we should all be allowed to conduct our enterprise without further handicap either of taxation or regulation, and upon the same equitable basis as other legitimate but less historic trades'.

There was some talk, nevertheless, of an expansion of the trade, and one well-known dealer urged an advertising campaign for wine along the lines of the much publicised advertising campaign for beer. 'A meal without Wine is a day without sunshine' was one suggested advertising slogan to counter 'Beer is Best', and a film about the work and life of the vineyards a suggested advertising medium. Finally, a spokesman of the Wine and Spirit Trade Defence Fund, himself an 'importer of fine wines and brandies', turned to what might be called the old Victoria Wine theme:

> I hope that during 1939 I shall be visited by Dukes and Earls who wish to lay down pipes of Port for the coming of age of their new-born grandsons and by millionaires who are wanting large quantities of Claret and Burgundy for consumption in the nineteen-fifties. But it will please me much more if I can do an equal volume of business with 'small' people. I have always argued that the future of wine requires a democratic more than an aristocratic or plutocratic basis. Despite the disproportionately high taxation of the less expensive kinds, merchants can supply genuine and mature wines at prices ranging upwards from half a crown a bottle. When once the less opulent classes understand that good wine, though dearer than it ought to be, is not out of their reach, they will cease to be wine shy. I am not suggesting that beer, our national beverage, shall be pushed out, but only that wine shall be brought in as a frequent alternative.
>
> Today, even our humbler folk are escaping from monotony in food; and the time has come for delivering them from monotony in drink. Therefore, instead of merely wishing for a multitude of 'small' customers in 1939, I shall try to make my wish come true by giving to the clerk and the mechanic a welcome no less hearty than that which I shall extend to the clubman and to the Peer of the realm.

None of the contributors to the symposium made any reference to the increasing links between the brewing industry, far more prosperous after 1933 than before, and the wine trade. Amalgamations encouraged takeovers not only of licensed premises but of off-licences, many of them selling wine and spirits as well as beer; and as bottled beers became more popular, for this reason, too, breweries often acquired bottling stores which had belonged to wine and spirit merchants.[42] Moreover, because of the cost of installing bottling machinery, large breweries were in a more advantageous position than small ones. There were stronger links, too, partly in consequence, between brewers and the soft drinks industry.

Many drinkers at home or in the 'pub' were unfamiliar with what was going on in board rooms behind the scenes or in warehouses and manufacturing plants, but they were fully aware of the slogans. 'Beer is Best', a slogan introduced in 1937 on behalf of the whole industry,[43] could be seen on all the hoardings of the late-1930s, along with the brilliantly contrived Guinness advertisements and their well-known slogan 'Guinness is good for you'. Yet nothing that happened in the board rooms then was comparable in scale or in drama with what was to happen after the end of the Second World War in 1945. It has been possible, indeed, not for a contemporary, but for a historian of business, to claim that 'before the Second World War, the brewing business was one of the most somnolent in the country.'[44]

The Second World War itself followed a different pattern in relation to beer, spirits and wine consumption than the First, just as it followed a different pattern in relation to the fighting itself. Indeed, the pattern of fighting directly influenced the pattern of production and consumption. Between September 1939 and May 1940 there were echoes of the First World War as the French wine market was described gently as 'fettered by transport difficulties and unjust demands'[45] and as prospects for the Christmas wine trade were said to be good. ('No man can live by bread and broadcasting.')[46] This was the 'phoney war', when one Company Director could offer more wine and spirits for Christmas festivities than ever before.[47]

From the summer of 1940 onwards, however, Britain was cut off from most of the continent of Europe where wine was produced, and it was not until after D-Day in June 1944 that the return of trade began. Wine consumption fell, therefore, from 21,228,028 gallons in 1940 to 4,373,122 gallons in 1945, while beer consumption actually rose from 19,275,646

---

[42] See Vaizey, *op. cit.*, p. 35.
[43] See *The Brewers' Journal*, 15 July 1933, for the background of the campaign, and for the result, see *Advertisers' Weekly*, 5 May 1938.
[44] G. Turner, *Business in Britain* (1969),

p. 271.
[45] *The Wine and Spirit Trade Review*, 13 October 1939.
[46] *Ibid.*, 3 November 1939.
[47] *Ibid.*

standard barrels to 20,090,422. The figure for spirits, which show an undramatic fall, are included in the following table:

| Year ended 31 March | Spirits | | Wines (Including British Wines) | Beer (Home-made and Imported) |
| | British | Foreign & Colonial | | |
	Proof Gallons	Proof Gallons	Gallons	Standard Barrels
1940	9,664,681	1,577,072	21,228,028	19,275,696
1941	7,662,456	2,345,625	18,762,589	18,848,232
1942	6,998,854	2,978,648	9,391,749	19,896,780
1943	7,732,684	2,942,439	5,097,729	18,715,199
1944	7,938,116	1,620,152	4,585,309	19,381,744
1945	6,763,781	1,579,339	4,373,122	20,090,422

TABLE 13 *Consumption of Wine, Beer and Spirits, 1940–1945*

The quality (and gravity) of beer deteriorated as it had done during the First World War. New substitute ingredients, like oats and potatoes, were introduced into its preparation, and excise duty on it rose from 24s a barrel to around £7. Yet the Churchill government refused to follow the same policies as Lloyd George had followed during the First World War. In 1943, for example, 'the Lord President's Committee unanimously recoiled' from reducing beer output or to closing pubs two days a week in order to save precious grain.[48] Bar prices rose from 5d to 1s 1d per pint – but there was no rationing and the flow of beer, though in places it became a trickle at times, was never to stop. There was also a move from the cheaper bars to the saloon bars by both men and women who might never have gone to the pre-war pub at all. 'The inn stands as the foremost social institution of the country in peace', wrote the *Brewing Trade Review* in 1940, the year of Dunkirk, 'and as one of real value to the nation in time of war.'[49] Inevitably there had to be a framework of national control, and it was more sophisticated than it had been between 1914 and 1918. It depended less on bureaucracy than on the close cooperation of the Brewers' Society.

As for spirits, which were usually harder still to come by, the Ministry

[48] See R.J. Hammond, *Food*, Vol. I, *The Growth of Policy* (1951), p. 268. Dried potato was suggested as a grain substitute: flaked maize and rice were among the commodities actually employed.
[49] Quoted in R.G. Wilson, *op. cit.*, p. 207.

of Food informed the whisky distillers as soon as war broke out that production would have to cease at the end of 1939 and six months' stocks of cereals were requisitioned. Thereafter, three permitted periods were allowed for distilling whisky between 1939 and 1944, although very short ones, and between then and April 1945 there was limited distilling. It was then Winston Churchill wrote his famous fighting *Minute*, 'On no account reduce the barley for whisky. This takes years to mature, and is an invaluable export and dollar producer. Having regard to all our other difficulties about exports, it would be most improvident not to preserve this characteristic British element of ascendancy'.[50] From a dedicated champagne and brandy drinker this was the highest praise.

Exports of whisky had reached £10,427,000 in the year of Britain's finest hour, 1940, and it was home sales of whisky which were reduced during and after the War: the biggest fall in the ration to wholesalers – 20 per cent of 1939–40 sales – came after the War ended. Indeed, the war-time allowance was 41 per cent.

Within this drinking pattern, influenced by Whitehall but not dictated by it, any hopes of an active home market for wine were bound to be hopes for the future. Yet small quantities of Australian, South African, Portuguese and Spanish wines were imported in every war-time year:

	1941	*1942*	*1943*	*1944*	*1945*
Australian	658	181	91	307	888
South African	202	120	110	276	639
Portuguese	436	414	218	320	399
Spanish	774	130	182	247	1,180
Other Wines	57	55	488	116	631

TABLE 4 *Wine Imports, 1941–1945* (000 gallons)

No Customs and Excise breakdown was provided for the year 1940 although, surprisingly, imports of 445,000 gallons of French wine were noted for the year of 1941 – from unoccupied France? – and 4,000 gallons for the year 1942. The figure for 1945 after the successful Allied invasion

---

[50] Quoted in Daiches, *op. cit.*, p. 108.

and the victorious end of the War was still very low – 43,000 gallons.

In fact, the annual consumption of wine and spirits had fallen from $9\frac{1}{2}$ million gallons to $7\frac{1}{2}$ million gallons, while beer consumption had increased. 'All in all the drink situation is bad', wrote Mollie Panter-Downes, the scintillating American war correspondent of the *New Yorker* in 1943. 'Those who like to drink out usually still can do so, at prices which range from the steep to the suicidal. The problem is more difficult for the person who wants to have the makings of a nightcap around or a bottle of something handy to bring out when friends call.' She added that even a glass of beer was 'hard to come by – especially in country districts whose population has been swelled by evacuated townsfolk and the military'.[51]

There were several other categories of consumer expenditure, including cigarettes and entertainment, the consumption in real terms of which had either been reduced very little during the war years or which had even shown increases. And while as far as beer was concerned, if alcoholic content had been taken into account, the sales figure for 1944 at 1938 prices would have been £194 million instead of £228 million, this was still an increase on 1939. In real terms consumption of wines fell sharply:

Year	Beer £ million	Wines/Spirits £ million
1938	180	88
1939	187	91
1940	186	82
1941	312	83
1942	215	67
1943	219	66
1944	228	60

TABLE 15 *Consumer Expenditure in Real Terms on Beer, Wines and Spirits, 1938–1944*

Not surprisingly, Mollie Panter-Downes anticipated an armistice with 'nothing more festive to drink than beer, perhaps diluted even

---

[51] M. Panter-Downes, *London War Notes, 1939–1945* (ed. W. Shawn, 1972), pp. 271–2.

below its present strength'. In fact, however, private bottles, hidden away, mysteriously reappeared on VE-Day. Soon afterwards, *The Wine and Spirit Trade Review* was looking beyond the 'immediate circle of trade affairs' to the more distant future and turning for guidance to a series of independent 'industrial surveys' prepared under the auspices of *The Economist*. On brewing it forecast that while 'the present high level of bar consumption' was unlikely to be maintained completely after the War, there would be a higher demand for beer – in conditions of full employment – than there had been during the 1930s: 'the trend of beer consumption will follow, at a distance, the curve of national income and surplus purchasing power'. On wine, it suggested that supplies, like those of spirits, would be 'subnormal' for some time.

This, however, would not be the case in the long run. The hope was that people would 'realise how good wine is and how poor civilisation would be without it; how there are hundreds of millions of gallons of it for sale, very cheap, by countries which would take our exports in exchange; how Chancellors of the Exchequer could get more revenue from low duties on a lot than from high duties on a little'. 'Experience has shown during the War,' concluded their declaration of faith, for that was what it was, 'that, to a larger extent than was suspected, the people of this country are wine-conscious, and if, in the fullness of time, the government can be induced to bring the duties back to a reasonable level there is little cause to take a pessimistic view of the future of the trade.'[52]

---

[52] *The Wine and Spirit Trade Review*, 3 August 1945.

CHAPTER SEVEN

The Evolution of a Company

1921-1945

The operations of Victoria Wine took place against this changing background, though in the first instance after 1921 there was an echo of the past rather than an intimation of the future.

When Frank Wood died, once again it was a widow, Helen Wood – Hughes's ward – who took charge of the Victoria Wine business. On this occasion, however, the regime was to be short-lived, and there was soon to be a complete change of control, very much in line with the general conditions of the times. Alive to the great potential of Victoria Wine, one of the most energetic businessmen of his generation, Sir Charles Edward Cottier, born in 1869, took over the concern in 1924 and turned it into a public company. One story is that he overheard a conversation in a train about its problems and prospects, was fascinated by what was said, and immediately took action.

For Cottier, however, there was nothing new in this kind of operation. A solicitor by profession, who qualified late in life, he was sole partner in Lane and Cottier, first of Plymouth and thereafter of Plymouth and London. More important, he was also Chairman by 1924 of Booth's Distillery Ltd and John Watney and Company. The former enterprise, which had established itself in the 1770s and had become a public limited liability company in 1897, had taken over the latter, a well established family firm of distillers at Wandsworth, in 1923.[1] Cottier was backed financially by Solly Joel and the firm of Barnato Brothers, and it seemed natural for him to move from the new combination to Victoria Wine

---

[1] See Lord Kinross, *The Kindred Spirit, A History of Gin and of the House of Booth* (1959), Ch. 4.

with its multiple retail outlets. There were cakes as well as ale (and spirits) in his bulging portfolio, too, for he was also Chairman of Buzzards, a famous cake shop in Oxford Street, which served teas as impressive as those which Mrs Russell had served at The Dell. Finally, he was Chairman of the Aëreated Bread Company, a huge concern which served a growing number of retail shops. It was three years older than Victoria Wine, having been founded in 1862, and it was concerned both with production and distribution.

Cottier's was an active and many-sided career, therefore, and he was knighted in the year Victoria Wine became a public company – in 1924. He was a Mason and a strong supporter of tariff reform, and it was no surprise that his name figured in Stanley Baldwin's resignation honours list. Cottier remained Chairman of Victoria Wine until his death in 1928, when his obituaries described him as 'a man who put fresh life into every concern with which he associated himself'.[2] By a coincidence, the business address from which Cottier planned his many business deals was the old wine centre of Tower Royal, Cannon Street, E.C., adjacent to the Three Cranes Wharf, where for many years London's wine stocks were landed and from which point they were distributed.

The new Victoria Wine Company paid the previous owner £588,000, of which £296,996 was taken in cash and the balance in ordinary shares. Frank Wood, therefore, had made an outstandingly good investment. Yet in return he had done much to extend the scope and secure the reputation of Victoria Wine, and £142,486 of the £588,000 represented good will. The freehold and leasehold properties were valued at £329,547.

The new company had an initial share and loan capital of £600,000, divided into 300,000 £1 shares and £300,000 $6\frac{1}{2}$ per cent First Mortgage Debentures. By its Memorandum of Association, dated 10 July 1924, it was authorised in the broadest terms 'to carry on the business of wine, beer and spirit merchants, licensed victuallers and manufacturers and dealers in drinks of all kinds (both wholesale and retail), growers and shippers of wine, producers of wines and spirits, brewers, and maltsters, distillers, importers, and manufacturers of and /or dealers in aereated mineral and artificial waters and other drinks'. It was free, too, to 'acquire and take over all or part of the business, property and liabilities of any business which this Company is authorised to carry on' and 'to

---

[2] See *The Wine Trade Review*, 24 August 1928; *The Times*, 23 August 1928.

enter into partnership or into any arrangement for sharing profits, union of interests, reciprocal concession cooperation with any person or company carrying on or engaged in or about to carry on or engage in any business or transaction which the Company is authorised to carry on or engage in'.

This was a comprehensive list of objects, and Victoria Wine Ltd also had the new power, much sought after by the retail business during the 1920s and 1930s, to increase its capital. The financial Press described shares and stock in it as 'a well secured investment', pointing out that average profits for the previous six years would have covered the interest on the debentures more than three times. In fact, at the end of the first year's operations there was a further increase in trading profits of £9,653. (Many of the new shareholders, it was reported, were clergymen.) Meanwhile, the Company had acquired two new freeholds and had opened five new branches, bringing the total of the latter to 104. Its new advertising slogan was 'Our Branches are Your Wine Cellar'. There was nothing new about the thought itself. What was new was the pithy mode of expression.

In 1927 the capital of the Company was increased to £400,000 by the creation of 100,000 new Preference Shares of £1 each. The preference shares were used, along with an allocation from the previous year's profits, to cancel almost half of the first Mortgage Debenture Stock. This cut down current liabilities and made the Company an even more attractive financial proposition. It was also more closely caught up in 'the trade'. In 1925, for example, it contributed ten guineas to the Wine and Spirit Trade Defence Fund and another ten guineas to the Wine and Spirit Trade Benevolent Society.

There were three other Directors besides Cottier – Edwin John Venner and Frederick Hutter, new to the business, and Vernon Frank Keeble, who had served it from early youth and represented continuity of management. Venner and Keeble, like Cottier himself, held 1,000 shares, and Keeble, who had previously received $2\frac{1}{2}$ per cent of net profits, now had his share increased to 5 per cent if profits exceeded £30,000. He had started in approved Victoria Wine fashion as an errand boy at Stroud Green and had worked his way up to become General Manager before 1924: his wife was a companion of Mrs Wood. Now, in 1924, he became not only Managing Director of Victoria Wine but a Director of the Aëreated Bread Company also. His niece was a shorthand typist at Osborn Street.

Keeble was described by one of his employees as the 'finest master in the trade', and he was also said to be the highest paid man in the wine business. The policies he followed, however, were cautious, more cautious than his Chairman's reputation might have suggested. The range of wines and spirits on sale was kept largely unchanged and there was little direct buying abroad. Samples were received from London agents, and there was no contact with foreign shippers. Nor was there any general strategy behind the acquisition or location of branches. All of them were still in the London area. One old senior employee still retained under the new reign was W.R. Hill, who in January 1926 had completed sixty years' service in the employment of the Company: he was called into the Board Room and presented with a gold watch. A unique letter addressed to him by William Winch Hughes still survives. It was dated 26 January 1883 and thanked him for the 'praiseworthy example' of his long service. On this occasion he had been presented with a clock. It is not known whether it was still ticking in 1926.

By that time, there was a small central staff of 20 at Head Office, where Arthur Pease remained as Cashier, ensconced in an office of his own. There was also a Sales Manager and Branches Superintendent, Harry Davis, to supervise the operations of seven Branch Supervisors. The Branch Supervisors made their rounds of the Branches by bicycle, and wines and spirits were delivered by pony and trap (one of these in the City was used for special deliveries), by horse-drawn carts or, again, by bicycle. The Branches, all of them with gold curtains in their windows, were still managed by Manageresses who, it is said, always knew on what day and at what time the Supervisors would visit their stores. Many Manageresses were described as Officers' widows: one was reputed to be a former nun. They were paid two guineas a week plus 7s 6d room rent. Miss Lilian Granger, who joined Victoria Wine in 1919 and retired as a Manageress after fifty years' service with the Company, has vividly recalled Miss Butterfield, her first Manageress, at Ealing Mall, where she went to work in 1921: among Miss Granger's first jobs was polishing syphons. Miss Butterfield wore a black dress and flannel petticoat, was a teetotaller, and had been at the same store for 48 years. She was a firm disciplinarian, and when on one occasion a relief Manageress arrived, Miss Butterfield complained that she looked as if she was going to a dance.

Another Manageress with a long record was Miss Smith, for 49 years Manageress at Dulwich. When she retired in 1928 she was granted a pension of 10s a week. Miss Butterfield's was 15s, later raised to £1, the amount paid to Mrs Parker, Manageress of the Stratford Branch, who retired in 1925. Further pensions were awarded on a more systematic basis in 1930, when action was taken also to systematise stock-taking procedures which had hitherto been remarkably haphazard.

Staff relations were a frequent item on Board agendas, and were equally frequently referred to at the annual shareholders' meetings. Yet the framework of human relations was not quite the same as before 1914. There were no more references to the reading room, and in 1924 there was the first mention of trade unions in the Victoria Wine records, when there was a report of an interview on 'wage levels' with the officials of the National Amalgamated Union of Assistants, Warehousemen and Clerks. Two years later, when deliveries were interrupted during what the Chairman called the 'disastrous' general strike of 1926, the staff was praised for its devotion: 'throughout the extent of the crisis no demands were made either at the distributing centre or at the depots which could not be as equally complied with as though we are carrying on under ordinary and normal conditions'. It was a sign that human relations remained good that in general bonuses figured more on the agenda than wages, and that they were increased in 1927 when workers in many other industries were facing wage reductions.

Manageresses, teetotal or not, never tasted the wines of Victoria Wine – at least on the premises – although the foremen at Osborn Street usually had a drink before they left and the office staff at Osborn Street, often working extra time, could take home wines and spirits to the value of £10 at Christmas, still very much the peak period of the year. This, in retrospect, might be the 'cocktail age', yet despite two 'Big Tree' mixed cocktails on the Victoria Wine list (Manhattan and Martini at 9s 6d a bottle), it was the cocktail age only for the few. The staple trade at Victoria Wine branches was still not dissimilar from what it had been before 1914. A wine list of the mid-1920s offered 35 ports, 5 of them Sandeman's. The cheapest, a soft ruby, was still selling at 42s per dozen, slightly less expensive than 'old and fruity' 'Victoria Optimo' at 51s. The dearest, a Raleigh Rogers, was selling at 126s per dozen (10s 6d per bottle). There were no crusted and vintage ports on the price list, however, and customers interested in them were told to apply for details. One port on the list was described as a 'specially shipped port' for Victoria Wine by Martinez, Gassiot and Company, with whom Victoria Wine had a special relationship. It cost 90s per dozen or 7s 6d per bottle. There was also a white port from the same firm at 5s 6d per bottle.

The continuing policy of offering basic cheap wines to the customer was strongly supported by a shareholder at the 1925 annual meeting. 'He did not know', he told the meeting, 'how at the low price charged by the Company they could sell their wines at a profit. He had on occasion tried other brands, but although the prices were higher, the quality was not comparable at all with that of Victoria wines.'

Sherries figured lower in the wine list than they had done before 1914, although there were still 18 of them, including a dry amontillado at 5s 9d per bottle, an old East India at 6s, and Harvey's Bristol Cream at 12s. Spanish red wine and Tarragona were still at the head of the wine list at 2s 9d per bottle and there was a long list of champagnes. The best Bollinger (1921) cost 19s 6d per bottle, the cheapest was a Blossier and Co at 8s. There were eight champagnes at less than 11s a bottle, all more expensive than the sparkling Saumurs. The list of clarets was limited to 12 – only three of them vintages – but there were now no less than 15 different Graves.

Clearly William Winch Hughes's opinion of the tastes of his customers was still valid in a new generation, although only rich customers of the 1920s would have chosen the Chateau d'Yquem (1923) at 13s 4d per bottle, less expensive, however, than a Mumm 1923 champagne at 14s. There were 15 burgundies, a few Riojas and a cluster of Australian burgundies ('purity and soundness guaranteed by the South Australian Government'), including Gilbey's Rubicon and Blancona, three Emus, and several wines shipped direct for Victoria Wine. The Stanley Wine Company of Clare, South Australia, was Victoria Wine's agent.

The number of rums had fallen to three (white Bacardi now among them), and of branded gins to five (with a 'triple-rectified' Victoria Brand – and Booth's – among them). Yet there was a striking range of whiskies, most at 12s 6d per bottle. Of 54, only Johnnie Walker's and John Dewar's had figured on the 1896 list, the former now offered in the red and black label varieties. Haig, Antiquary, Claymore, Queen Anne, Teacher's Highland Cream and Vat 69 were among the new names, with Dimple at 13s 6d and Old Parr at 15s among the few more expensive varieties. Irish whiskies were selling at the same price, while brandies ranged from 15s 6d per bottle (Otard, Dupuy) to Denis Mounie's 1875 Grande Champagne at 33s.

The Warnink Advocaat agency had been renewed in 1924, and relations between the British and Dutch firms remained close: indeed, in 1927 a temporary financial advance was made to Warnink, free of interest, when the Dutch firm had cash problems. (In the same year a Victoria Wine advertisement appeared offering a sample of Advocaat for a nominal price.) Advocaat was selling then at 13s a bottle – it was sold in half bottles too – and Akvavit at 15s. South African Van-Der-Hum had made its appearance too (along with South African wines) at 15s 6d.

There was a very wide variety of mineral waters, which now included 'Quinine Tonic', Vichy, Celestins, Contrexeville, Evian, Vittel, and 'Farris Waters', the London agency for which was acquired in 1926. There were many 'cyders' also. In 1896 there had been only one cider, the Company's Devonshire Cyder, on the list: it cost 5s per dozen then, and now cost twice as much. Now in addition, however, there were four Bulmer's ciders and four Whiteway's, not to speak of a gold-seal 'anti-uric' cider, 'specially blended for its anti-rheumatic qualities'. Apart from one whisky ('Pountain's Pure Natural Scotch for all medicinal purposes'), and Martinez Invalid Port, 'robust and invigorating', this was the only item on the list with a health tag attached to it. There was now no reference to teas or coffees, and there were no other grocery items on sale.

The pattern of wine lists – and of wine prices – had not changed significantly by the mid-1930s, although 'Golden Galleon' became a registered trademark in 1934 and there were now more items marked 'Victoria', like Victoria Tarragona at 3s 3d per large oval bottle, Victoria Old Fino Sherry, Victoria Rich Austral, and even Victoria Ginger, and 'Empire products' (like Australian Ophir, Red or White, at 5s per flagon) benefited from the system of imperial preference. Victoria Optimo Port was still 5s per bottle, but Haig's whisky was up from 12s 6d per bottle to 14s 3d, Booth's gin from 12s to 13s 6d, and Martell's three-star brandy from 17s to 18s 3d. Bisset's Gold Label whisky, in which Victoria Wine specialised, cost 12s 6d per bottle in 1935, and its Black Label version 13s 6d. Meanwhile, at least one Victoria Wine branch (Clapton) now placed cocktails, not Tarragona, at the head of its list, and offered Zip, Here's How, Double Tops, Royal Salute, Segavin, Odds On, Eleven O'Clock, Golden Griffen, Late Night Final, Skyscraper, Green Goddess, Whoopee 'and many more in stock' at prices ranging from 2s 10d per bottle (Zip) to 6s 3d (the very popular Green Goddess).

Victoria Tarragona, old staple, cost 3s 3d per large oval bottle, and there were 15 white wines on a 1935 Jubilee list, three of them Chateau-bottled (Chateau Filhot, 1923, at 9s, and Chateau d'Yquem 1924 and 1928 at 15s 6d and 12s 6d respectively). Chateau Beychevelle St Julien at 4s 6d per bottle was among seven vintage clarets, the oldest of which were 1924s and the most expensive of which was Chateau Pichon Longueville Pauillac at 6s. The cheapest, Cotes de Blaye, cost 2s per bottle, as against the cheapest Macon at 2s 6d. There were seven vintage burgundies, including 1926 Pommards and Volnays at 5s 6d and a 1923 Chablis Clos des Hospices at 7s 9d. Graves and Sauternes were said to be less in demand than they had been, and the taste in sherry, ranging in price from 3s 6d per bottle to 8s – Sandeman's Brown Bank – was moving at last, it was said, towards drier brands.

With the new interest in mixers, the price of Martini and Rossi rose from 3s 3d per large bottle to 5s 6d and of Noilly Prat from 4s 8d to 7s, and there was now a British vermouth ('French' at 3s 9d per large bottle and 'Italian' at 3s 3d). There was also an unsweetened cocktail gin at 11s per bottle, 14s 6d per magnum. The Warnink Advocaat agency had been renewed in 1934 for fourteen years (with reduced margins and with a new rider that no Advocaat other than Warnink's should be stocked). Yet the employment of a specialist Advocaat traveller, G. Hardy, was no longer felt to be warranted, and there was a flourishing sub-agency system for Advocaat sales in shops outside the Victoria Wine trading areas. (Advocaat was in greatest demand in the North and the Midlands.)

There was one champagne, Jules Laroche (not on the 1920s list), said to be 'shipped exclusively to us and equal to many advertised brands sold at much higher prices', at 10s per bottle, while 1920 vintage ports, bottled in 1922, ranged from 72s per dozen to 102s (Sandeman's). Most 1927 vintages cost 60s. Their quality was praised rather than their price or their possible effects on the health and well-being of those who drank them. Yet the invalid element had actually been reinforced in the list. Buckfast, Hall's Phosferine, Sanatogen, Vibrona and Wincarnis now all figured on it. So also did beers – among them 44 bottled beers and seven lagers, including Carlsberg, Dressler's Bremen Export, Pilsner Urquell and Munich Löwenbräu. Yet as far as domestic beers were concerned, Taylor Walker and Company was now in the centre of the picture. This was because in 1929, one year after Cottier's death, Taylor and Walker, which had become a limited liability company as recently as 1927,[3] acquired control of Victoria Wine, the first brewery to show an interest in doing so, by obtaining 59.6 per cent of the Ordinary Shares, shares previously held by Cottier. The takeover came as a surprise to the Victoria Wine Board, which had elected Keeble as Chairman in 1928 – he took the Chair at only one meeting – at the suggestion of a new Director, W.A.S. Hewins, who had been nominated by Cottier himself

---

[3] See F.A. King, *The Story of the Cannon Brewery* (1951).

when Cottier was ill. Indeed, before the Managing Director of Taylor, Walker and Company was appointed a member of the Victoria Wine Board, the old Directors, taken unawares, sought legal advice as to their own position.

Nonetheless, there was no major change before May 1929, when Commander Redmond McGrath, a sportsman of Irish descent with a good war record and a friend of Churchill and Lord Birkenhead, became Chairman of the Board. McGrath had been drawn into Taylor and Walker from the City by John Bradshaw, its Chairman, and succeeded him as Chairman. It was he who is said to have been responsible for suggesting the take-over, and his nomination to the Victoria Wine Chairmanship was proposed by A. Chiles, Warehouse Manager, who had been appointed a Director in October 1928. At the same time, May 1929, the appointment of F. Bromwich, who in Cottier's time had been made an Administrative Assistant, was terminated with compensation. Keeble, who was continued in office for two years in 1928, remained as Managing Director until 1933. He had resigned from all his other Boards (including ABC) in 1929 so as to enable him 'to devote his whole time to the interests of Victoria Wine', and in the same year Hewins resigned 'owing to his other interests occupying too much of his time', with A.M. Geesing taking his place.

It was Keeble who reported to the new Board in July 1929 that he had completed negotiations with Taylor, Walker and Company as to the terms on which their beers were to be supplied to Victoria Wine. They were to pay Victoria Wine for advertising facilities at the branches, while Victoria Wine was to pay a commission of 5% to them in respect of wines the brewing firm bought for sale in their tied houses. Yet there was no tied policy in relation to beers sold by Victoria Wine. Guinness was always stocked, and in addition to British beers it was agreed in 1931 to add Tuborg lager to the Company's lists. Two years later an agency was offered for Löwenbrau.

Seventeen shareholders had attended the annual general meeting at Winchester House, Old Broad Street, in 1929, when the new Chairman pointed to 'satisfactory trading in a difficult year'. National imports of wines of all kinds were down by a quarter, he noted, but Victoria Wine was thriving, and he went on to praise Keeble for his 'acumen' and his staff, as in the past, for their 'industry'. The year 1930, when the duties on beer were increased, was even more difficult, and the Chairman told the twelve shareholders who were present at the annual meeting that 'trade throughout the country during the past year has been such as to affect adversely businesses such as ours', and 'up to the present there appears to be no indication of any improvement'. He went on to urge the shareholders – and he could not have been concentrating on those who were present – 'to become customers of this Company and also to recommend their friends to do the same. In this way you can all help "to paddle your own canoe".' The following year, he took up the same point again, 'If all our shareholders would try to persuade their friends to deal at our shops it becomes a sort of rolling stone: if we can only satisfy them and they try to get another person to come, our business would be absolutely enormous'. Yet shareholders were not granted discounts as some of them wished.

When the range of Victoria Wine business was extended in 1934 to include a tobacco and cigar section – not all stores were licensed to sell tobacco – the Chairman explained that despite an improvement in confidence, justified by Treasury and employment returns, spirit duties had not been reduced. The tendency of Victoria Wine customers then was 'to buy the lower-priced types of wines', while still expecting 'quality'. It was doubtless as a result of meeting this demand that Victoria Wine continued to pay a dividend throughout the depression, even though on ordinary shares it fell to four per cent in 1933 and 1934. (Dividend on preference shares was then eight per cent.)

When times were hardest economically, one of the shareholders pointed to favourable social forces operating in favour of the Company – particularly the rise of housing estates and the number of house owners. There, he said, the demand for wines and spirits would be likely to rise, particularly when, because of falling prices of other goods, real wages (and salaries) were going up even in a period of depression. It is notable that debentures were reduced even in bad years like this and that a 'trustees' redemption fund was gradually built up,. The culmination of this policy came in 1933, when the whole of the debenture stock was redeemed and £2,000 in annual interest charges was thereby saved. Meanwhile, extended credit was often granted to Victoria Wine by suppliers, who recognised that it would take time for new stores to show profits. On balance, there was always more emphasis on expansion than on retrenchment, and as the number of branches increased – there were eight added in 1933 itself – new infusions of capital were necessary.

The policy of expansion was pushed harder after Keeble retired in 1933. The Board, which appointed a small committee 'to take steps for efficient conduct of the business on his retirement', selected Eric Fisher from Slater and Bodegas as General Manager, and he was to remain in the position until 1948, becoming a Director in 1937. Under Fisher, there was a more systematic approach to store location, management and control and a more vigorous approach to advertising. The changes began in December 1933 with the replacement of contract transport – six five-ton Leyland lorries and one one-ton Ford van – for Victoria Wine's old carts, vans and bicycles. 'Have you seen our new vans running about London?', the Chairman asked the shareholders at the next Board meeting. 'Yes' was the reply. 'And what is your opinion?' he went on, to which one shareholder gave the right answer, 'admirable'. 'Now that is just one thing which I think is a step in the right direction,' Commander McGrath added, 'It is an advertisement which costs us nothing except keeping it up.' He had seen 'all seven' go by the previous week, holding up the traffic, and he had been delighted.

Not all advertising cost nothing. A campaign of unprecedented cost was launched in 1934, when 18 new branches were opened: it included canvassing of new blocks of flats. And when new branches were acquired, particular attention was now placed on locating them in streets near to underground stations. This was only the beginning. By Christmas 1937 the scale of advertising was such that three whole columns were taken in eighty local newspapers throughout the Company's area, setting out basic details of what was on offer, and 70,000 circulars were dispatched to all the Company's customers. A second edition (50,000 copies) was prepared of 'Here's How', advertising cocktails: the first in 1934 had proved highly successful. So, too, were special window displays, not least in a new branch opened in 1936 in New Oxford Street.

Even more costly than advertising was the modernisation of other branches. Every effort was made during the 1930s to acquire full Justices' Licences, which allowed beer as well as wines and spirits to be sold, and whenever possible premises tried to display all the best of their wares, including bargains. 'Of course, if we modernise outside, we must modernise within' one shareholder observed in 1937. 'I feel the Board are pursuing the right policy in modernising. On the public house side one sees modernising proceeding at quite a rapid pace, and the same applies to the off licence.' 'It is always a pleasure,' the same shareholder said the following year, 'to pay tribute to the efficient management and the tasteful conditions within which our shops are maintained.'

Within the modernised shop, he went on, it was 'the personality of the manager and the staff' as well as 'the quality of goods' which counted. And there had been changes here too. Under Fisher, managers rather than manageresses were usually appointed to run branches, and standard instructions were now sent out from the central office as to how they should carry out their duties.

Price list cover design for Etablissements Nicolas
by Alfred Latour, 1932

Price list cover design for Etablissements Nicolas
by Joseph Hecht

W. Glendenning's price list for Christmas, 1931

Two days' notice had to be given for orders from Head Office. All cash was to be entered immediately in a day book and had to be paid into the bank 'as often as possible'. Monthly statements were to be 'properly filled up'. Invoices were to be checked and return notes given to the carmen who delivered. The same number of empties had to be returned as received. 'On no account' was a Manager 'to buy bottles from the shop boys, or dealers in bottles', and 'great care' had to be taken to avoid sending 'oily' bottles back with empties: 'only an occasional bottle causes endless trouble'.

Wines and Spirits were 'not to be placed too high in the shop', and all stock was to be sold in the order in which it was received. 'On no account sell anything that is doubtful.' 'All Wines, also Cyder, must be kept lying down: Spirits, Liqueurs, Mineral Waters and Beers Standing up.' Syphons should be checked to ensure that the glass was polished and all water in them 'bright and clear'. Not more than six bottles of the same kind of spirit could be sold without an excise permit and (underlined) *'no Spirits should be sold to a retailer for resale'*. At the same time, 'The smallest quantity of Spirits or Liqueurs that you can sell at one time is the reputed quart bottle, and the largest quantity one dozen reputed quart bottles or two gallons'.

'The smallest quantity of Wine that you can sell at one time [no hint of the old trade by the glass] is one reputed pint bottle, and the largest quantity two gallons, or one dozen reputed pint bottles.' 'You cannot sell Beer in greater quantities than a $4\frac{1}{2}$ gallon cask (a pin), or two dozen reputed quarts, four dozen reputed pints, three dozen Imperial pints, six dozen half-pints, or one and a half dozen quarts at one time.' Bottles of beer should not be opened to put into customers' jugs, nor corks drawn. No child under the age of fourteen years could be served with wine or beer in any less quantity than one reputed pint (half-bottles of wine were reputed pints) and if spirits one reputed quart. *'All vessels must leave the premises with seal intact.'*

Not inappropriately, one of the last points – Number 45 out of 50 – was that 'a holiday of two weeks will be given to Managers who have been in the service for one year.' Number 49 was: 'Managers are not allowed to telephone other Branches', and Number 37: 'Wines, Spirits, Beers and Mineral Waters of our own bottling should always be recommended first'. William Winch Hughes would have been interested in Numbers 30 and 38: 'Should a Carman meet with any accident to his horse, van or motor, while conveying the Firm's goods, Managers are authorised to advance an amount not exceeding five shillings', and 'In the event of an accident outside the premises, Spirits can only be given with the consent of a Police Officer. Doctor's authority is not sufficient'.

While there was more emphasis in instructions of this kind on efficient management, the Board itself – with Fisher as an additional member after 1937 – interested itself in much of the detail. It consisted, as one shareholder put it, of 'practical men', who had recognised Fisher's value to the business by raising his commission in 1935, and his salary in 1936. In the year Keeble retired, Chiles had retired from the Board also and two new Directors were appointed – A.R. Deering and V.H. McNamara, both of whom were said to have been 'connected with the trade' all their business lives. When the latter died in 1935, he was replaced by W.H. Kingsmill, and a year later, when 'times were improving', the Marquis of Carisbrooke joined the Board.

In 1937 Commander McGrath became Managing Director as well as Chairman. His concern for the detail of the business can be illustrated from one of the last minutes of the Board before War broke out in 1939. There would be a number of 'major reconstructions of shop fronts and fittings' during the following year, 'each of which had been or would be considered by him individually'. In the previous year, a difficult one when 'world politics affected every phase of our lives and business', 19 new branches had been opened. A decade of business change through growth was drawing to a close.

There were changes in warehousing also between 1933 and 1939, including the installation of a new conveyor system, the introduction of new washing machines, the dismantling of the mineral water factory, and the purchase of new bottling plant 'to cope with the increasing trade in British wines'. The changes, Fisher told the Board, all made for greater productivity. In the winter of 1936/7 the number of employees at Osborn Street had been reduced by 38 and output had increased. The number of motor vehicles in use increased too. In 1937/8, 22 additional ones were acquired.

A number of incomplete returns of takings from individual branches exists for the 1930s. In 1935 Victoria Wine held 147 licences, only three of them outside a fifty-mile radius of London – Margate, Boscombe and Southsea; 128 licences were full Justices' Licences for wines, beers and spirits, 18 Excise Licences for the sale of wines and spirits only, and one a full Justices' Licence for beer and an Excise Licence only for wines and spirits. The branch with the highest takings in 1935 was Purley (£17,848), followed by Baker Street (£14,880). In the rather fuller 1934 list there were only three other branches with takings of over £10,000 – Golders Green, Hampstead and Sutton.

From a series of annual takings figures between 1930 and 1935 it is clear that most old branches were less prosperous at the end than they had been at the beginning. The depression had obviously taken its toll in places like Brentwood, Brixton, Peckham Rye, Wembley Hill, Charleville Road and Holloway Road. Yet there were exceptional branches where business had boomed – among them Boscombe, Bristol Gardens, Brompton Road, Chelsea, Chingford, Kenton, Upminster and Windsor, and, outstanding among this group, East Grinstead, where takings increased each year between 1930 and 1935. Surbiton was also in this group, while in Norbiton takings fell in 1931 and 1932 and had not reached the 1930 figure by 1935. At a few places, including Tooting and Weybridge, there were virtually no sales variations from year to year.

For one branch, 920 London Road, Thornton Heath, where takings in 1935 (£4,986) were lower than in 1930 (£6,524), there are monthly returns which reveal the seasonal pattern of sales in 1935. That the returns exist is a matter of accident: they were filed with the Licensing Authority as part of an attempt to secure a removal of a three-bottle restriction, and attached to the request was a note that Victoria Wine had never sustained a conviction in respect of its business in the whole of its 75 years of existence. To the nearest pound the returns were:

January	407
February	363
March	398
April	361
May	396
June	420
July	352
August	355
September	335
October	384
November	398
December	786

TABLE 16 *Monthly Takings at a London Branch, 1935*

The branch had been opened in 1913, and the manager had been in charge there since 1924. The average monthly gallons sold in 1935 were beers 347, wines 65, and spirits 53. The year 1933 was particularly bleak there: takings fell to £4,761.

The introduction of the price list for 1939/40, headed 'In Spite of All Things', emphasised how little things had changed. Services were 'practically unimpaired'. Because of petrol rationing there had had to be an economy on the method of delivery of supplies, but 'all Wines, Spirits, Beers, Table Waters and so forth' were on offer 'at pre-War budget prices'. 'We have more than 3,000 lines from which you can make your choice.' They included the first olive oil at 4s 6d a bottle, thin wine biscuits at 7d per ½lb packet, and liqueur chocolates at 10s per lb.

Cocktails, which now headed the list, cost 4s 6d (Here's How), 5s 6d, 6s 3d (Green Goddess) or 7s 6d (Pink Lady) a bottle. Pimms Number 1 Cup cost 14s. Votrix was among the vermouths at 4s 3d. Angostura cost 14s 6d, Booth's gin 13s 6d and the main Scotch whiskies (of which there were 20 on offer) 14s 3d. There were 47 ales, beers and stouts, including four Fremlins and four Tollemaches, four Hammertons, four Mann's and Bass, Truman's, Whitbread's, Worthington's and Younger's Scotch Ales. There were six Taylor Walker's, including a barley wine, and two Ind Coope's and Allsopp's (with no intimation, of course, of the role Ind Coope was to play in the history of the Company after the War).

Among the wines, a Margaux, a Château Durfort Vivers 1934, cost 60s per dozen bottles and a 1928 Château Cos D'Estournel 78s per dozen. Château Haut Brion 1928, cost 108s and among the burgundies Gevrey Chambertin 1933, 72s per dozen. Clos des Hospices 1934 was selling at 108s per dozen and Chambertin 1921, the oldest vintage on the list, at 120s per dozen. There was a non-vintage Châteauneuf du Pape at 48s per dozen and a Chablis at 54s, but a striking feature of the first war-time list was the new emphasis on vintages. Indeed, it included a nostalgic list of 'the best vintages today' (see Table 17 opposite).

Amongst these vintages the oldest port on the list was then the 1920 at prices varying from 90s to 108s per dozen, and the oldest champagne was 1928, at prices ranging from 120s to 168s. Of the quarter bottles of champagne selling at prices from 32s to 43s per dozen, it was touchingly noted that they were 'supplied largely for use in illness' and could be re-corked after pouring out one glass, and a second glass drunk later in the day. It was noted also that according to the Licensing Acts quarter bottles might not be sold singly. There was another more curious note. 'A number of London householders may have noted among their communi-

Champagne	1926	1928	1919	(1934)
Port	1904 1920	1908 1924	1912 1927	1917 (1935)
Hock and Moselle	1929 1937	1933	1934	1935
Bordeaux	1920 1929	1923 1934	1924 (1937)	1938
Burgundy	1921 1929	1923 1933	1926 1934	1928 1937

TABLE 17 *Vintage Years*

cations lately delivered to their doors envelopes impersonally addressed to the Butler or Parlourmaid.' These, the note went on, came from particular champagne networks, and if the messages were traced back they pointed to 'the threads of a vast subterranean organisation' which had been in existence for at least fifty years, but had 'of late burgeoned exceedingly'. It is remarkable that this was the first subterranean organisation to be identified during the Second World War.

The same lists had a note on German wines. 'No matter what his attitude towards the ideology of present-day Germany, the true wine-lover acknowledges the quality of the products of the Rhine and the Moselle vineyards. Accordingly, we include a list of the stocks of hocks and Moselles, which, purchased long before the outbreak of war, are still available at pre-war prices.' The hocks at prices quoted 'subject to disposal of stocks', included one 1929 – a Forster Jesuitengarten at 126s per dozen – and one 1921 Moselle – a Piesporter Goldtropfchen Auslese – at 120s per dozen. There were three 1935 hocks and three 1935 Moselles at prices ranging from 48s to 90s per dozen.

At the 1940 meeting of the shareholders McGrath was not present: he was 'fighting with the Army in France'. 'The wine trade,' it was reported then, 'was very difficult owing to the increase in cost, freight and insurance, plus the possibility of not being able to produce certain wines at all.' Fortunately, large stocks had been built up 'because we never know what is going to happen in the future with regard to supplies'. The next year showed. Wines and spirits were both 'very difficult to obtain'. And during the year that followed patience and determination counted for more than enterprise. By 1942 it was stated that in spite of the prohibition of imports of both foreign and Empire wines, an 'extensive trade in home produced beer and spirits had been maintained'. In 1943, when 900 employees were serving in the Forces, there was 'a sound level of turnover' and dividends to shareholders were doubled from 5 to 10 per cent, a level held in 1944.

Some shops had had to be closed because of 'evacuation of the population and shortage of managers due to the call up'[4], and in February 1943 Arthur Edwards became Deputy Manager when it seemed likely that Fisher himself would be transferred to other war duties.[5] He retained the title when Fisher was allowed to stay in post, and a month after his appointment Fisher played a prominent part in the acquisition of a chain of E.A. Mitchell stores, a shrewd and far-sighted deal. They were run by a General Manager, later a Director, responsible to Victoria Wine, which controlled their policy. Since they held large quantities of South African wines in their cellars, they provided immediate reinforcements for the Victoria Wine stores.[6]

These were hard times, however, as many Victoria Wine shops were closed as a result of enemy action, among them 18 King's Road, Southsea, the first to go in September 1940, 269 High Street, Lewisham, 47 Upper North Street, Poplar, and 136 Tachbrook Street, London, SW1. Most serious of all, the Osborn Street depot was bombed in May 1941, and five people were killed.

Such destruction faced post-war management with many problems, but in a period of tough physical controls there was little scope for replacement. Nor, indeed, was there much possiblity of immediate expansion. The future wine supply position seemed more promising than that for whisky or gin, but a lack of bottles was even more frustrating than a lack of what to put inside them. The shelves were bare. There was little sense then, therefore, of what a huge transformation there would be in the first twenty years of peace.

---

[4] Victoria Wine Board, *Minutes*, 24 July 1941.
[5] *Ibid.*, 10 February 1943.

[6] Note by T.G. Bloomfield, 28 September 1980.

CHAPTER  EIGHT

Victoria Wine within a Trading Empire 1945-1980

The story of Victoria Wine during the last forty years of its history is even more dramatic than its story during the pioneering days of William Winch Hughes. It tells, however, not of one man's enterprise but of the enterprise of many men, and it is part of a far bigger story of business amalgamations, a narrative which has never yet been fully told. The bigger story is more concerned with beer for sale – Britain in the 1960s was the third largest market in the world for beer – than with wine, for it was brewing experience and prospects, national and international, which led in 1961 to the creation of the large-scale brewing amalgamation, in its origins defensive, of Ind Coope, Tetley Walker and Ansell.[1] These were the three principal subsidiaries in Allied Breweries within which an enlarged Victoria Wine, the shop window of the amalgamation, was another. Yet within this trading empire wine sales rose to new heights. What had started defensively did not long remain so, and within ten years Allied Breweries, having acquired many new interests, was said to be the largest 'drinks group' in Europe, and its interests, very actively promoted, included soft drinks as well as wine.[2]

Four years after the first sweeping and exciting moves had been made, a wine merchant wrote in *The Wine and Spirit Trade Review*, that 'although of great age and tradition, the wine trade could not expect to isolate itself from the prevailing radical tenor of the period'.[3] He was thinking of a period longer than four years or even 40, as his memories stretched back to the First World War. It is fair and correct to comment, however, and it

---

[1] For earlier amalgamations, see J. Vaizey, *The Brewing Industry, 1886–1951* (1960), pp. 45–6.

[2] *Beer, A Report on the Supply of Beer* (HMSO,

1969), p. 21.

[3] H. Caplan, 'Half a Century of Change' in *The Wine and Spirit Trade Review*, 1 January 1965.

127

would have been so at the time, that at no stage in its history would Victoria Wine, product of a more recent and less leisurely history than some of the oldest (and smallest) firms in the wine trade, ever have wished so to isolate itself. Joining the Allied Breweries Group made no difference to its stance.

Long before 1961, long before 1945, in prosperity and depression, Victoria Wine had set out, as we have seen, to break the old and treasured image of the wine merchant as an experienced consultant working contentedly alongside the solicitor and the doctor, with the solicitor and the doctor among his chief clients. From the beginning, even when new houses had cellars, the company had sold wines primarily not for the cellar but for the house above, often the small house where the wine was kept in the kitchen or under the stairs. It had been concerned from the start with turnover, not with status, and it had always been keen to advertise. Moreover, it had never hesitated to sell spirits, beer, and soft drinks as well as wine. Ease of access to Victoria Wine's shops meant that over the years it had appealed not only to many British travellers who had learnt what they knew of wine in foreign climes, but to people who had never left the shores of Britain and had no experience of wine being delivered to their homes. It had appealed also on account of its range and its prices to foreign tourists to London, including visitors from France who knew a great deal about wine before they came. The Company was operating, of course, before the supermarkets, and it sold carefully chosen wines of quality as well as cheap wines. Yet it was never satisfied with the market for wine as it actually stood. It was always looking for more customers.

Well-established managers of Victoria Wine stores would have found nothing new, therefore, in the headline of an *Observer* article of 1967 which read 'Wine Trade shakes off some of the Cobwebs'. Nor would they have found anything new in the description which followed of the 'attempt to lift Britain's wine trade out of its mystique-laden past'. As they read on, however, they would have appreciated that the article referred to the latest episode in the history of their own firm – the first full-scale television campaign to sell 'cheap branded table wines'.[4] In this case, the five wines on offer belonged to the clearly labelled Nicolas range, which, it was claimed, already accounted for three-quarters of the

---

[4] *The Observer*, 29 October 1967. There had been an earlier attempt by Harveys to sell 'Club One' in 1963, but the wine was thought to be too expensive and the campaign was said to be 'ahead of its time' and did not succeed.

French market, the largest market for wine in the world, which had never been handled institutionally in the same traditional way as the British market.

Four years earlier, Grants of St. James's had formed a Company, Nicolas–Grants Ltd, with Établissements Nicolas S.A., which had been founded in Paris in the Rue Saint Anne in 1822. The new company planned to import Nicolas wines into Britain and to export whisky and sherry to France.[5] Pierre Nicolas was its Honorary Chairman. Grants were linked also with the German producers of the Goldener Oktober range of wines, St Ursula Weingut und Kellerei, makers of what were said to be Germany's first branded wines. The Nicolas Wines were imported in bulk and sold at 8s 3d a bottle, well below the ceiling of 10s which it was then thought allowed for a sales breakthrough.

The expensive television campaign of 1967, which cost £250,000, was launched by Grants who by then, like Victoria Wine, were a subsidiary of Allied Breweries, and the language used by Derrick (later Sir Derrick) Holden-Brown, then their Deputy Chairman – and Chairman of Victoria Wine – was certainly without the slightest tinge of mystique. The campaign, he stated, was part of a long-term plan designed to encourage people to identify and pick up from the shelves 'a cheap no frills table wine' as 'readily as they now buy a bottle of ketchup'.[6] Holden Brown hoped to sell 250,000 cases a week. He was seeking 'brand leadership'.

Grants of St. James's, a company with a new name but a long pedigree, was the immediate successor to B. Grant and Company, which had been formed in 1904 to take over the Wine and Spirit Department of Ind Coope and Company Ltd eight years after Ind Coope moved into such business. The first manager's name was Bernard Grant Holden, after whose middle name the name of the Company was taken, and its activities were limited at first to supplying the tied customers of Ind Coope, a brewery which owned a large number of tied public houses. Its sales increased substantially after 1934, however, when Ind Coope merged with Samuel Allsopp and Sons Ltd. By 1939, its turnover was over £1 million, and 15 retail shops had been acquired.

---

[5] Établissements Nicolas was renowned in the 1930s for its price lists, illustrated by well-known graphic artists. It also made a well-known cartoon film, *The Sleeping Beauty*, in 1935. In 1972 it held a worldwide auction sale of some of its finest wines to celebrate its 150th birthday. The proceeds were given to the 'Venice in Peril' fund.

[6] *The Observer*, 29 October 1967. See also an article in the *Observer Magazine*, 9 September 1979, by Derek Cooper, 'Wine Thrives in the Chains'.

There were no links of any kind at that time with Victoria Wine. Nor were there any links between Ind Coope as brewers and Victoria Wine. The links were forged as the result of the mergers of the late 1950s and early 1960s, when many other new links in the chain were being forged as well. In 1959, eight years before Derrick Holden-Brown made his statement about the Nicolas campaign, Ind Coope, which had already begun a series of much publicised take-overs two years before, had acquired Taylor Walker Ltd, the parent company of Victoria Wine.[7] The genealogies are as intricate as the genealogies of medieval manors, and spirits were often a part of the deal, as well as wine. Thus, Ind Coope acquired not only Victoria Wine, but the Curtis Distillery Company, which had its distant origins in Mile End in 1769, almost a hundred years before William Winch Hughes started Victoria Wine not very far away. John Curtis had been apprenticed as a distiller as early as 1722.

In 1958 the Curtis Distillery Company, from which Victoria Wine was already buying spirits,[8] had itself taken over the wine and spirit business of J. and W. Nicholson and had changed its name to Curtis Nicholson; and two years later the name of Grants of St. James's became the name of the new business unit when in April 1960 B. Grant merged with Curtis Nicholson. Within the new set-up of 1961, only later to be called Allied Breweries, most of the foreign wines sold in Victoria Wine shops were shipped and bottled by Grants of St. James's which thereafter became Victoria Wine's 'sister company', operating as four regional companies within the old Ind Coope, Tetley Walker and Ansells areas. Meanwhile, 46 of the old B. Grant and Company shops were transferred to the Victoria Wine chain. And through this and other transfers Victoria Wine, as part of a bigger and still expanding Group, became a far bigger concern in itself, merging with other retail businesses. By 1965, one hundred years after its foundation, it had as many as 630 shops. In 1977, for a time it had over 1,000.

Equally important, through the operations of the Allied Breweries Group, it became associated during the 1960s with many other businesses, some of which, like Harveys of Bristol, founded in 1796, had even longer histories of their own, older even than Établissements Nicolas. The then Managing Director of Harveys, Michael McWatters, was the great grandson of the first John Harvey, who joined the

---

[7] See above p. 117.
[8] When in January 1953 whisky bottled with a Curtis Distillery label was difficult to sell because of the 'steady improvement in

proprietary Scotch whisky' supplies, the Victoria Wine label was used instead (*Minutes*, 29 January 1953).

Company in 1822. Yet the history of Harveys during the 1960s was even more dramatic than that of Victoria Wine. In 1966 it was taken over by Showerings Ltd of Shepton Mallet, which had been incorporated as a private company in 1932 and had gone public in 1959. Showerings were producers of 'Babycham', the popular new drink of the 1950s made from pears, which had first been produced in 1946, winning a prize under the traditional name 'perry' at the Three Counties Agricultural Show at Worcester in 1950, and which after a run of further prizes became known as 'baby champ'.[9] Orders came in so fast during the 1950s that demand is said to have exceeded supply by twenty to one.[10]

The rapid increase in sales of 'Babycham', given its name in 1953, owed much to television advertising; and it was after the Showerings takeover that an equally lively advertising campaign in foreign markets succeeded in pushing sales of Harveys' Bristol Cream in the United States to the point in 1968 when it accounted for one-third of the American market for imported sherries.[11] The Showerings sales force of nearly five hundred men was the biggest in the drinks business, and the profitability of Harveys rose by 40 per cent in the first year after the take-over.[12]

There was very sharp competition in the wine and spirits business, notably with International Distillers and Vintners, and there was a further increase in the size of the bloc within which Victoria Wine operated when a massive deal later in 1968 led to the merging of Showerings with Allied Breweries. Already before that date, Showerings had become a big bloc in themselves, having acquired R.N. Coates and Company, cider makers, in 1956, Jules Duvall and Company, wine dealers, in 1959, William Gaymer and Sons, Britain's oldest cider makers, Vine Products, Britain's largest producers of British Wines,[13] and Whiteways Ltd in 1961.

In 1969 Francis Showering became Chairman of the Wines, Spirits

---

[9] In 1952, seven years before going public, Showerings decided to 'brew their last barrel' of beer and concentrate on the production of cider and perry. (*Morning Advertiser*, 21 August 1952.)

[10] See *The Grapevine*, March 1983, which includes a highly informative article by Clive Smith, 'The Life and Times of Francis Showering CBE' along with many other articles about the history of the business.

[11] *The Times*, 18 May 1968.

[12] *The Observer*, 9 July 1967, 'Hard Sell Hits the Cellarman'. In 1962 Harveys had taken over the whisky firm, Stewart and Son of Dundee, makers of 'the Cream of the Barley'.

[13] Vine Products had been founded in 1905 four years after Alexander and Minos Mitzokadis had established their Crown Grape Company in Fulham. In 1954 it had entered the soft drinks market and had acquired Britvic. The secret negotiations with Showering in 1961 led to the naming of the amalgamated company Showerings, Vine Products and Whiteways.

and Soft Drinks Division of the new Allied Breweries Group. 'When two live wires come together', Francis's brother Herbert remarked, 'there are bound to be sparks', and the new division prospered from the beginning, after nine years becoming one of three such divisions, along with Beer and Food, the third created in 1978 after the acquisition by Allied Breweries of J. Lyons and Company. 'Sparks there were', Sir Derrick Holden-Brown, now Chairman and Chief Executive of Allied-Lyons, was to recall in 1983, 'but out of the sparking process there flowed agreed and identical objectives: a determination to ensure that the business was profitable, soundly based and expanding, with long-term growth changes in mind'.[14]

In consequence of these and other moves, wine for sale acquired a radically different business orientation in the 1970s from that which it had in the late 1940s, when Eric Fisher still managed the Victoria Wine concern as part of the Taylor Walker Group. Fisher's emblem was a screw press: a new emblem might have been a clearly labelled bottle on a television screen. Yet the result of the merger, which began with beer – Allied Breweries owned around 9,000 public houses – was a huge increase in sales of wine. Indeed, as Allied Breweries grew in strength, its financial stake in wines, spirits and soft drinks became as large as its stake in beer.[15] There could be greater profits here also. By 1980/81, when turnover in each of its three divisions was almost identical at just under £800 million, trading profit margins on wine, spirits and soft drinks (7.4 per cent) were higher than those on beer (5.9 per cent) and food (4.1 per cent). So, too, of course, were advertising expenditures. At the same time, since the business structure of the huge Group reflected a deeply rooted belief in decentralisation (and 'a decentralised management style'), Victoria Wine, as a very profitable component of the total business within the Group, retained through all the successive phases of amalgamation and reorganisation a distinctive identity of its own.

Recent Allied/Lyons Reports and Accounts, very different documents in appearance and scope from the Reports of Victoria Wine during the 1930s and 1940s, have described succinctly the most recent changes in the fortunes of Victoria Wine against a background of 'intense competition in the High Street and a reduced total market'.[16] Yet the total market by the early 1980s was far bigger than it had been a

---

[14] *The Grapevine*, March 1983.
[15] *Beer, A Report on the Supply of Beer* (HMSO), (1969), p. 21.
[16] Allied/Lyons, *Report and Accounts, 1982*, p. 16.

generation before. Hughes would have appreciated the significance both of the retail growth and of the keen competition required to sustain it. He would doubtless have been delighted also to be told in 1982 that 'the light wine market is the growth area, and it is the Company's aim further to improve its position here'.

Commander McGrath would not have dissented either, although he would perhaps have been even more delighted, given his own particular interests, in a further remark that 'Victoria Wine branches are maintained to very high standards, and it is also part of their strategy that trading sites be continually reviewed and improved'. During the Second World War he had been anxious to secure West End premises 'to deal with the high class trade now being done',[17] and 3 Clifford Street had been acquired. And he had insisted after the Second World War, as before it, on carefully supervising acquisition of all new premises. He would have detected a logic in the process whereby Victoria Wine has been transformed, and he would have noted with special pride the presence of his nephew, Brian H. McGrath, Master of Wine, on the Board of Directors of Allied/Lyons.[18]

It is unwise, nonetheless, to trace the history of a business in terms of the kind of logic which is derived only from today's hindsight. In fact, the end of the 1970s and the 1980s have no claims to be special vantage points. The business continues to change, and some of the tendencies of recent years have not yet established themselves as trends. There were many surprises in its story after 1945. In January 1948, for example, when Commander McGrath was still Chairman, Eric Fisher was killed in an air crash *en route* to Bermuda in the air liner Star Tiger. Three years later, the death of Arthur Edwardes, joint Managing Director of the Company, came as a distressing surprise too, although there was no surprise in the ensuing appointment of the Assistant Manager, H.N. Harris, an accountant, as joint Managing Director of the Company. He had joined it in 1936.

What is never surprising in the wine trade – or in brewing – is the kind of continuity represented at the top by Brian McGrath's directorship and 'lower down' in the persons who work in offices, warehouses and shops. There are always people with a very long record of service. In 1981, for example, there were 24 people still employed by Victoria Wine with 40 years or more of service and another 26 with 30 years or more,

---

[17] Victoria Wine Board, *Minutes*, 20 October 1943.
[18] *Ibid.*, 27 September 1955. Brian McGrath joined the Company at the age of 21.

each one with his or her own story to tell. Miss Granger, for example, joined the Company in 1919 at Goldhawk Road and had later served as Manageress at St John's Wood, was still employed at the Finchley headquarters fifty years later and could recall every change of style in the business. Fred Hale, who started as a boy on a bicycle at the Hampstead Road shop in 1925 and went on to serve as Fisher's chauffeur until the latter's death, was to go on to spend 14 years with Allied Breweries.

In the pre-merger period from 1945 to 1960, most of the changes which took place in Victoria Wine were of a pattern. First, there was an improvement in organisation in 1946, when a Sales Supervisor was appointed: hitherto there had been no close contact between the shops and headquarters, and the only regular dealings were routed through the orders office. Second, there was a continuing emphasis on expansion, which was given considerable publicity in 1948, the year of an important new Companies Act, when the Company's Articles of Association were revised. As a result, further chains of shops were acquired in different parts of the country. In 1956, 13 years after the take-over of the E.A. Mitchell chain, 11 shops were acquired from Bartlett and Hobbs, to be followed in 1958 by the acquisition of 11 shops from Clifford Nichols and Company in South Wales. Third, decisions were taken to devote increased expenditure to advertising: the budget for 1953, for example, was £16,800, and 'roof cards' in underground railways among the places chosen for advertisements. The scale of advertising was far less than it was to be during the late 1960s, but the objects were the same.

Fourth, and perhaps most important, the business began to look increasingly attractive to outsiders interested in possible take-overs. At the time of a flotation of 600,000 new Ordinary Shares in 1949, Commander McGrath held the largest number of individual shares, 5,000, and there were three other shareholders each holding 4,000, but Taylor, Walker and Company held more than 50 per cent and it was on them that the gaze was fixed. In June 1958, McGrath retired from his Chairmanship, to be replaced as Chairman by his then Vice-Chairman, W.H. Kingsmill, but Kingsmill did not serve as Chairman for long, for in July 1959, when there were only three other Directors, he was replaced after the Ind Coope take-over by an Ind Coope nominee, Derek William Pritchard. The strand of continuity was obvious, however, since Brian McGrath served as Joint Managing Director and Commander McGrath himself remained as a Director.

The turnover figure for 1959 – on the eve of the merger – is not available, but trading profits then were £97,688 (well down on those of

1957, £278,259), and a dividend was paid of 7½ per cent.[19] Fixed assets in property were then valued at £1,062,676 – £251,847 up on 1957 – the kind of increase which attracted outside attention. E.A. Mitchell Ltd., with 25 retail shops, all in Bristol or in the surrounding area, and Clifford Nichols and Company were described as subsidiaries at this time. So, too, were Taylors (Wine Merchants) Ltd and London Wine Importers Ltd. There were then 88 Victoria Wine shops in London and 88 outside, the furthest away at Bletchley, Bognor Regis, Boscombe, Cambridge, Canterbury, Eastbourne, High Wycombe, Slough, Tenterden and Westcliffe-on-Sea.

The wine lists of the pre-merger years reveal first an increasing range of wines, spirits and beers on offer after the end of post-war austerity and, second, rising prices, although the price rise was not comparable with that of the 1970s, when the base price for a bottle of table wine doubled in five years. A 1948 'austerity' list set out details in its first column of eight ports on offer, alongside seven Spanish sherries, three Empire sherries (including a Cyprus, medium dry) and one British sherry ('Canterbury Tales'). The cheapest port then cost 18s a bottle and the dearest 60s, but there was a difference of only 2s between the cheapest sherry at 20s and the most expensive at 22s. There were 17 white Bordeaux ranging from 9s 6d to 14s – most of them were 'medium rich' or 'rich' – and only five clarets, the most expensive a St Julien 1937, at 17s 6d. There were three white and three red burgundies: Meursault 1942 cost 21s, and Beaujolais 1949, 11s 6d.

Vintage 'Grande Marque' champagne cost 25s 6d and non-vintage champagne 22s. There was a sparkling Saumur at 18s 9d and a South African 'Vin Mousseux' Style at 17s 6d. Cheap Australian 'burgundies' included Company brands of the familiar type at 9s and an 'Austral Ruby' at 14s 6d. Compared with this lean list, there was a long list of 20 imported liqueurs, headed with Advocaat at 25s 6d and including green Chartreuse at 61s 9d. 'Standard brand' whiskies cost 33s 4d and 'de luxe' qualities 35s 4d. Gin was slightly less expensive at 32s 4d and brandy more expensive, with Martell, Hennessy, Girand, Courvoisier, Calvet and 'all other French brands' costing 42s.

Prices had fallen in a 1949 Christmas Price List, following important tax changes,[20] so that St Julien 1937 now cost only 15s 6d, and there were

---

[19] Statement of Accounts for the Annual General Meeting, 19 November 1959.
[20] See below p. 153.

were two Mouton Cadets, 1945, at 9s 6d and 1943 at 12s. The price of the cheapest port was now down to 17s 6d and the cheapest sherry to 18s. In both lists there were Algerian wines, a new import, at 6s 9d. Bottled beers included, in addition to Taylor Walker (pale ale, brown ale, stout, reserve ale and barley wine), Bass, Mann, Crossman, Tollemache, Watney, Whitbread, Worthington and Guinness.

Ten years later in 1958, when stocks at cost stood at over £1 million, the list was far more comprehensive. Indeed, the proud slogan of E.A. Mitchell, the Victoria Wine subsidiary, a very competitive business in Bristol, was 'Mitchell's have Everything'. There is no surviving list for 1958/9, but the list for that year of Tyler and Company, a firm with which Victoria Wine was to merge,[21] set out no fewer than 29 vintage ports and 26 sherries. There were 29 clarets, too, only five without specifications of chateau and vintage. Prices had fallen further too. The cheapest port was now 16s and the cheapest sherry also 16s. The cheapest claret was 7s, the oldest, two 1947s. The cheapest red burgundy was 7s 9d and the most expensive a Musigny at 28s 6d. There were six Italian wines, including a sweet Lacrima Cristi and an Asti Spumante, three Hungarian wines, three Portuguese and one Algerian at 7s 6d.

It is clear from other evidence that Victoria Wine had many suppliers at this time – among them Cockburn Smithes and Company[22] and Martinez Gassiot for port; Barton and Company; Bouchard Ainé; Brega and Rossi and Egidio Vitali Ltd for Italian wines; Simon Brothers and Silva and Cosens for Bordeaux and Burgundies; Lessner and Company for Hungarian wines; Jarvis and Halliday for South African wines. Vine Products and Harveys, which, following the Showerings merger, were both to become part of the Allied Breweries Group, supplied respectively British wines, including 'Canterbury Tales', and sherries (as did Gonzalez Byass). The boom in British wines had not yet begun, however,[23] nor the fashion for home wine-making.

Immediately following the merger, the surviving wine lists did not look very different, although the range on offer was advertised far more widely than ever before. Considerable latitude was left to McGrath in wine buying and to Harris in matters relating to shop premises.[24] They were now subject to Group budgeting controls, but ample room was left for a distinctive Victoria Wine strategy. In particular, expansion was still

---

[21] See below pp. 138–9.
[22] Cockburn Smithes y Cia Ltd went on to become a part of the Allied Breweries Group.

[23] See J.H.C. Abbott, *British Wines* (1975).
[24] Note of 20 June 1960.

A modern Victoria Wine Company shop (exterior)

A modern Victoria Wine Company shop (interior)

the order of the day. Thus, it was stated specifically in an Ind Coope *Minute* that while 'expenditure on new projects could not be accurately forecast ... a bid should nevertheless be submitted to the Committee (of Management) to cover anticipated outlay in respect of (new) individual projects likely to arise in the financial year', and an estimate of £150,000 was duly submitted.[25]

The same procedure was followed in 1961, by which time Victoria Wine had acquired a large number of new retail shops as part of the giant merger, some of them only recently taken over by Ind Coope, like Beverleys Ltd with 44.[26] On the eve of this change, the expansion of the Victoria Wine business was said to be greatest in the West Country,[27] but all the Cluff and Pickering shops were within 25 miles of the centre of Manchester, and there was now expansion everywhere.

The result of the increase in the number of shops and their new geographical scatter was a basic reorganisation of Victoria Wine itself, which was now divided into four 'divisions' – London, Northern, Western and Scottish. The possibilities of expansion for each division were now considered separately as part of the budgetary process: they were also related to other aspects of group strategy, particularly the development of Grants of St. James's which was selling wines not only to Victoria Wine but to other customers.

E.A. Mitchells, now with about a hundred shops, were fully incorporated into the Company in October 1961 to become the Western division, and on the same day the nucleus of the Scottish division was provided when the retail trading concern of J.J. Blanche and Company, which had been acquired by B. Grant and Company in 1960, was also taken over.[28] Later in the year, the John Murray and Son group of shops in Glasgow was added to the Victoria Wine chain. Meanwhile, Beverleys and B. Grant provided the foundation of the Northern division[29], and J.R. Phillips, a firm of wholesale wine merchants in Bristol, taken over in

---

[25] Victoria Wine Directors' Meeting, *Minutes*, 10 May 1960, with cross reference to an Ind Coope *Minute* of 3 March 1960. The capital Reserve Account then stood at just over £1 million. There were only two Directors besides the Chairman, Derek Pritchard, and the Secretary was A.L. Ament.

[26] In 1953 Seagar Evans had bought the share capital in Beverleys: they sold out to Ind Coope in 1959–60. William Cluff had started his business in 1904 at Deansgate, Manchester, and entered a partnership with his clerk, Rupert Pickering, in 1917. Cluff

also sold out to Ind Coope in 1959–60.

[27] Report of the Board of Directors, 17 November 1960. The profit on the 53-week year 1959–60 was £351,078.

[28] Victoria Wine Board, *Minutes*, 2 June 1961.

[29] Other smaller chains incorporated in the Northern division included five P.G. Ward shops which had been acquired by Ind Coope; R.P. Brindley with J. and L. White shops, which had been acquired by Tetleys; Favell and Cockayne of Sheffield; Fountains of Derby; and nine shops in Hull.

1961, provided a warehouse, a bottling plant and later the headquarters of the Western division. In addition, ten other shops from associated companies and 51 from 'outside sources' were acquired in 1961/2, and six shops were closed.[30]

The total value of licensed and other properties, leaving out shop furniture and equipment, now stood at £1,869,339, and, not surprisingly, it was reported in November 1962 that 'great selectivity' was now being shown in the policy of acquiring properties coupled 'with the aim of avoiding large payments for goodwill'. It was reported also that there was greater concentration on expansion in areas where there was a reasonable chance of securing a full Justices' licence, and that special attention was being paid to new housing development areas and new towns. Hitherto, none of the Company's bids for premises in the new towns, where shop leases were open to tender, had been accepted.[31] They were to be key places on the map in the future of the business.

Expansion never stopped during the 1960s. In 1963 the chain of 38 shops owned by W. Glendenning & Sons of Newcastle upon Tyne was acquired, and two years later, in 1965, a particularly exciting year, 83 shops trading as Bristol Vintners Ltd were acquired from Harveys of Bristol. Glendenning had held the Cointreau agency since 1906, when the family first met Edouard Cointreau at Angers: in 42 years, Garth Glendenning wrote in 1948, there had 'never been the smallest vestige of disagreement between the two Houses'.[32] As for Bristol Vintners, they themselves were a widely scattered group geographically, the result of take-overs – with A.J. Smith and Company of London, Byron Gulliver of Hertfordshire, Connelly and Oliver in the Midlands, Sidgwick & Cowell of Ipswich and, not least, Matthew & Son of Cambridge, known to generations of Cambridge undergraduates. The name 'Bristol Vintners' was retained for 61 of the shops in 1963,[33] but four shops were transferred to the Northern division of Victoria Wine, two to the Western division, and 16 to Tyler and Company, which merged financially with Victoria Wine in September 1965 to form Victoria Wine-Tylers Ltd.[34]

Tyler and Company was a large and successful concern, founded at Woking in 1902, with 163 shops in 1965, most of them in Surrey, Sussex and Hampshire. Indeed, although it had not been in direct geographical

---

[30] Report of the Board of Directors, January 1963.
[31] Board *Minute* of 1 November 1962.
[32] G. Glendenning, 'Notes on the Cointreau Agency,' 1948.

[33] Until 1964 the names over their shops remained the same as they had been before the Harvey's takeover.
[34] Victoria Wine Board, *Minutes*, 8 April 1965.

competition with Victoria Wine, it had been in a real sense a competitor as far as standards and achievements were concerned. The new merger, the most important of all Victoria Wine's mergers, was the result of a take-over acquisition by Allied Breweries earlier in 1965 of Friary Meux, one of their own old rivals in the brewing industry, and this itself the product of an amalgamation of 1956.[35]

During the 1930s Tylers, with an enterprising wine list and a range of 'Shakespearian' sherries, including 'Twelfth Night' and 'Dogberry', had pioneered wine shops as part of 'pubs'; in 1946 they opened a shop in Wigmore Street, London[36] and during the 1950s they had broadened horizons and moved north-westwards to Cheltenham, Upton-on-Severn and Tewkesbury. In 1959 they had acquired 43 shops (and a brewery) from G. Peters and Company, two from James Brown which gave them a footing in Oxford, and four from J.K. Munger and Son Ltd, one of which was in Leighton Buzzard (where there was also a Victoria Wine shop). When they were taken over as part of the Allied/Friary Meux merger, they were accounting for between 30 to 40 per cent of the profits of the Friary Meux group. They were renowned too for their pioneering attitude to store management. Since 1951, for example, they had been operating a system of self-service.

There was remarkable continuity in the Tyler enterprise also, for W.O. Crawt, who became Managing Director in 1954, had been appointed Company Secretary in September 1931; and it was he who became Managing Director of the new Victoria Wine-Tyler Ltd, with Derrick Holden-Brown as Chairman and Brian McGrath first as Vice-Chairman and then as Chairman. At the same time, the old Friary depot at Slyfield became a Grants of St James's depot. The two partners, Victoria Wine and Tylers, continued to trade under their own names, but it was Crawt, the former competitor, from his head office at Finchley who had to deal with the three biggest changes in the wine business since the nineteenth century – changes in licensing rules; the end of resale price maintenance; and the growth of supermarket competition.[37] Moreover, it was these three changes which influenced the merger movement of the

---

[35] Friary, Holroyd and Healeys Breweries, of which Tylers was a subsidiary from 1908 onwards, merged in 1956 with Meux Brewery to form Friary Meux Ltd.

[36] Tyler and Company, *Minutes*, 3 January 1945. Tylers had built up good stocks before the War. In March 1944 stock in hand was set at £85,000 as against £100,000 a year

earlier. (*Minutes*, 27 April 1943). At that time Tylers were still running a number of grocery shops also, notably in Leatherhead, Three Bridges and Cranleigh. The Cranleigh branch had received the Royal Warrant to Edward Prince of Wales, later King Edward VIII, when he lived at Fort Belvedere.

[37] See below, p. 143.

1960s which in turn left the wine trade in a very different position at the end of the decade from that at the beginning.

There had been one important earlier change in licensing rules in 1949, which had the effect of multiplying the number of off-licences at a time when the number of 'pub' on-licences was diminishing. Already by 1950, the number of public houses had fallen from over 100,000 fifty years earlier to less than 80,000, and the number of off-licences had almost doubled from 18,000 to 32,000, of which 19,000, however, were for beer only and not for wines and spirits. There were changes also within the 'pubs' themselves, many of them owned by the large breweries, both in their appearance, their pattern of sales and their style of service.[38] Tenanted pubs were a distinctive feature of the British social scene.[39]

Far bigger changes came during the 1960s, beginning with a new Licensing Act in 1961, the first general revision of the licensing law for forty years, and a further consolidating Act of 1964 which is the basis of the present law. In the latter year, Edward Heath committed the Government too to the abolition of resale price maintenance which he deemed 'in general' to be 'incompatible with the objective of encouraging effective competition and keeping down costs and prices'.[40] With the rapid growth of supermarkets, now able to sell wines and spirits like any other commodity, at all times when they were open, competition became keen enough for Crawt to describe as 'vicious' some of the price cutting which he had to face.[41] Indeed, before Victoria Wine-Tylers was formed, he had been in consultation with McGrath about the business consequences of new retail developments.[42] Profit margins were being reduced, and many well-established smaller wine stores were either closing or facing the threat of closure. 'The wine trade has started a marketing war', Roger Eglin wrote in *The Observer* in May 1968, 'with an intensity that smacks of detergents rather than Mouton Rothschild.'[43]

The consequence was a sharp break in style in the amalgamated business in 1967. Hitherto almost all wine shops, whether Victoria Wine or Tylers, had operated on what had become by then a 'traditional' style,

---

[38] Vaizey, *op. cit.*, p. 120. By the early 1950s sales of wines and spirits in bigger houses already accounted for 20 per cent or more of their turnover; and while sales of food rarely exceeded 2 per cent to 3 per cent of sales, it was obvious that as this proportion increased there would be a growing demand for wine – and soft drinks.

[39] See H.A. Monckton, *The Story of the British Pub* (1983).

[40] See 'Boldness in Competition' in *The Economist*, 18 January 1964.

[41] Tyler and Company, *Board Minutes*, July 1965.

[42] *Ibid.*, 25 March 1965.

[43] *The Observer*, 12 May 1968.

with counter service, credit and delivery facilities, and a wide range of stock on display. Now 'Wine Markets' began to appear, working on a cash-and-carry basis with a limited range of stock on offer at highly competitive prices. The new system, which had something in common with the system first developed by Hughes, favoured the sale of branded wines. Moreover, it was easier as a result of it to integrate the activities of the individual shop into the large-scale structure of national amalgamations competing increasingly through national advertising.

Grants of St James's, a key component in the integration process, launched its Nicolas sales drive at this point, pushing at the same time a Don Cortez range of Spanish wines, in conditions of hard selling in a growing market.[44] One competitor was Peter Dominic and Westminster Wine, the retail arm of International Distillers and Vintners, who had themselves taken over many smaller chains and were running an enthusiastic Wine Mine Club with its own magazine.[45] Others were Arthur Cooper, linked with Courage, and Threshers Limited, linked with Whitbreads. But it was the competition from groceries and supermarkets that speeded up the merging of the big groups – with Grants themselves selling wine to well-established grocery businesses like Liptons and Maypole and to new firms like Victor Value and Tesco. In such circumstances the management of Victoria Wine had to take stock of every move: it could not afford to look 'staid'. It had to push its wines with the help of national as well as local advertising, to compete in the presentation of 'special offers' and, above all, to establish its own image. It also had to deepen the knowledge of its managers about wine if image and reality were not to diverge.

One other response was to increase further still in size. In the same year, 1967, as its first changes of style took place, 96 shops operated by Castle and Company, a subsidiary of George G. Sandemans and Company Ltd, the port shippers, were acquired,[46] along with eight shops of P.G. Ward and Company. Castle and Company, which had started as a theatre bar company in 1898, brought a new strand into the Victoria Wine-Tylers inheritance, although the Company had gone into the off-licence trade as early as 1918 and, after their purchase by Sandeman and Company in 1925, had acquired several chains of local shops in

---

[44] See *The Economist*, 1 June 1968, 'A Matter of Taste'.

[45] The Autumn 1962 number began with a memorable article by J.B. Priestley, 'Some Tots and Sips': its sub-title was 'Are you a Mediterranean or a Baltic Type?'

[46] In 1961/2, Allied Breweries had acquired a shareholding in Sandeman and had entered into a long-term trading relationship with it. At the same time, Sandemans acquired a one-third stake in J.R. Phillips, as did the House of Seagram.

South Wales and Lancashire.[47] Many Castle shops had been rivals of Tylers. They had sold Sandeman ports, while Tylers sold Gonzalez Byass sherries. Such old rivalries were forgotten in 1970, however, when a group of Sandeman shops was acquired by Victoria Wine-Tylers and when Ansells, one of the three breweries which made up the beer division of Allied Breweries, transferred a chain of 128 'My Cellar' shops around Birmingham, which had previously traded under their own name, to Victoria Wine-Tylers.

In 1971 there was a change of management when Crawt retired as Managing Director and Eric Colwell took his place – with Brian McGrath as Chairman. Colwell had entered the business by a different route from any of his predecessors. He had been the Accountant of one of the firms taken over by Ind Coope before 1959 – Bartlett and Hobbs, a small local wholesale wine and spirit business which he had joined in 1957 – and he was now to serve as Managing Director of Victoria Wine until 1984 through another period of striking change in the character of the business. Promotions within the bigger businesses of the day often pushed to the top men who had been associated with smaller units of the giant amalgamations. Thus, it was Keith Showering who rose to the top of Allied Breweries. He was to receive a knighthood in the Queen's Birthday Honours List of 1981 in the year before his sudden death.

The first big change in Victoria Wine when Colwell took over in 1971 was structural. It was decided in 1973, after detailed research, that all shops should henceforth trade as 'Victoria Wine' in order to take full advantage of the Company's dominant national position. The decision followed the acquisition of the enterprising Wine Ways chain of 160 shops, a concern built out of the old-established Valentine Charles business and selling wines at highly competitive prices. It had been very profitable during the years 1970–72 and brought into Victoria Wine an up-to-date retailing organisation.[48] In such new circumstances in 1976 Victoria Wine-Tylers Ltd reverted to the old name, Victoria Wine Ltd. There were then eleven directors, including Keith and F.E. Showering, along with David Bedford, G. Davies, J.W. Dunnington, A.B.H. Edwards, I.T. Glendenning, A.O. Hunt and F.C. Roberts.

The second change was financial, and it reflected new social and cultural trends in a period of national economic and political upheaval. The 1970s was a more difficult decade than the 'swinging' 1960s,

---

[47] The Welsh stores belonged to Hallinan and the Lancashire stores to Bradshaws.

[48] See E. Colwell, 'The Off-Licence' in *The Grapevine*, March 1983.

beginning with the news that during the first six months of 1970, after a decade of remarkable growth in the wine trade, the British were drinking less wine than they had done during the first six months of 1969.[49] There were to be many problems during the decade, particularly those associated with an unforecast coexistence of unprecedented inflation and mass unemployment. Nevertheless, the wine trade as a whole did not languish,[50] and Victoria Wine turnover increased year by year in what also was unprecedented fashion:

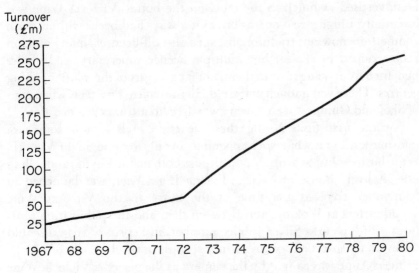

TABLE 18 *Victoria Wine Turnover, 1967–1980*

This remarkable increase in turnover was achieved in the face of continuing inroads by the supermarkets into the retail wine business.[51] While Victoria Wine prospered, there were many smaller firms which went into the red and some which slid into oblivion. *The Times* had pointed to one of the essential ingredients of success in its introduction to the decade, even if it rested on a somewhat dubious presupposition, 'Too often the inflexible efficiency of big business can discourage a creative personality and eventually deter the layman from venturing into wine-drinking. It is significant that the retail chains which have wine departments showing good profits are those where interested individuals provide personal service.'[52]

---

[49] *The Times*, 12 November 1970.
[50] See below, p. 165ff.
[51] See below, p. 166.
[52] *The Times*, 12 November 1970.

In 1973 *The Sunday Times Magazine* congratulated Grants of St James's for providing the three best wines on the table in a competition between chains and supermarkets – among them a St Emilion, the best among 21 wines and selling at 74p a bottle – a verdict often repeated.[53] Grants were selling, too, of course, to Victoria Wine's retail competitors, so that it became increasingly important to train Victoria Wine managers 'to give the customer confidence' and focus on the corporate 'personality' of the Victoria Wine business.[54] In consequence, the name on the shop began to be advertised as much as the label on the bottle. Victoria Wine was essentially a high street operation, as it always had been, with its main competitors now not traditionalist specialist off-licences, many of them now grouped in chains, but multiple licence supermarkets. Its sales benefited from being near to them, not far away from the main shopping centres. There was a touch of the old Hughes spirit, however, when cans of Skol and Guinness were given away free 'to attract customer flow'.[55]

For the first time during these years there is a new source of information about what was happening not only to trends in the Victoria Wine business but to attitudes – attitudes both on the buying and selling side. A lively house magazine, *Victoria Wine News*, was launched in September 1973 at the time of the move to the Victoria Wine headquarters at Woking, and between then and the publication of its twenty-fifth issue, a Silver Jubilee number, in February 1979, it could claim many so-called 'coups', if not scoops, in its chronicle of events. Princess Anne was caught by the camera as she passed a Victoria Wine shop at the opening of Port Talbot's Aberfan Centre, and the comedian Dave Allen had a front page picture showing him buying two cases of Moët & Chandon. The Jubilee number, which featured, as previous numbers had done, the 'old and the new', showed pictures of the Surbiton shop, which was already there in 1896, and of Frank Potter, its Manager, who had been with Victoria Wine for thirty years. It also had a picture of the King's Road, Chelsea, branch, originally a house converted into a jeweller's shop during the 1800s and radically transformed since the 1950s: its manager, Paul Giddy, who had been at the branch for 21 years, recalled more recent history too. He had had to board up the windows every Saturday morning during the 1970s, anticipating fights between 'Punk Rockers' on the King's Road.

---

[53] *The Sunday Times Magazine*, 2 December 1973.

[54] See E. Colwell, Speech at the Supermarketing Conference, 4 November

1981, reprinted in *Supermarketing*, 6 November 1981.

[55] E. Colwell, 'The Off-Licence' in *The Grapevine*, March 1983.

The same Jubilee number announced details of the latest Victoria Wine Education Scholarships scheme which was open to all employees of Victoria Wine, grouped in different categories, with Shop Managers first. They had to complete a difficult questionnaire and went through different stages 'in a fun way' until the winners reached regional semi-finals and national finals.[56] All twelve finalists were to win travel scholarships; the top four were to visit European wine growing areas and the other eight, Highland whisky distilleries. As the business became more sophisticated, the necessary knowledge required in order to master it grew at every level. Training schemes became increasingly important, therefore, and a school at Stockport was opened in 1978.

A 1977 Commemorative Jubilee Wine List to celebrate Queen Elizabeth's Silver Jubilee compared prices then with prices at the time of Queen Victoria's Golden Jubilee in 1897. There were informative notes by John Arlott and an addendum, 'Victoria Wine regrets that these prices no longer apply'. In 1897 there had been 21 Spanish sherries and six montillas on the list, compared with 24 and three in 1977 and 27 ports (plus two 'Spanish ports') compared with 12. There were also in 1897 madeiras and marsalas in profusion, rich dessert wines (for the morning as much as for the evening), a Spanish red wine 'Tent' from Alicante, and a 'Canary' wine which disappeared in the twentieth century. There had been no French wines from the Rhone, Alsace or from the Loire in 1897, except for Saumur: now there were more than 12. Only two vineyards had been specifically mentioned in 1897 (Château d'Yquem and Moulin à Vent) and no vintage years, except in the case of champagne, were listed. Now, despite the new emphasis on blending, individual vineyards were frequently mentioned, as were years. Yet even in 1897 'wholesome and bloodmaking' Californian 'Big Tree' had been actively promoted, and there was a prominent place, too, for Australian and Canadian wines. There was to be a boom in sales of Californian wine in Britain during the 1980s,[57] but already during the 1890s the London wine firm of Grierson, Oldham and Company had begun importing wines from California on a substantial scale, and on the eve of the First World War there were Californian accounts of a 'vogue of Californian wines' in London.[58] Indeed, the British have been described as the pioneers of the

---

[56] 'The change we want to see in Victoria Wine,' Colwell wrote when introducing the scheme, 'is an improvement in our sales of Table Wines ... One good way of doing this is to study and enter for the Wine Scholarship.'

[57] *Pacific Wine and Spirit Review*, 30 June 1912.

[58] For the beginnings, see J. Robinson, 'Taste of Richness from the Gold-Rush State' in *The Times*, 9 July 1980.

Victoria Wine Branch Directory May 1982

Californian wine industry, Victoria Wine active among them.[59]

Continuities in the business were as much stressed in 1977 as contrasts. In 1977 there were 14 Victoria Wine shops still open which had been open in 1897, and photographers were approached to collect pictures of historic sites like Shad Thames, The Dell and 10 Catherine Court, Tower Hill. Shops with a long history included 104 Brixton Hill, 160 Ebury Street, which had been closed in 1941 as a result of enemy action, 51 The Broadway, Wimbledon, 62 High Street, Hampstead, and perhaps most appropriately named of all, England's Lane, Belsize Park.

Some of the most successful shops, however, were not only new shops but were new shops in new places. The new town of Milton Keynes (headquarters of the new Open University) came fifteenth in the list at the beginning of the 1980s and was to head it in 1982/3, as one of two shops having a turnover in excess of £1 million. Others in the top ten in 1982/3 were to include Penarth, Deal, Largs, Chiswick and Tower Hamlets, an extraordinarily varied list both geographically and socially. All in all, there were by then 77 Victoria Wine shops with takings in excess of £500,000. No attempt was being made to increase the number of shops for its own sake. Indeed, there were to be fewer shops in 1982/3 (916) than in 1977 (972). The peak figure was 990 in December 1975.

Lay-out was changing considerably, but was still conceived of as 'traditional'. 'Flashing lights and chromium plated signs' are not 'the style for the wine merchant' was the considered opinion of Dan Keough, the Company's marketing director, who had joined Victoria Wine from Grants of St James's in 1972. 'You can't be a specialist easily if you are operating in a warehouse ... Think of other specialists, like jewellers, and look how they operate ... If you increase a shop size, it doesn't necessarily mean there will be extra sales.' 'Our ability to perform profitably is dependent on our ability to project ourselves as wine specialists. An ideal site for one of our shops would be to have a supermarket either side. It would mean enormous customer flow.'[60]

National advertising, reinforced by market research and increased attention to packaging and display, assisted the activities of the store managers. The corporate image of the business became nationally well-known through such promotional activities as the Rugby Team of the Week Award in the *Sunday Telegraph*, begun in 1979/80, the Cricketer of

---

[59] See W.T. Heintz, 'Heintz on History', his monthly column in *Wines and Vines*, May 1981.
[60] *Drinks*, June 1983.

the Week, which began three years earlier, and the Cricketer of the Season, begun in 1978. Meanwhile in 1978, David Bedford, Master of Wine, launched his first *Wine News Letter*, modestly described as his 'last scribbles',[61] setting out invaluable personalised advice to customers. The last number before the end of the decade ended with the words:

> If we could have another vintage in 1980 like 1979, it would have a beneficial effect on prices and then, please Lord, could we have a 'Vintage of the Century' in 1981?[62]

The clarets had to wait until 1982, which some observers compared not only with 1961 but with 'the fabulous 1929s'.[63]

---

[60] *Drinks*, June 1983.

[61] *Wine News Letter*, Summer 1978.

[62] *Ibid.*, March 1980. There were several wines on the list which cost less than £2 – among them a French Dry White at £1.89, an Orvieto at £1.95 and a Yugoslav 'Sauvignon' at £1.69.

[63] *The Times*, 2 March 1985.

CHAPTER NINE

The Supply and Demand for Wine 1945-1980

The story of Victoria Wine between 1945 and 1980 is part of a far bigger national story. 'There has been a great deal of talk recently', Hugh Johnson, one of the most knowledgeable and authoritative authors of books on wine, wrote in 1974, 'about how wine consumption is on the increase in Britain'. 'Certainly the percentage increases over the last few years have been impressive,' he went on, 'but we have a long way to go before we can be called a wine-drinking nation. Compared with the French, the Anglo-Saxon countries scarcely touch it. The following are the total wine-drinking figures for the United Kingdom and France – every man, woman and child in the United Kingdom – 7 bottles a year: every man, woman and child in France – 142 bottles a year'.[1]

This was an old, indeed the old, comparison. Yet the increase in the British figures after 1945 was strikingly impressive. Total consumption of wine in 1945 was 4,373,000 gallons, when the trade, hit, as it usually has been, by 'the crippling burden of taxation', was finding consolation in 'small mercies', like the fact that modest concession shipments of wine had begun to reach Britain.[2] In 1974, the year when Johnson's book was published (when the Allied Breweries Group was the biggest and most comprehensive beer, wine and spirits organisation in Britain), the figure was almost twenty times as great – 83½ million gallons. Nor was this the peak year of the 1970s, a decade not of economic growth but of economic difficulties and doubts: the figure for 1979 was 94½ million gallons. Indeed, by then the consumption figure for British-produced wine (as

---

[1] H. Johnson, *Wine* (1974), p. 19. The top three beer-drinking countries in 1970 were Czechoslovakia, West Germany and Belgium, and Australia, New Zealand and Austria also came before the United Kingdom.

[2] *The Wine and Spirit Trade Review*, 28 December 1945.

against imported wine) was more than 12½ million gallons, nearly three times the figure for total wine consumption in 1945, double the 1946 figure, and more than the 1949 and 1950 figures; this figure, too, was to be exceeded again in 1981, 1982 and 1983.

Year	Imported	British Wine	Total
1945	1,638	2,735	4,373
1950	8,092	3,662	11,754
1955	11,783	5,075	16,858
1960	16,597	6,827	23,424
1965	27,404	9,570	36,974
1970	32,541	10,999	42,640
1975	62,610	16,762	79,372
1979	92,004	12,573	104,577

TABLE 19 *Total Wine Consumption, 1945–1979*
(Thousand gallons)   (Year Ending 31 March)

The prelude to the present, the long period of peace or relative peace between 1945 and 1980 within which this unprecedented upward trend is traceable, falls, when more closely examined, into distinct shorter phases, each with its own identity, like the shorter phases in the history of Victoria Wine. There were at least five of them between 1945 and 1980. The first phase, from 1945 to 1950, in contrast to what came later, was one of continuing austerity, when there were worse privations in relation to the availability of many articles of consumption (including bread and potatoes) than there had been during the War. There was a 15 per cent cut in beer production in the year ending September 1945, and in August 1945 a further 10 per cent cut was imposed on average gravities. Bread rationing did not end until 1955. The second, a phase of steady, if not spectacular recovery and growth, culminated in the year 1959, a vintage year for wine, when Harold Macmillan reminded and warned the electors that they had never had it so good. The third phase from 1959 to 1967 saw a continuing increase in production and consumption, while the fourth from 1967 to 1974, with Britain's entry into the European Economic Community in 1971 standing out as a landmark, saw a far more remarkable growth, reaching its climax in 1974, one of the most difficult years in the history both of the British economy and of the British political system. In the last phase, there was a falling off in the consumption of imported wine in 1975 and 1976, but a continuing upward trend after that date.

Within each phase there were peak and trough years. 1949, 1953, 1966 and 1970 were trough years and 1948, 1974 and 1979 peak years. Yet in every year between 1958 and 1965 total consumption rose. Meanwhile, total beer consumption, which was higher in 1946, when beer cost a shilling a pint, than in any year since 1920, fell markedly until 1950, and stayed on a plateau, gently rising during the early and late 1960s, until the 1970s, when it rose again in the last few years of the decade to record figures (with light lager beer, which it had long been thought would never become popular, dramatically increasing its share of the market). The lowest year of *per capita* consumption in bulk barrels per head of population – and most sections of the population were now thinking in terms of bottles per head, as they were to think later in terms of cans – was 1959.[3] Spirits consumption, however, showed an upward trend, like the trend for wine, with a peak in 1951, the year of the Festival of Britain, which was not reached again until 1955, and at the end of the whole period a huge increase in 1979:

(Beer in Bulk Barrels: Spirits in Thousand Proof Gallons)

Year	Beer	Spirits
1945	31,797,416	8,029
1950	26,780,892	9,179
1955	24,647,966	10,962
1960	26,646,775	13,715
1965	29,907,803	18,677
1970	33,463,444	17,567
1975	39,108,762	32,420
1979	40,953,000	40,733

TABLE 20 *Consumption of Beer and Spirits 1945–1979*

---

[3] For the relevant statistics, see the invaluable *U.K. Statistical Handbook* published by the Brewers' Society.

Turning to the different phases in the history of wine consumption one by one, during the first five years after the end of the War there was still little wine available which was old enough for current consumption, and the rate of growth in consumption was slow – with wine imports actually falling in 1948, 1949 and 1950 from a 1947 post-War peak:

Year	Total	From France	From Portugal	From Spain	From Australia	From South Africa
1945	3,892	63	399	1,180	888	639
1946	8,204	766	1,820	1,677	1,486	1,444
1947	10,052	879	2,046	2,414	1,735	2,199
1948	9,959	767	1,470	1,604	1,907	2,447
1949	7,627	563	2,548	2,339	1,100	775
1950	8,228	1,062	1,956	2,562	625	1,270

TABLE 21 *Wine Imports, 1945–1950*
(Thousand gallons)

There were no imports from Germany during this period, and Italian wines did not reach this country until 1950, when 455,000 gallons were imported.

The severe strains and pressures of these years did not encourage sound prediction about the future. 'Less wine at table' ran a headline in *The Times* in January 1949. 'It is now safe to assert,' the writer, 'a Special Correspondent', maintained, 'that the people of this country have almost given up the habit of drinking table wines with their meals.' 'In the circumstances of today British wine importers are affected not only by the inability of the "landed gentry" to replenish their cellars, but also by the lack of such custom as once came from middle-class customers.'[4] Only champagne had retained its hold, the writer suggested, and he went on to describe the increasing habit of people drinking gin before meals rather than wine with them. He also suggested that sherry was losing its popularity as an *aperitif* because, unlike gin, it could not be diluted.

---

[4] *The Times*, 22 January 1949. Mark Abrams in his Bureau of Current Affairs pamphlet *The British Standard of Living* (1948) suggested that among the working classes also the 'real' consumption of alcoholic drinks was 10 per cent down on 1938.

The spirits figures did not bear the writer out, although no one challenged him. Indeed, in 1949, the year when he was writing, consumption both of home-produced and imported spirits actually fell. Imports of brandy rose each year between 1945 and 1950, but imports of rum, which were to fall dramatically during the 1950s, were significantly lower in 1949 and 1950 than they were in 1948. Vodka had not yet then suggested that it would seriously compete with gin.

The third annual general meeting of the Wine and Spirit Association, which was held later in the same year, was more optimistic than *The Times* Special Correspondent, probably as a result of Sir Stafford Cripps's budget of April 1949 which reduced the duties on cheaper kinds of table wines – 'light wines imported in cask'. Moreover, Cripps's welcome move was not just an 'adjustment'. It was a deliberate means of assisting trade with France, which was in economic difficulties, and with the wine-producing countries of the Commonwealth. The Cripps reduction by 12s a gallon meant that there would now be some cheap wine available at 8s a bottle. Cripps had been urged earlier in the year to emulate his great Victorian predecessors, Gladstone and the radical Cobden who had wanted to improve Anglo-French trade and who in retrospect, at least, was almost as austere as Cripps himself;[5] and he responded positively to the challenge while keeping the rates of duty and surcharges on other wines at the same rate as before.

Cripps calculated that if there were no increases in consumption the initial effect of his measure would be to reduce the revenue by £1 million. Yet he believed that such a fall would be unlikely, and he was proved right. Imports of still light wines increased in 1949/50 from 1,218,600 gallons to 1,667,400 gallons and total French imports from 563,000 gallons to 1,062,000 gallons, and the rise continued in the following year.[6] Cripps had also taken 1d a pint off the price of beer in 1949 – with the effect of reducing the cost of living index by about seven-tenths of a point.[7] In this case, however, there was no increase in total beer consumption in 1950, although the permitted gravity was raised and sales of imported beers increased.

The writer of *The Times* article on wine consumption made much of the influence of price on British drinking habits, although if he had

---

[5] See *ibid.*, 22 January 1949.
[6] The volume of French wines imported in bulk doubled between 1948–49 and 1950–51. The phrase 'mis en bouteilles au château' became a connoisseur's phrase at this time as many bottles of French wine bottled in England were exported.

[7] He had increased the duty on beer in 1947 and in 1948 so that the price increased by 1d a pint. There was a fall in beer production in 1947 and 1948 and a further reduction in gravity.

looked comparatively across the Atlantic at the pattern of American gin drinking, he might have been more cautious. He was clearly a lover of claret, and it was with claret in mind that he surveyed the wine scene. The fact that a bottle of champagne cost no more than a bottle of claret and less than a bottle of very good claret was his most serious concern. Yet the only reason that champagne had retained its popularity, he suggested, was that there had been a reduction in the relative duty on champagne in 'an adjustment made under a convention' rather than as a result of deliberate fiscal policy. Before the War, a reasonably good bottle of claret had cost 2s 6d at a retail wine shop or 4s 6d to 5s at a restaurant, with the better vintages fetching up to 10s and 20s respectively. Now, the tax on a bottle, which had risen six times since 1938, was almost as high as the pre-war restaurant price had been. A reasonably good bottle of claret at the retail shop that cost 2s 6d before the War now cost 8s and at a restaurant 18s, while the better qualities fetched up to 22s and £3 respectively. These figures seemed to him sufficient in themselves to explain why claret and similar wines had 'disappeared from English dining tables'.

Yet there were many other reasons. Until the beginning of 1949 British importers were still not free to buy wines as and when they could – within their controlled allotment of sterling – and to sell them for what price they could fetch in the British market. They had to accept a framework of price schedules and margins agreed by the Ministry of Food.[8] Now, from January 1949 onwards what was left of control in the trade – and it was still substantial – was placed in the hands not of the Ministry of Food but of the Board of Trade.[9] And the change had taken place after much 'thorny and complicated', but nonetheless effective, discussion behind the scenes between industry and government.[10] Both *The Economist* and *The Wine and Spirit Trade Review* welcomed the Cripps reduction in duties as a further instalment of sanity, although the latter insisted, as the Victorian reformers had insisted, that 'it would need a very large reduction to break the social tradition which dictates that the British as a whole prefer beer to wine'.[11]

A well-informed forecaster would have wanted in 1949 to look beyond the economics of the control system and Cripps's fiscal changes to likely changes in the habits of society. It might well have been partially true

[8] See 'Freedom for Wine' in *The Economist*, 8 January 1949.
[9] 'Wake up call to Trade' in *The Wine and Spirit Trade Review* 1 July 1949.
[10] See *Ibid.*, 28 December 1945: 'the voice of the trade must be strong, and forceful if it is to shake off some of the fetters that bind it.'
[11] *The Economist, loc. cit.*

that 'any taste for wine acquired by the occupation troops was soon destroyed by the Chancellor of the Exchequer with the successive increases in the excise duty'.[12] Yet Cripps himself knew that it was not entirely true. Nor in a post-war age of severe financial controls on private travel did he overlook the possibility that if the foreign travel habit became more popular – as it was to do in unprecedented fashion – a taste for wine might be one of the peacetime by-products of it.[13] Food habits might change too, of course. In 1949 'eating out' was treated as a grim activity in a fascinating *Mass-Observation Bulletin* which did not mention wine at all,[14] but would it always be so? Another *Mass-Observation Bulletin* discussed the little examined question of home drinking, suggesting that as much as £80 million a year was being spent on it. Was there not a great opportunity for retailers here? Already by 1950 there were 32,000 off-licences as against 18,000 in 1900.[15]

Of every 100 people 'observed' who kept beer in their homes, over half kept at least four other types of alcoholic drink as well. As many as 90 had whisky, 88 sherry, 82 gin, 70 brandy, 57 port, 51 other wine and 49 rum (40 kept cider). The appeal of 'pub' life was strong – and was to remain strong – but one-third of home drinkers actually objected to 'pub' life, and the party habit had spread to all sections of the population. At one working-men's 'demob' party in the North of England, for example, in 1949 five bottles of 'best port' were consumed at 25s per bottle, eight bottles of red wine at 7s 6d per bottle, two bottles of 'fine, old sherry', two bottles of whisky, and several quart bottles of Guinness and Brown Ale. It is interesting to learn that there were no objections to 'pubs' on this festive domestic occasion, for most of the men and some of the women 'went round to the local in the course of the evening'.[16]

'How did retailers fare this Christmas?' asked a writer (also called 'Observer') in *The Wine and Spirit Trade Review* a few weeks later. 'My inquiries prompt me to suggest,' he concluded, 'that the "off-trade" fared better than the on-trade as regards extra demand', although the extra business was mainly limited to the ten days or so before Christmas.

---

[12] *Ibid.*
[13] The number of new passports issued in a year more than doubled between 1947 and 1966. In the former year only 3.3 per cent of the population spent holidays abroad. See A.H. Halsey, *Trends in British Society* (1972), pp. 549–50. There is no chapter in this useful book on food and drink.
[14] *Mass-Observation Bulletin*, May 1949, 'Eating Out'. One person in five, a mass-

observer reported, alleged that food was not only cooked unimaginatively but badly. It was around this time that Raymond Postgate contemplated a 'Society for the Prevention of Cruelty to Food.' (See R. Postgate, 'How *The Good Food Guide* Began' in C. Ray (ed.), *The Compleat Imbiber* 7 (1964)).
[15] Williams and Brake, *op. cit.*, p. 212.
[16] *Mass-Observation Bulletin*, 1 April 1949, 'Home Drinking'.

'Today drinking is expensive, especially if one has company, and as a result . . . more and more people are drinking at home instead of visiting their "local", where they may meet a few pals, necessitating a round of drinks.'[17]

As it was, retail stocks both of spirits and wines were rapidly depleted – 'whisky was almost non-existent' – as the effect of the reduction in the price of light wines was felt. So, too, were beer supplies, particularly as far as bottled beers were concerned, as the result, it was claimed, of the reduction in the tax on beer. There can have been few households, therefore, that were in a position to toast Sir Stafford Cripps with appropriate enthusiasm. Later in the year, however, there was more generous scope for wine drinkers. 'The general picture (in the wine trade) is of a market of improving health in which the buyer is in a stronger position than he has been for a decade', *The Times* remarked in November 1950. Sound French wines were then selling at 7s or 8s a bottle, and Yugoslav riesling at 7s. And now there were new villains. 'In the rear of the advancing column of the fellowship of the wine trade', *The Times* writer went on – was he the same 'Special Correspondent' as in 1949? – 'trailing along slowly and even reluctantly, are the hoteliers and restaurateurs.'[18] After the War, the price of wines in restaurants had been kept higher to provide the profit which could not be made on the controlled-price 5s meal, and wines that sold at 7s per bottle in the shops were being offered by the wine waiter at 27s. Could this continue for ever? There might be a demand for 'blended wines' also, the 'Special Correspondent' suggested, 'for a number of fixed standards which might be classified in order of price and alleged quality'.[19] At this point, not fully developed, the forecasting, which was essentially social rather than economic, was beginning to be more focused: blended wines, like the Nicolas range, were to have a remarkable future.

Two years later, near the beginning of what can be recognised, in retrospect at least, as a new period of growth, when talk of austerity gave way to talk of affluence, Stephen Potter, a favourite writer of the period, was able gently to satirise 'wine gambits' and to include 'winemanship' in his advice on 'gamesmanship'. There were certainly far more books and articles on wine in circulation, some of them justifying Potter's formula – 'how to talk about wine without knowing about it'. The first

---

[17] *The Wine and Spirit Trade Review*, 12 January 1950.
[18] 'Science and the Vintner' in *The Times*, 25 November 1950.

[19] *Ibid*. The writer noted how 'wine had reaped advantages from biology and analytical chemistry ever since the revelations of Pasteur.'

edition of Raymond Postgate's *The Good Food Guide* – in his own words 'a Frankenstein's monster or a fairy beanstalk' – appeared in 1951 with what came to be a familiar challenging preface dealing with wine as well as with foods, 'advising, warning and praising'.[20] And his *Plain Man's Guide to Wine* was to run through many editions.

For *The Economist*, sensitive as it was to new tendencies in eating and drinking as well as in thinking and feeling, 'full employment and the redistribution of income' had at last brought wine within the means of 'an entirely new public'. Yet it noted that the amount of wine withdrawn from bond in 1950–51 remained less (even for light wines) than it had been in 1938–9. Heavy wines had suffered most, it suggested, largely for reasons of taxation, so that consumption both of port and of sherry (taxed at 50s per gallon compared with 8s before the War) was well down – sherry by 25 per cent in quantity, port by more than 50 per cent. Yet there were other reasons also, it went on. Port had been a drink for the rich at one end of the scale and the poor at the other, but there were now far more people in between who did not like it. And 'port styles', including Australian 'port styles', had suffered in particular as the taste for drier drinks had been widely canvassed. Meanwhile television, still in its infancy, was increasing the demand for bottled beer, gin consumption had increased at the expense of both whisky and sherry, and in restaurants people were being pressed, not for the first time, to drink expensive liqueurs.[21]

While *The Economist* was observing and interpreting and recalling what it had said a hundred years before,[22] the Wine and Spirit Association, financed by a levy on its members, was seeking to persuade restaurants to sell wine by the glass and to invite wine merchants to offer wine tokens on the same lines as book tokens. By the end of the 1950s, indeed, more money was being spent on advertising of drinks other than beer than on beer advertising itself.[23] In the long run, however,

---

[20] See Postgate, *loc. cit.* and Christopher Driver (ed.), *The Good Food Guide, 1971*, for a retrospective look, ending with the advice (p. xix), 'So eat, drink, and be thankful – but also, please, be critical'. In the same year *Egon Ronay's Guide* had reached its fourteenth edition. See also R. Postgate, *The Home Wine Cellar* (1960). One of Postgate's professed objects was to prove that Australian clarets could be good.

[21] *The Economist*, 'The Vintner's Custom', 20 December 1952.

[22] See *ibid.*, 9 October 1852: 'Wine is a cordial, a restorative, a medicine. It seems peculiarly adapted, like tea, to invigorate the nervous sensibility exhausted by the sedentary avocations of civilized life ... The people of Britain rich as they are, unable to procure it at its present exorbitant price, consume the cheap substitute manufactured at home.'

[23] See Williams and Brake, *op. cit.*, pp. 199–200. A Wine Education and Publicity Fund was launched after a *Morning Advertiser* survey of 1950 had suggested that of the people who drank alcoholic beverages on the day before the count 86 per cent had tasted beer and only 1 per cent wine.

reorganisation of the business was to prove more dramatic in its consequences than advertising, and *The Economist* was already noting an increasing tendency of both chain shops and breweries to cut out middlemen and to buy wine direct from the shipper or the grower. A firm of chain stores, it reported, 'had hopes' that by an agreement with the Bordeaux growers it would be able to sell wine at less than the usual prices and 'so create a new wine-drinking public in the British working class'. There was, of course, nothing more new in this hope than there was in *The Economist*'s own suggested schemes for the future development of the industry. It might have looked back not only at what its own editors were saying a hundred years before but at what was actually happening – amalgamation of businesses, spanning all sections of the 'drink trade', including soft drinks, and increasing sales of wine in multi-product chain stores and supermarkets (the word was still new) which had not previously sold wine in their range of goods on offer.

Throughout the late 1950s, as sales of refrigerators, washing machines and television sets climbed upwards, so, too, did sales of wine – with the exception of port and of champagne (highly priced after a disastrous vintage in 1951):

Year	Imported Wines			Total	Total British Wine	Total Wine Consumed
	Still		Sparkling			
	Heavy	Light				
1950	5,937	1,667	476	8,092	3,662	11,754
1951	6,439	2,684	560	9,683	4,451	14,133
1952	6,078	3,233	519	9,831	4,672	14,503
1953	5,639	3,157	394	9,191	4,411	13,602
1954	6,102	3,556	427	10,084	4,537	14,621
1955	6,531	4,787	465	11,783	5,075	16,858
1956	6,768	5,404	500	12,672	5,489	18,162
1957	6,794	6,345	518	13,658	5,750	19,407
1958	6,611	7,319	580	14,510	5,438	19,948
1959	7,027	7,035	571	14,634	5,632	20,270

TABLE 22 *The Pattern of Wine Imports, 1950–1959*
(Thousand gallons)

There was no sign, however, during these years, of a breakthrough in wine sales camparable with that in sales of refrigerators, washing machines and television sets, indicators of a new society and culture.

Indeed, in 1959 itself British people were still drinking no more wine than they had drunk before the Second World War. By 1960, however, when the French were being subjected to an anti-alcohol campaign, there were signs that something new and different was happening in Britain, and *The Economist* was not alone in discerning a tendency to regard wine more 'as a business and less as a connoisseur's hobby' and in suggesting that if the expansion of wine-drinking continued at its present pace 'commercialism' would represent 'the shape of things to come'.[24]

It was in 1960 and 1961 that the giants in the 'drinking industry' began to grow, with Bass and Charrington coming together – they had a subsidiary, Bass-Charrington Vintners – alongside Ind Coope, Ansell and Tetley Walker.[25] Although Britain with a *per capita* wine consumption of one third of a gallon remained far behind not only France (with a *per capita* consumption of 30 gallons per head) but countries like Italy (24 gallons per head), the huge brewery concerns were beginning to be more interested in wine than ever before in their history. They were more interested than ever before in off-licence shops also, for these were still increasing in numbers; and they were investing, sometimes heavily, in the modernisation of pubs, the numbers of which were falling.[26] Nor was the wide gap between Britain and other countries as wide as it had been. British consumption was behind that of Germany too (2 gallons per head), but was already above that of Holland (0.16 gallons).

During the early 1960s it began to be noted in Britain for the first time that cheap table wine at 7s to 9s 6d a bottle, cheaper than it had been in 1949, was providing keen price competition for beer: a 'light Chianti', indeed, cost only 6s 6d. It was also noted at this time that whisky was winning the day against gin ('gin and orange' was on its way out); that vodka was on its way in;[27] and that a range of wines from 'Babycham' to genuine French white wine, still not sold very generally by the glass, was beginning to attract customers, female as well as male. It was a sign of change, too, that at this critical point, when Spanish Rioja was 'kept by

---

[24] *The Economist*, 28 May 1960.

[25] The story of the giants is sometimes said to have begun with the bid of an 'outsider', Sir Charles Clore, for Watney Mann in 1959. At that time the five largest brewing enterprises were responsible for 23 per cent of output: by 1965 the percentage was 64 per cent. (See R.G. Wilson, *op. cit.*, p. 223.) See also K.H. Hawkins, *A History of Bass Charrington* (1978) and K.H. Hawkins and C.L. Puss, *The Brewing Industry, A Study in*

Industrial Organisation and Public Policy (1979).

[26] For a critical and dated study of the process, see C. Hutt, *The Death of the English Pub* (1973). See also M. Lovett, *Brewing and Breweries* (1981) and Cmnd. 4227, Report of the National Board for Prices and Incomes, *Beer Prices* (1969).

[27] See Prys Williams, *Social Effects of the Ending of Resale Price Maintenance of Alcoholic Beverages* (1968).

every wine merchant'[28] port, and particularly, 'port-style wine' sales remained low. Indeed, withdrawals of Australian 'port-style wines' from bond in 1960 were a tenth of what they had been in 1938, and by 1965 France, surprise of surprises, was importing far more port from Portugal than Britain was.[29] Sherry, however, had survived well, and sales of Spanish sherry had increased by about eight per cent a year during the previous decade.

The two most important business changes of the 1960s – the end of resale price maintenance and the growth of supermarket sales – were preceded by the Licensing Act of 1961, the first major revision of licensing laws for forty years, which set the keynote for the decade. It enabled off-licence shops to open during normal shop hours, not just during 'permitted hours' determined by local justices; and one of its inevitable, if not fully foreseen, consequences was an increase in the number of supermarkets (relatively new types of retail units) selling alcoholic drinks straight from the racks like any other commodity. Another, more deliberately intended, was a restriction in the discretion of local justices to refuse to grant on-licences to restaurants and residential hotels, and the number of such licences substantially increased.

Four years later, the end of resale price maintenance, abandoned publicly by the distillers in February 1965, three months before legislation came into force, increased competition between the different retail outlets.[30] For a time there was a flood of cut-price liquor, particularly spirits, on display in the shops, as prominent supermarket chains, some with 200 branches or more, cut prices of a bottle of popular branded whisky by as much as seven shillings (from 44s 6d to 37s 6d) or of gin by roughly the same proportion (from 42s 9d to 36s). As a result, one supermarket at Waltham Cross took more in cash between 8.30 a.m. and midday on the Tuesday when it cut its prices than it usually took in a whole week. 'We did not think people would go for it like this', was the delighted comment of one supermarket spokesman after his company was almost sold out.[31] Yet some 'loss leaders' involved too great losses and margins in general were sometimes cut 'beyond the bone'.[32] Sherry sales

---

[28] 'Wines of the World,' a *Guardian* survey, 21 November 1962. Russian wines figured in this article: they seem 'destined', the author said, 'to take their place in the English market alongside those of France and Spain'.

[29] *The Wine and Spirit Trade Review*, 1 January 1965.

[30] *The Economist* hailed the move away from 'price fixing' as 'the beginnings of a new economic policy'.

[31] *The Times*, 25 February 1965.

[32] *The Wine and Spirit Trade Review*, 5 January 1965.

benefited greatly from such price cutting although other table wines benefited far less, if at all, and canned beer sales were as yet a highly profitable trade only for the future.[33]

Although the flood soon receded, it left many supermarkets (which hitherto had been without licences) in the business of selling beer, wines and spirits. Only 102 such stores possessed licences in 1966 (Sainsbury's acquired theirs in 1962): by the end of 1967 the figure was 264.[34] There had been no reference at all to supermarket sales in John Vaizey's *The Brewing Industry* published in 1960. In 1967–8, however, when supermarket licences still accounted for only one and a half per cent of the total, fears were being expressed by the Wine and Spirit Association, which included many of the 15,000 off-licence outlets not controlled by breweries, that too many off-licences had already been granted.[35]

All in all, during the ten years from 1960 to 1970 the total number of off-licences, including those granted to chain stores specialising in the sale of beer, wine and spirits, rose from 23,679 in England and Wales to 27,910. A year later, in 1971, the figure was 28,166, as against figures for on-licences of 64,087 (52 of them for wine only and/or cider), for registered clubs of 23,985, and for restaurants and residential hotels of 11,228. The big wine and spirit chains, which had resisted drastic price reductions at first, were clearly in a long-term position – through selective price-cutting and special offers – to increase their own share of the future trade.[36] 'The customers prepared to shop around for bargains should make savings of up to 5s, and sometimes even more, per bottle of most spirits, wines and even the more expensive sherries', a *Times* correspondent wrote in 1967.[37]

This was a marketing revolution indeed, and not surprisingly, there were increasing pressures towards business amalgamation during the 1960s as the 'drinks trade', including the soft drinks trade, became increasingly profitable. In 1968, the year of the merger of Allied Breweries and of Showerings Vine Products and Whiteways, Watney Mann, another of the brewing 'Big Six', acquired a 38 per cent interest in

---

[33] The official price index was no longer based on information from manufacturers. 'In this month's sampling', wrote *The Economist* (13 March 1965), 'whisky and gin will be priced in the shops for the first time . . . Nor, for gin, is the previous cost of a nip in the pubs good enough'.

[34] Prys Williams, *op. cit.*, p. 5.

[35] *The Times*, 4 January 1968. See *ibid.*, 26 December 1965, for the comments of John Finney, then Chairman of the Association: 'If the retailer should lose a major proportion of his spirit trade, or be compelled to cut prices on the whole of it his net profit margin will disappear'.

[36] See *Which*, November 1965, and *The Economist*, 11 December 1965.

[37] *Ibid.*, 11 May 1967.

International Distillers and Vintners Ltd. Brewery combines, 'largely unnoticed' according to *The Times*, now accounted for roughly three quarters of the wine trade.[38] Meanwhile, the marketing director of the wine subsidiary of the third big brewing group, Bass Charrington, was confident enough to claim that 'the wine habit was growing so fast that there was more for everybody'[39] – for supermarkets as well as for specialist wine, spirit and beer stores. Just as the Distillers Company, by far the largest producer and exporter of Scotch whiskies, now had sizeable interests in gin and vodka production, so the great amalgamations were placing themselves strategically to deal with all sections of an expanding market, international as well as national.[40]

A 'small is beautiful' reaction led to talk by 1970 of a 'private sector' in the wine and spirit retail trade – with at least one firm of wine merchants having broken away from a combine the year before to resume trading as an independent firm.[41] Indeed, despite high taxation, with four increases in duty between 1964 and 1968, the last of them substantial in the case both of wines and spirits,[42] there was a wider range of active wine marketing agencies in the early 1970s than ever before. Each type of supplier was providing a different range of facilities for the growing number of wine drinkers. At one end of the spectrum were specialist wine merchants – and there were still regular new entrants to the trade – who were prepared, as in the past, to meet the needs of limited, known, but growing clientèles and to offer unblended wines in limited supply, some of them from small-holder vineyards producing less than fifty casks a year.[43] At the other end of the spectrum were wine chains, like Augustus Barnett, Peter Dominic and Victoria Wine, and supermarkets that were dealing in large quantities of cheap wines and were turning more and more to blended wines, 'red', 'white' or 'rosé', and relying on market research, large-scale advertising and more sophisticated modes of packaging. One of the last giant entrants into the trade, Marks and Spencer, started (without advertising) to sell wine in 1973, beginning

---

[38] *The Times*, 12 May 1968.
[39] *Ibid.*, 4 January 1968.
[40] Amalgamations were international too. Thus, Seagram, the Canadian whisky firm, controlled Mumm Champagne, Brolio Chianti and Chivas Regal. In 1976 Showering Vine Products and Whiteways acquired Teacher (Distillers) Ltd.
[41] For the reaction, see *inter alia* W. Davis, *Merger Mania* (1970), particularly Chapter 1, 'Togetherness'.
[42] *The Times*, 21 March 1968. There was a wine trade recession as a result of these

measures. The Chancellor in 1968, Roy Jenkins, was warned also by Jasper Grinling, Managing Director of International Distillers, that 'he could well be killing his classic golden goose'.
[43] One pressure on the specialist firms was the demand for discounting which was itself publicised during the 1970s. See, for example, Pamela Vandyke Price, 'Go for a discount on that Christmas Wine' in *ibid.*, 25 December 1972.

with eight wines and four sherries on sale in 12 stores. They would have used the St Michael label had it not been that this registration had been used by a small wine company within the Allied Group.[44]

It was a consolation doubtless that there seemed to be an endless supply of wine and an endless range of wines. 'Are there many different table wines?' was the first question posed at the opening of *What about Wine?* by André Simon, the most traditionalist of interpreters. 'As many as there are stars in the heavens' was his answer. 'This is surely an exaggeration,' the questioner went on. 'Far from it', Simon replied, 'It is more likely to be an understatement.'[45]

Certainly far more varieties of wine were available during the 1960s and early 1970s than there were varieties of beers, including continental beers. Indeed, the varieties of beers had declined sharply as a result of amalgamations, a shift which encouraged the campaign for 'real ale' which was launched in 1971 after four English journalists who had just visited Ireland returned determined to restore old English tastes, 'the simple drinking habits of the English people'.[46] In 1881, 16,798 excise licences to produce beer had been in operation: in 1967 there were 244. Within less than three years the Campaign rallied 30,000 members, each paying an annual subscription of £4. There were other changes of taste too. The demand for mild beers, which accounted in 1959 for 42 per cent of all beer consumed, had fallen to 13.3 per cent by 1975, and there had been an even sharper fall in the demand for brown ale from 12 per cent to 2.6 per cent. Meanwhile canned beer, in the words of Lord Monckton in 1969, was 'moving steadily, if slowly forward':[47] four years later it had moved forward far more dramatically as more homes acquired refrigerators, and more supermarkets sold cans in packs. The marketing revolution affected beer as much as wine.

The changing business context which directly linked marketing and production was investigated by the Monopolies Commission in 1966; and after consideration for two years as to whether or not the tied house system of retailing beer constituted a monopoly, it reported in April 1968

[44] In 1980 the Chairman of the Allied Breweries Group presented Lord Sieff, the Chairman of Marks and Spencer, with the trademark.

[45] A. Simon, *What About Wine?* (1953), p. 1. For contemporary attitudes to wine in the late 1960s, see *Wine Mine*, published by Peter Dominic. It appeared twice a year and had 110,000 readers. See in it, for links with the past, John Arlott's article on 'The Professor of Drink, John Saintsbury' (Summer, 1969).

For the early 1970s, see *inter alia* Pamela Vandyke Price, *Wines and Spirits* (1972) which begins with a chapter 'Wine is Fun'.

[46] See *The Penguin Guide to Real Draught Beer* (1979). For the story of brewing, see H.S. Corran, *A History of Brewing* (1975). See also C. Gregory and W. Knock, *The Beers of Britain* (1975).

[47] Quoted in Williams and Brake, *op. cit.*, p. 212.

that within the existing framework of licensing legislation, which it considered archaic, there was no means of breaking it. The Commission presented a very full account of the trade, including the entry of the brewers into the wine and spirits trade, but its philosophy of free competition – advocacy of 'the sale of alcoholic drinks for on and off consumption, by any retailer whose character and premises satisfied certain minimum standards' – raised social as well as economic issues;[48] and a further Departmental Committee, chaired by Lord Erroll, was appointed by the Home Secretary in 1971, to review the licensing laws in their social context. Its unanimous Report, which appeared in December 1972, was as illuminating as the Monopolies Commission Report. It followed the Monopolies Commission as far as off-licences were concerned, but in relation to on-licences refused to accept the conclusion that the sale of intoxicating liquor is so similar to other forms of retail activity as to justify complete freedom from control. Noting the increase in the consumption of 'all types of intoxicating liquor' since 1960, including the dramatic increase in wine consumption from 0.68 gallons per head in 1960 to 1.14 in 1970, it summed up concisely the 'drinking situation' then and in the past as follows:

> The picture we get, particularly over the last twenty years, is of rising over-all consumption, accompanied by increases in alcoholism, death rates and in offences of drunkenness, all of which, however, are still below the peak levels reached towards the end of the last and the beginning of this century.[49]

Breathalyser tests were a landmark in the story, introduced in the Road Safety Act of 1967. During the first three months of the breathalyser road casualties dropped by 16 per cent and road deaths by 20 per cent.[50]

At the time when the Erroll Committee reported, the public was demonstrating that there were changes not only in its attitudes to on-licence 'outlets' – pubs, clubs and restaurants[51] – but to what was being

---

[48] See *The Times*, 29 April 1969, which argued that the licensing laws were the envy of foreign governments and 'ought not to be relaxed out of an impulse to promote free-er competition.'

[49] *Report of the Departmental Committee on Liquor Licensing* (1972). The report also asked for more research, and since it was published the volume of research has been substantially increased, particularly on alcoholism, on 'problem drinkers', on advertising, and on the effects of taxation on over-all consumption.

[50] G. Prys Williams, *1968 – The First Full Year of the Breathalyser* (1968).

[51] In October 1977 Marplan carried out on behalf of *The Sun* a poll of what the British thought about their pubs. The picture was favourable, although only one in three women named the pub as her favourite place for a drink. Fewer than two adults in ten (17 per cent) never went to the pub for a drink. There were some complaints from the over-40's that pubs were now 'ruled by teenagers and loud music'.

ordered both there and in the off-licence outlets. Indeed, the statistics speak for themselves:

Year	Imported Wine (million gallons)	British Wine (million gallons)	Beer (million bulk barrels)	Spirits (million gallons)
1969	34.1	11.4	32.2	17.1
1970	32.5	10.0	33.5	17.6
1971	47.4	11.0	35.0	19.7
1972	43.8	11.6	36.1	21.7
1973	52.1	12.6	36.6	24.4
1974	67.9	15.6	39.2	32.0

TABLE 23 *Consumption of Wine, Spirits and Beer, 1969–1974*
(Year ending 31 March)

Immediately before and after the Erroll Report, between 1970 and 1974, wine sales rose each year, and during the last three years dramatically, while beer sales increased only slightly. For the first time in a period of increased drinking the wine and beer curves (per head of population) were diverging sharply, a pattern which was to be repeated at the end of the decade. Moreover, the change preceded Britain's entry into the European Community, a move which would doubtless have met with Cobden's genuine, if qualified, approval:

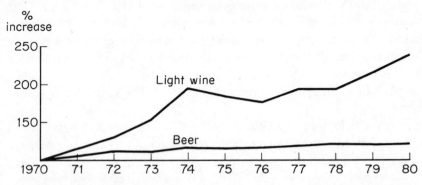

TABLE 24 *Percentage increase in consumption of light wines and beers, 1970–*
1980
(per head of population)

It was on the eve of Britain's entry into the Community that *The Economist* reported that Britain's joining would be greatly welcomed by the Community's vintners, who noted that international trade accounted for only 10 per cent of the total wine harvest, and that 'it was always the more expensive, better quality and more profitable wines' that were exported. They were aware of the fact, it pointed out, that Britain was already consuming 60 per cent of the world's sherry and was still the second largest outlet for port, and they wanted to tap this market. *The Economist* noted also, however, that there were some tensions in the Community as Italy, a country which had greatly expanded its international trade in wine – without quality control standards – continued to place a higher excise duty on imported wines than on home-grown ones. Finally, it feared that as the 'peasant crop' became 'decreasingly profitable' throughout Western Europe, 'cheap wines' would become progressively scarcer. 'Within a decade', it speculated, 'wine could be toppled as Europe's everyday drink, pricing itself off the table. But the future of wine as a luxury drink seems assured.'[52]

The decade was to follow a different pattern, as the price of some of the most coveted 'luxury wines' continued to rise sharply. Thus, first-growth Lafite, which had doubled in price between 1962 and 1968, doubled again between 1968 and 1974, and yet again between 1974 and 1976, while Corton Charlemagne doubled in price between 1968 and 1970, 1970 and 1974, and 1974 and 1976. Meanwhile, the price of second-growth clarets climbed only slowly until 1973. Wine was becoming an increasingly fashionable commodity for investment during the early 1970s, when there was even talk of assembling 'portfolios' of wine.[53]

It took time for the riskiness of this limited approach to become apparent and for it to become even more apparent that the greatest business potential lay, as it had done for decades, with low-cost, high-volume trade. In 1973, a year when the price of some of the best vintage clarets fell, the gallon-of-imported-wine-per-head figure was broken for the first time in the century. '73 was a good year for the vin ordinaire', was the title of an article by Patricia Tisdall in *The Times* in November 1972.

In her article, Patricia Tisdall turned to forecasting and referred not only to sparse harvests but to the introduction of a system of reference

---

[52] *The Economist*, 'Sour Grapes', 4 July 1970. Cf. *ibid.*, 29 December 1969. 'Over the next decade, grain-based drinks seem likely to capture a slightly greater share of the market at the expense of drinks made from grapes.'

[53] Johnson, *op. cit.*, pp. 40–1. See also *The Economist*, 29 December 1969.

prices for non-EEC low-price table wines which might push up the price and to the likely effects of the Common External Tariff which would come into full effect in July 1977.[54] In fact, sales from outside the Community of Spanish wines in Britain increased from 4.2 million gallons in 1971 to 5.8 million gallons in 1975 and the range of wines on sale from outside Europe was widened every year. 'A good London wine list is a compilation of the best that is made in every corner of the globe,' Johnson wrote.[55] 'As we have no viniculture of our own to speak of', a different observer wrote in 1974, 'a greater variety of wine can be found here than anywhere else on the globe.'[56]

There were social changes, too, however, which were making for a greater interest in all ranges of wine, among them the growth of wine bars, 'the hottest thing in the liquor trade since own-brand plonk'[57] – in the North of England as well as the South-East – evidence, therefore, of 'UK calculation' as much as of 'continental modishness'.[58] There had been wine bars even in the nineteenth century and they were a familiar feature of the urban scene in Yorkshire and Lancashire.[59] Now, however, they became profitable as well as 'new style', and some at least were linked in chains, like Wolsey's and Wild Angus Wine Bars of Manchester. The former offered wines ranging in price from £1 to £50 per bottle. More significant, perhaps, in relation to drinking trends was that it was now acceptable to ask for wine in pubs and clubs, many of which were 'new style' too, contrasting sharply in appearance with the old pubs and clubs where 'crates of empty bottles were stacked in every nook and cranny behind the bar and the barmaids . . . were frequently the only women there'.[60]

The fact that grocery outlets – usually, in the first years, with wine in the corner – were becoming more common in the trade was important too as far as women's buying was concerned. So, too, was advertising increasingly devoted to women, as Showerings had recognised during the 1950s. Between 1971 and 1976 the consumption of vermouths and aperitifs among women went up by 66 per cent and among men by 40 per cent, and there was a similar trend in the demand for liqueurs. Moreover,

---

[54] *The Times*, 23 November 1972.
[55] Johnson, *op. cit.*, p. 19.
[56] *Observer Magazine*, 6 October 1974. In 1973 *The Sunday Times* had founded a Wine Club with Hugh Johnson as President.
[57] R. Milner, 'A Gallon Per Head Helps the Wine Bar Boom', in *The Sunday Times*, 12 May 1974. Thirty London wine bars were listed in *Egon Ronay's 1971 Guide*. One was described as an 'ultra-modern basement', another as having 'plenty of Victorian atmosphere from the sawdust on the floor.'
[58] *Ibid.*
[59] See above, p. 27.
[60] 'Changing Face of Britain, No. 11, Drinking'. (*The Times*, 20 August 1976).

at least one of the wine bars was organised by and deliberately designed to appeal to women customers. It is interesting to note that in 1975, when imported wine sales fell from their 1974 peak and beer sales dropped also, spirits consumption increased, as did consumption of British wines, some of which particularly appealed to women.

In that year, at home or away from home, the 'nation was drinking 201.2 pints of beer per head compared with 186.8 in 1945, 6.6 pints of spirits compared with 1.9, and 1.3 pints of wine compared with 0.7'. And within the spirits figures rum was back in favour again: consumption, 3.5 million gallons, had doubled between 1970 and 1975. Vodka consumption, however, had risen even more sharply from 0.8 million gallons to 2.6 million gallons. 'Lightness' was increasingly appreciated in rum and in whisky (with increasing demand for single malts)[61] – and in beer, as well as in wine, and there were many observers who were pointing out that lager beers, which in 1959 had accounted for only 2 per cent of the market, and at the end of the 1960s only $3\frac{1}{2}$ per cent in England, now accounted for 19.9 per cent. 'Tastes in beer do not transplant easily', Graham Turner had commented in 1969.[62] By the mid-1970s, it was clear that they could.

As far as light wines were concerned, there were substantial increases not only in the sales of Italian and of German light wines, as had been predicted, but in the sales from outside the European Community – for example, from Yugoslavia:

	1970	*1974*	*1979*	*1980*	*% Growth 1970–80*
France	46	36.7	36.9	36.2	+ 175
Germany	10	10.8	18.3	21.5	+ 660
Italy	4	14.3	18.2	17.6	+ 1440
Spain	22	19.0	13.6	12.1	+ 95
Yugoslavia	4	4.9	6.3	6.1	+ 435
Portugal	6	3.8	2.4	2.1	+ 25
Others	8	10.4	4.3	4.4	+ 95

TABLE 25 *Light wine consumption by country of origin, 1970–1980*

[61] See also above, p. 152.
[62] Turner, *op. cit.*, p. 269. He pointed out, however, that the share of lager beer in Scotland was already nearer 20 per cent.

White wine was increasingly favoured as against red – and rosé – and fashion trends, backed by sophisticated marketing, began to be more prominent:

	1970	1976	1978	1979	1980
Red	42	36	35	34	32
White	49	54	58	60	63
Rosé	9	10	7	6	5

TABLE 26 *Light wine consumption by colour, 1970–80*

There was a place in the picture, too, for English wines from new or old vineyards. An English Vineyards Association, proposed at a meeting in 1965 and formally instituted in 1967, had over 100 members by 1970:[63] its first object was 'to propagate, graft, grow, cultivate, purchase and sell grape vines and to develop new varieties of grape vines' and its second was 'to buy and sell and to process whether for the making of wine or grape juice . . . grapes from vines planted in the United Kingdom'.[64] The total yield of the 1969 harvest was just over 2,000 bottles. Müller-Thurgau and other vines designed to stand up to the rigours of the English climate had been planted in forty vineyards, and there was great optimism about the future.[65] The further trend has been described in terms of 'energy replacing amateurism' and 'respect replacing mockery'.[66]

By the time the Chancellor of the Exchequer introduced alterations in alcoholic duties – lower excise duties – to coincide with the introduction of Value Added Tax in 1973, there was already an active British wine-producing interest. 'The future of the English vineyards', wrote Jack Ward of Merrydown, 'must be the concern of the British Government if they are to survive. Events have shown that the present revival cannot be dismissed as a triviality.'[67]

In April 1974 the European Economic Commission published an

---

[63] See *The Times*, 12 November 1970.
[64] See H. Barty King, *A Tradition of English Wine* (1977), esp. Ch. 6, 'Transformation Scene, 1945–1967'. In 1952 Sir Guy Salisbury-Jones, first President of the Association, had planted a vineyard at Hambleden, and ten years later Jack Ward of Merrydown had begun to make wine from

grapes. See also R. Barrington Brock, *Planting a Vineyard* (1964). For the earlier history, see E. Hyams, *The Grape Vine in England* (1949).
[65] *The Times*, 9 July 1980. See also G. Pearkes, *Growing Grapes in Britain* (1969).
[66] Barty King, *op. cit.*, Ch. 7.
[67] *About Wine*, February 1973.

official list of the varieties recommended and authorised for cultivation in England, part of designated Zone A, which included the Northern areas of Germany and Luxembourg. The Commission had already encouraged European countries to identify specifically 'quality wines produced in different regions', turning for guidance to the development of the 'appellations d'origine' system in France before and after the introduction of a Wine Code in 1936. Before agreeing in 1976 on a labelling system, it also had been compelled to take account of 'traditional' differences between French, German and Italian interests and of a long history of international negotiation.[68] It has been claimed that the English were able to drink 'real Beaujolais' for the first time during the 1970s and that the British Wine Standards Association, which published its first report in 1974,[69] was as big a domestic landmark as any of the great dates in the history of the Vintners' Company. Yet despite the fact that wine-making in Britain had now surpassed that of the Middle Ages, the role of Britain was still primarily that of an importer, and merchants wanted a say in any future arrangements along with growers. For merchants, as for customers, the price of wine in the bottle mattered profoundly, and the picture of change in wine habits is incomplete unless further attention is paid to price, both in the years of highest inflation – when oil prices influenced wine prices – and later. Indeed, price changes were so great during the mid-1970s that in seeking to establish real consumption trends in Britain it is essential to examine more closely what was happening to drinking habits on the basis of constant prices. The relevant figures show an upward trend in expenditure on all kinds of alcoholic drink and in their share of total consumer expenditure down to 1980, when there was a fall, but a less consistent picture in relation to their share of total consumer income (see Table 27 opposite).

Within these overall statistics there was no doubt that, even allowing for constant prices, the demand for 'other alcoholic drink' was rising more sharply than the demand for beer and that only the demand for telephones in a selective but representative list of consumption items was rising more sharply than the demand for wine. By

---

[68] A brief but complete and influential account of the French and other systems and of Community efforts to 'harmonize' was prepared by the Institute of Masters of Wine in 1970 with the title 'The Protection of Names of Origin'. The first Community rules were promulgated in 1962, five years after the signing of the Treaty of Rome. The first international agreement relating to wine had been signed in Paris in 1883 at a conference attended by representatives of 40 countries.

[69] *First Annual Report, Year Ending 31 August 1974.* Chapter I deals with its origins and establishment.

Year	Total Disposable Income	Total Consumer Expenditure	Total Expenditure on Alcoholic Drink	% of Total Expenditure	% of Total Income
1970	100 (£63,141m)	100 (£57,496m)	100 (£3,676m)	6.4	5.8
1971	103	103	107	6.6	6.1
1972	111	109	115	6.7	6.0
1973	117	115	130	7.3	6.4
1974	119	113	133	7.5	6.5
1975	117	113	132	7.5	6.6
1976	116	113	134	7.6	6.7
1977	115	112	137	7.8	6.9
1978	124	119	145	7.8	6.8
1979	133	124	152	7.8	6.7

TABLE 27 *Trends in consumer income and expenditure at constant prices, 1970–1980*

comparison the demand for books, like the demand for food and fuel and light, was more or less constant (see Table 28 overleaf).

The picture reveals, therefore, that the annual increase in light wine sales in real terms, as in money terms, was beginning to justify for the first time in the twentieth century the kind of dreams William Winch Hughes had enjoyed in the nineteenth century. And they were dreams best expressed in bottles – or in glasses – rather than in millions of gallons (see Table 29, p. 173).

Meanwhile, as the demand for light wines increased, demand for sparkling wine kept up too, without showing as great an increase, while the demand for fortified wines fell slightly. And the demand for British-made wines rose. Whisky held its market share in the spirits increase – 51 per cent in 1970 and 1980 – but the share of gin (19:13) declined and that of vodka (5:12) increased. The share of cognac fell (7:4), but that of brandies went up (1:3). The share of liqueurs doubled from 2 to 4, their total consumption increasing three times ('Irish Cream' being prominent among them).

There were marked regional and class differences in the picture. Market research suggested that while total consumption of wine was

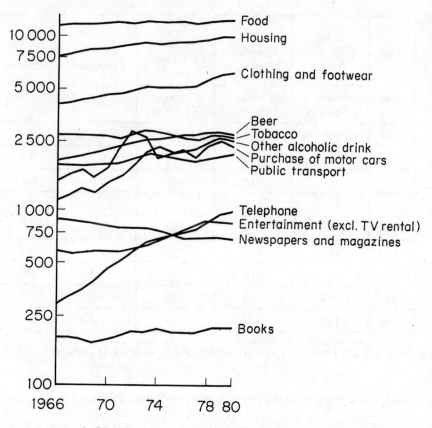

TABLE 28 *Changes in selected consumption patterns at 1975 prices*
(United Kingdom)

highest and remained highest in the South of England, wine-drinking in
Scotland increased more than in England as a whole during the decade
between 1970 and 1980. The increase started from a lower level, but
helped to restore the balance of earlier centuries when Scotland had been
renowned for its taste in claret. There was a marked increase, however, of
10 per cent in Victoria Wine's own original territory of London.

The increase should always be put in perspective. There were said to
be still only 21 million wine drinkers out of 41 million in the adult
population in 1980, and the first five wine-drinking countries in the
world were still France, Portugal, Italy, Argentina and Spain – in that
order – with Britain standing only thirteenth in the league table. The
total increase in wine-drinking between 1970 and 1980 amounted only to
the equivalent of one extra glass of wine each week for each adult in the
country. The Gladstonian dream had not yet become a reality.

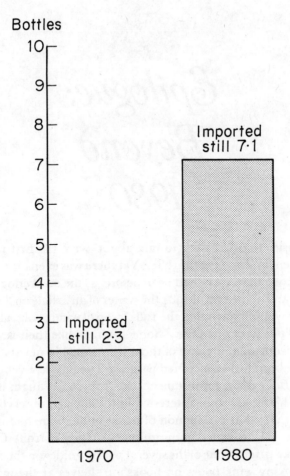

Bottles

TABLE 29 *Consumption of still Wines in 70 cl bottles per head of population of fifteen or more years of age*

Epilogue: Beyond 1980

'Wine is easier to drink than to talk about' were the first words of an advertisement in *The Times* in 1984.[1] Yet there was even more talk about wine after 1980 than there had been before, as the marketing revolution continued, and at the end of 1984 the writer of an article on 'laying down a library' of wine claimed that the 1984 'crop of wine books' almost made up for the 'indifferent vintage'.[2] Some of them, like their reviews, were written by women, and many of them were noted in newspapers which would have been little concerned with wine twenty-five years before. It was in the *Daily Mail*, for instance, that Auberon Waugh, not the first member of his family to be interested in the subject, observed, again at the end of 1984, that production of books about wine had outstripped even the growth in wine consumption.[3] Already in 1981 Christopher Fielden had written in one of the several pocket guides on the subject that 'there are many wine books on bookshop shelves at the moment and there are probably as many again that have not found the publisher bold enough to invest in them'.[4]

The books of 1984 included the latest edition of Hugh Johnson's bestselling *Pocket Wine Book*, first published in 1977: it was described by Waugh as 'simply indispensable for all serious wine drinkers, however grand or however poor'. The 'grand' could turn to Michael Broadbent's *Great Vintage Wine Book* and the 'poor' to *Webster's Wine Price Guide*. Michael Broadbent also wrote a *Compleat Wine Taster*. There were, in fact, wine books of many different kinds, including serious studies of

[1] *The Times*, 2 July 1984.
[2] Alice King, 'Laying Down a Library' in *The Field*, 22 December 1984.
[3] Auberon Waugh, 'Unlocked, Secrets of the Best Cellars' in the *Daily Mail*, 20 December 1984.
[4] *Harvey's Pocket Guide to Wine* (1981) p. 4.

particular wines, like Rosemary George's *The Wines of Chablis*, the first book on the subject since 1935, Graham Chidgey's *The Wines of Burgundy*, and Pamela Vandyke Price's *Alsace Wines* and *The Wines of Champagne*. Antiquarians could turn to R. Dumbrell's *Understanding Antique Wine Bottles* and the up-to-date to Johnson's *Wine Video: How to Handle a Wine*. There was also a new edition of the *1985 Which? Wine Guide*, first published in 1981, a Consumers' Association product, like the *Good Food Guide*, with Jancis Robinson as its first editor,[5] to place alongside *The Sunday Telegraph Good Wine Guide*; and Grants of St James's published its second *Wine Diary*, the text written by Angela Muir, their Buyer.

It would be a mistake, however, to identify a general movement of wine from the cellar to the library as the main theme of this epilogue. The marketing revolution was at the centre of change, and it was not bookstalls, but supermarkets that mattered most. Women as customers were more significant than women as writers, and it was with customers that Kathryn McWhirter, the new editor of the *1985 Which? Wine Guide*, was directly concerned: on her second page, before turning to specialist shops, to chain stores and supermarkets and to auctions, she noted as the basic fact of the trade that over half the wine bought in Britain was now 'selected from supermarket shelves'.[6]

The *Guide*, like all other guides, focused on the wide range of places where you could taste, drink or buy wine to take away; and in choosing the right places there was no shortage of persuasion as well as of information. 'The British wine buyer is one of the most assiduously courted customers in the world today', wrote David Rutherford, Chairman of the Wine Development Board, in 1980. The Board consisted of 'senior men in the trade' who gave their services to 'the cause of promoting wine' yet theirs was now a creed which had no shortage of evangelists outside as well as inside the business. Wine clubs, local and national, increased in numbers and in membership, seeking to demonstrate to their members that each of the wines they offered, including their cheapest house wines, had 'its own authentic, delightful and genuine personality', while there were probably more wine tastings – both in London and elsewhere – than at any previous period in history.

People in the trade tried sometimes to explain what was happening, rather than simply take advantage of it. Thus, S.W. Dodd, Marketing and Sales Director of Grants of St James's, generalised in 1983 that

---

[5] The first sentences of the 1981 *Guide* read 'Why, it may reasonably be asked, a *Which? Wine Guide*? For there is no lack of information available to drinkers at all levels of quality and price'.
[6] *1985 Which? Wine Guide* (1985), p. 10.

'whereas twenty years ago wine was enjoyed by an élite who preferred traditional clarets and burgundies, lifestyles have now changed, and people of all age groups and from all walks of life are now enjoying wine. For both men and women, wine-drinking is socially acceptable, and there has been a steady increase in the number of occasions when wine is served. In many households, a bottle of wine now makes a regular appearance on the Sunday lunch table, and in pubs and clubs the number of people asking for a glass of wine has more than doubled in the last five years'.[7]

Explaining is more than describing, of course, and the social historian has to consider recent changes in élites (some, old or new, still prefer 'traditional clarets' or, if they can afford them, burgundies) as well as in the habits of 'people of all age groups and from all walks of life'; and in considering the latter, like the market researcher, he has to look at the influence of region, education, sex, age, income and travel on individual and family preferences. There remain marked differences in habits between, for example, East Anglia and the South-East, between university graduates and early school-leavers, between women and men, between the young and the old, between those in socio-economic groups AB and CF, between those who flock to the Mediterranean and those who do not. There are differences too in what is consumed at different times of the year. Changes in what is deemed 'socially acceptable' or 'civilized' in part reflect the general influences. So, too, do the practices of institutions as well as of individuals. Wine has always had its institutional as well as its family use, not least in Oxford colleges.[8] Its 'business use' has varied and still varies: in November 1984 eleven of the country's leading accountancy firms competed, for example, in a wine tasting competition for a St James's Wine Trophy offered by Grants.[9]

Perhaps an even more basic fact than Kathryn McWhirter's is that consumer spending on alcohol accounted in 1980 for over 8 per cent of total consumer expenditure – there were estimates that it would rise to 8.8 per cent by 1986 – and that given such circumstances the most interesting question for the wine trade relates to the share of wine in that total and, within that general share of wine, the share of particular wines. There often remained an element of status-seeking in the search for and

---

[7] Press Release, July 1983.
[8] In 1798 *The Times* (19 February) reported a question addressed by a lady to 'the late sagacious Dr. Warren'. 'To which university should I send my son?' 'Madam,' replied he, 'they drink, I believe, near the same quantity of port in each of them'. The university scene is now far more varied in 1983 than it was in 1798, in 1865, or in 1955.
[9] Press Release, 'Accounting for Taste', November 1984.

choice of wine, but while the 'lure' remained – and it could be attractive rather than off-putting – 'consumer awareness' was undoubtedly changing. 'You don't have to be a connoisseur' had already been the reassuring slogan in 1971 in an advertisement of a shipper of what were called 'the quality wines of France',[10] but by the 1980s there were far more genuinely knowledgeable connoisseurs than there ever had been, people who were able to cope with what Hugh Johnson called 'a mountain of information'.[11]

Statistics of wine sales and other sales of drinks during the early 1980s registered change. There was a slump in beer sales – and production – in 1981 and 1982, and, though there were few cider connoisseurs, a boom in cider sales.[12] Indeed, beer production in 1982 was at its lowest since 1972, while cider production leapt by 20 per cent. There was talk too of 'a rejection of traditional regular and heavy beer consumption'.[13] The volume of whisky sold in Britain fell also by 15 per cent between March 1979 and March 1983, when there was a further increase in taxation. The fall in 1982 alone was 6 per cent.[14]

It is obvious that the incidence of taxation, which was raised significantly in 1980, still had much to do with demand for particular kinds of alcoholic – and non-alcoholic – drinks. Cider, for example, was exempt from duty until 1976, and in 1982 was carrying a duty of only rather more than 4p per pint as against the duty on beer of 14p per pint. Not surprisingly, there was pressure for changes in taxation as the trade worked out interesting and revealing figures relating to 'pence to be paid per centilitre of alcohol by product category' (see Table 30 overleaf). The reduction to a common denominator in the nineteenth century would have been a subject of interest only to teetotallers.[15]

Table wine sales were up 6.5 per cent in volume in 1982, but each bottle was further taxed by 5p in 1983, when the tax on fortified wines, the demand for which had further decreased in 1982, was increased by as much as 7p per bottle in the case of sherry and 8p per bottle in the case of port. It is ironical that the 1982 increase was made on the eve of Britain's tenth anniversary of membership of the European Common Market, when more than two-fifths of British exports went to the EEC; it was

---

[10] *The Guardian*, 20 March 1981.
[11] H. Johnson, *Hugh Johnson's Pocket Wine Book* (1982 edn.) p. 4.
[12] The slump was particularly plain in relation to bar sales. Beer in many parts of the country was still bought over the bar in rounds.

[13] *Harpers*, 13 January 1984.
[14] *Ibid.*, 2 December 1983.
[15] It was noted as part of the research that the man hours required to purchase alcoholic beverages had declined compared to other commodities.

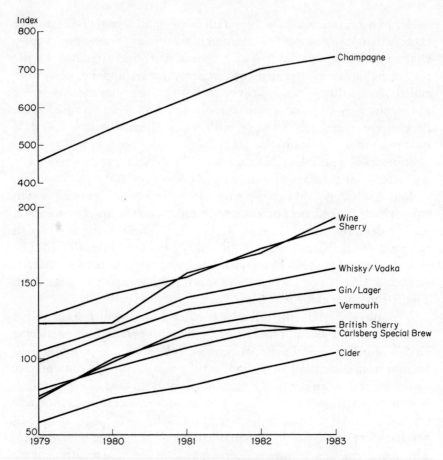

TABLE 30 *Index of pence per centilitre of alcohol by product category, 1979 to 1983*

followed by an additional increase in 1983 of 5p on a bottle of table wine, 7p on a bottle of sherry, 1p on a pint of beer, and 25p on a bottle of whisky. It was left to *The Economist* to decide how far by then Britain had 'gone European' (see Table 31 opposite).[16]

A little earlier, wine was said to account for only 2.1 per cent of the value of Community agricultural production as against 15.5 per cent for veal and beef and 19.5 per cent for milk. Nonetheless, it played a 'determining role in the regional balance within the Community',[17] and

---

[16] *The Economist*, 25 December 1982.
[17] Commission of the European

Communities, *A Future for Europe's Wine*, July 1980.

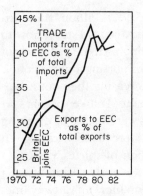

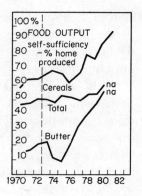

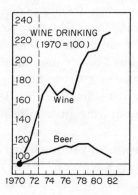

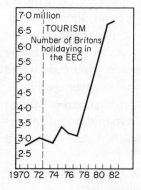

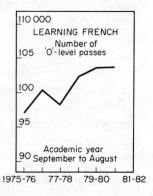

TABLE 31 *How Britain went European, 1970–1982*
(Source: *The Economist*, 25 December 1982)

discussion of Europe's wine surpluses was noisy enough to hit British headlines in 1984. 'Alcohol causes headaches', wrote *The Economist* in March 1984; 'Europe's alcohol industry has three now: how to drain the

European Community's surplus "wine lake" [2.7 billion standard bottles]; how to cut fermentation/feedstock costs; and, old story, how to deal with the French.'[18] France was said to be annoying its neighbours not only by subsidising its own producers but by importing pure alcohol.

Paradoxically, the French were gradually decreasing their consumption of wine while that of the British was increasing. In twenty years *per capita* consumption fell by a third. Office workers were said to be drinking less wine at lunch; the rich and ambitious were concentrating on '*appellations d'origine controlées*' – and consumption of spirits was going up.[19] It was a sign of frustration when during the early spring of 1984 wine-growers in the Languedoc-Roussillon region blew up railway lines and cut telephone wires in protest against falling wine prices, against an EEC proposal to cut subsidies for short-term storage, and the decision to allow Spain to enter the Community.[20] The wine-growers did not note how since 1980 the EEC as a whole had taken the place of the United States – increasingly a wine exporter to Europe – as the biggest buyer of bottled Scotch whisky – with France in the lead.[21] Nor did figures of increasing British imports of wine attract the attention in France which they deserved.

The statistics were conveniently summarized in the autumn of 1983 by Arnold Tasker, the Deputy Chairman of the Wine and Spirits Association, who pointed out that August sales of 'light wine' were then running more than 10 per cent ahead of the previous year, following an increase in the previous year of over 7 per cent on the 1981 figure. 'In my view', Tasker went on, 'this points to a significant new increase in the number of wine consumers'. He was confident that the total had now topped the 25 million mark. 'The time is getting nearer when light wines will have more consumers than any other alcoholic beverage in the country.' His statement was accompanied by comparative August figures for 1981, 1982 and 1983, now expressed not in millions of gallons but in hectalitres.[22] The light wines included 'wines, table wines and

---

[18] *The Economist*, 3 March 1984. Wine cost about four times as much to make as synthetic alcohol. Meanwhile, according to the *Daily Telegraph*, 11 May 1984, European wine surpluses were being sold to the Soviet Union for less than 7p a litre. There were other European headaches, for example, an Italian whisky war which it was claimed in December 1984 had at last ended, with apologies (*Financial Times*, 7 December 1984).
[19] *The Economist*, 27 April 1983; for the

position in the United States, where 90 per cent of American wine was made in California (with 540 vineries), see *ibid.*, 25 December 1982. California also accounted for 70 per cent of the wine drunk.
[20] *The Times*, 27 March 1984.
[21] *Daily Telegraph*, 11 May 1984.
[22] Customs and Excise changed its calculations from gallons to hectalitres in January 1980, a historic moment.

quality wines', the medium wines sherries and vermouths, and the heavy wines ports:

	1981	*1982*	*1983*
Still Wines (up to 15 per cent)	238,271	246,963	270,984
Medium Wines (15–18 per cent)	75,323	65,976	96,938
Heavy Wines (over 18 per cent)	4,636	4,052	4,069
Sparkling Wines	14,605	13,409	16,673
Total[23]	332,835	330,400	388,684

TABLE 32 *Sales of wine totals based on quantities of duty paid*

In 1983 and 1984 further figures revealed, notwithstanding, that while wine sales were increasing – and there were hopes of 30 million consumers by 1990[24] – the traditional place of beer in the British drinking pattern had not been undermined. After the significant fall of production in the years 1980, 1981 and 1982 – 13.5 per cent on an annual basis – there was evidence of increased consumption in the latter months of 1983 and the first months of 1984. Cost-cutting exercises, some of them drastic, on the part of big brewers, most of them increasingly diversified with greater interests in 'leisure industries', had been accompanied by increased investment in pubs; and according to surveys made in 1983, a year when beer consumption still fell, pubs were still visited at least once each month by seven out of ten men and four out of ten women.[25]. Meanwhile, 'eating out', often with wine, was still on the increase, despite economic restraints. *Social Trends 15* identified 'going out for a meal' as the third most common leisure-time activity in Britain. Forty per cent of the sample had eaten a meal out in the month preceding the

[23] Excluding 'British-made wines', which included 'fruit wines, British sherries and similar wines'.

[24] Wine and Spirit Association, Press Release at the Opening of the International Wine and Spirit Trade Fair at Olympia, 29 May 1984.

[25] *The Times*, 18 June 1984, 'Beer keeps its head high'. A financial survey by Inter Company Comparisons on 'Brewers, Bitters and Soft Drink Manufacturers and Distributors', published in January 1984, dealt with the trends of the previous three years, including a rise in the demand for 'real ales' which protected regional brewers from some of the worst effects of 'the slump'. See also p. 163.

survey. Only those who gardened (44 per cent) and those who listened to tapes or records (63 per cent) were more numerous in the leisure categories.

The general picture in 1984 seemed to be that the extent both of home drinking and of pub drinking was increasing and that in each case beer and wine were part of the *repertoire*. There were signs as early as late 1983, wrote *Harpers*, a magazine 'open for discussion on all subjects of general interest to the wine, spirit and allied trades', that consumers were willing to increase their spending on 'all alcoholic beverages, including beers and spirits just as much as ciders and wines'.[26] The same magazine forecast 'a new period of prosperity during the late 1980s',[27] and took comfort in a Campbell Neill report on the Scotch whisky industry, running to more than 100 pages, in which Alan Gray forecast a 3 per cent increase in consumption rates in the years up to 1990.[28] Undoubtedly hot weather in the summers of 1983 and 1984 contributed to a boom which extended to soft drinks – and even to milk.[29]

The overall pattern was as follows:

| | Spirits | Light Wines | Fortified Wines | British-Made Wines | Beer |
		million gallons			bulk barrels
1980	54.8	58.7	29.6	11.6	41.5
1981	52.0	69.0	26.2	11.2	39.4
1982	49.0	73.2	23.6	11.6	37.1
1983	50.4	82.1	23.7	12.1	36.9

TABLE 33 *United Kingdom consumption of alcoholic drinks, 1980–1983*

The split of wines consumed between different regions of production showed an increase in the proportion of German wines – a sign perhaps of the still increasing preference for white wine – but France more than held its own against Spain and Italy:

[26] *Harpers*, 23 December 1983.
[27] *Ibid.*, 16 December 1983. See also *ibid.*, 9 December 1983 for an article headed 'Food and Drinks Forecast predicts healthy five years for wines, beer and spirits'.
[28] *Ibid.*, 2 December 1983.
[29] See *The Standard*, 8 September 1983, 'Milk is the toast as pub sales soar'. Nonetheless, 'the beer market remained difficult', as the Allied/Lyons *Annual Report* put it in 1984, 'and total volume increased only marginally in spite of a heat wave in July and August'.

	1980	*1981*	*1982*	*1983*
France	37	39	40	39
Germany	20	21	24	26
Italy	18	17	16	16
Spain	13	11	9	9
Others	12	12	11	10

TABLE 34 *Wine imports by country of origin, 1980–1983*
(percentages)

The influence of fiscal policy on British drinking patterns was a matter
of continuing debate after 1980 even though in 1979 the Advocate
General of the European Court of Justice in Luxembourg, Gerhard
Reische, had concluded that the difference in duties had not actually
deterred the British from drinking wine or led them to drink beer instead.
Indeed, he had accepted also the argument of the British Government
that the duties on wine, when related to alcoholic strength, were only half
as high again as those imposed on beer and that the difference was not
enough to amount to 'indirect protection' for beer. The British budget
changes in 1983 marginally eroded still further the already diminishing
initial ratio of four to one in favour of beer, but there was pressure inside
the Community for a significantly smaller ratio of three to one and
'parity' within six years. A further verdict in the European Court in
1983, fought by the British Government and lost, contended without
qualification that Britain was protecting beer by taxing it too highly (4 to
1 it was claimed) in relation to wine. The British system had the effect,
the Court ruled, of 'stamping wine with the hallmarks of a luxury
product which, in view of the tax burden which it bears, can scarcely
constitute in the eyes of the consumer a genuine alternative to the typical
domestic beverage'.

When the really important fiscal change came in 1984, it was no
surprise to the trade, although the Chancellor of the Exchequer told the
Commons that how to relate EEC 'rules' on alcoholic drinks to British
budgeting had confronted him with his 'most difficult decision'. He had
'complied with the Court's judgment' and increased the duty on beer by
the minimum amount needed to maintain revenue – 2p on a typical pint
of beer, including VAT – while at the same time reducing the duty on
table wine by the equivalent of 18p per bottle, again including VAT.
Duty on cider was to go up by 3p a pint; the duties on British 'made-wine'
were to be aligned with those on other wine; and the duties on sparkling

wines, fortified wines and spirits were to rise by about 10p a bottle, including VAT.[30] In a lively budget the Chancellor's comments on beer and wine were far less eloquent than those of Gladstone in 1860. Nor did they contain any message other than that of 'harmonization', fitting British taxes to those of the Community system and hoping that the Italians would be as responsive in relation to whisky policy.[31] Nonetheless, as the Wine and Spirit Association gratefully noted, in the response to the change there was a growing recognition that as Britain was one of the member states of the Community where alcohol was 'more highly taxed', the United Kingdom 'could hardly fail to benefit from harmonization of duties'.[32]

It was perhaps a sign of the optimism that can come from harmonization that Welsh whisky, which had figured in early Victoria Wine catalogues, reappeared in the headlines in 1983 when 'Swn y More' Chwisgi – 'sound of the sea' whisky, blended and bottled in Brecon – was said to be crossing not only the Channel but the Atlantic. There was a touch of optimism too for New Zealanders, who had benefited little from harmonization, in the inclusion in the Victoria Wine summer lists for 1984 of 'New Zealand Dry Red'. Yet the French should have found even greater pleasure in a special number of the by now handsomely printed *Wine Newsletter* by David Bedford for May 1983 which introduced a special French Wine Festival with words that would have cheered Cobden even more than Gladstone:

> For the month of May we are pleased to feature all things French and in the case of wine nearly 40% of all wine imported into this country is French – traditions die hard in our preference for wine![33]

The *Newsletter* also told readers about 'this marvellous aperitif' Kir: Regnier Creme de Cassis cost £6.65 per bottle, but 'only a small dollop in the bottom of the glass' was necessary to give light white wine a new flavour.[34]

---

[30] *Hansard*, 14 March 1984.

[31] In *The Financial Times* (22 December 1984) Edmund Penning-Rowsell advised wine buyers to replenish their stocks on the grounds that in the next Budget the Chancellor 'would be more than likely to try to recover some of the £2m. a year that he was obliged by the EEC to give away last year.'

[32] Wine and Spirit Association, Press Release, 13 June 1984, Statement by the Chairman, Guy Gordon Clark.

[33] Victoria Wine, May 1983 *Wine Newsletter*, No. 22. There were five issues of the *Wine Newsletter* in 1983, beginning with Number 21 which had articles on 'bin ends' and 'Christmas favourites'. There were also two numbers concerned with 'Wines for summer', a sign that the seasonal balance of drinking remained of great importance.

[34] There had been an earlier description of Kir in the *Wine Newsletter* for August 1980, when it was described on a cold and wet Wimbledon day as 'a personal blending preference drink to suit yourself.'

Memorandum dealing with a transport problem, 1916

PLEASE ADDRESS ALL COMMUNICATIONS TO THE FIRM.

MEMORANDUM.

TELEGRAMS: "WITHWINE, LONDON"
TELEPHONE No. 3818 LONDON WALL

AVENUE 5838 (2 LINES)

FROM : :

**The Victoria
Wine Company,**

12 to 20, OSBORN STREET,
LONDON.

VICTORIA WINE COMPANY·LONDON
ESTABLISHED
1865
TRADE MARK.

20th Sept 1916.

Mr A. E. Taylor
41 High Street
East Grinstead.

Dear Sir

We are sorry to hear about the death of the
Pony, as we cannot send you another just at present
please hire in the neighbourhood for the time being.
We remain
Yours Faithfully
The Victoria Wine Co
per MCH

Horse-drawn delivery
carts about to set off from
Harveys original Bristol
premises, 1920

Austin 10 delivery van, mid-1930s

Modern delivery van

Christmas advertisement, *The Pictorial World,* 1880

PORT

	Per Dozen Bottles.
CARRADOR PORT	42/-
VELHO PORT, Tawny	48/-
A.D., Tawny Port	54/-
RED SEAL, Invalid Port	54/-
WHITE LODGE, full fruity	60/-
TAWNY PORT, fine old	66/-
COCKBURN'S, light ruby	66/-
SPECIAL QUINTA, a full wine, vintage style	69/-
EMBASSY, fine wine, medium full	72/-
PRINCE, beautiful old wine	78/-
ROYAL CROWN, a fine old tawny	80/-
KING'S, superb old wine	80/-
EMPRESS, very old in wood, slightly tawny ...	84/-
SPECIAL VINTAGE CHARACTER, a full, fine old blended Port	90/-
OLD MOSCATEL, finest old tawny, with Muscatel flavour	96/-
EMPEROR, elegant old, tawny, medium dry, a perfect wine	102/-
REX IMPERIAL, superb old tawny	120/-

WHITE PORT.

WHITE PORT, One Diamond	54/-
WHITE PORT, Three Diamond	60/-

Single bottles can be supplied at per dozen rate.

Half-bottles of above Wines in stock.

Our Cash Register seizes up on Christmas Eve.

Our hire-powered delivery vans cope with our Christmas rush.

Rush of out-patients during our Christmas consulting hours.

7

A page from W. Glendenning's 1931 Christmas list,
which was illustrated throughout by Pont, the
well-known *Punch* cartoonist.

Cover of W. Glendenning's 1932 Christmas list, also
illustrated by Pont

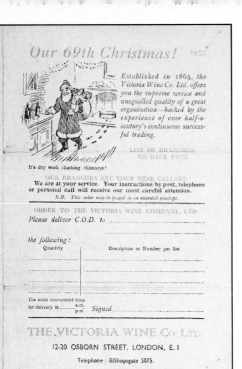

Victoria Wine Company

Tyler and Company

Two price lists from the 1930s

PRICE LIST, 1936
No. 8

THE VICTORIA WINE CO LTD

CHIEF OFFICES
12-20 OSBORN ST, LONDON, E.1.
Telephones: BISHOPSGATE 5875 (Eight Lines)

DELIVERY TO YOUR DOOR

LONDON'S WINE MERCHANTS SINCE 1865

SPEEDY DELIVERY
TO YOUR DOOR

THE VICTORIA WINE CO. LTD

CHIEF OFFICES:
12-20 OSBORN STREET, LONDON, E.1
Telephones: BISHOPSGATE 5875 (Eight lines)

In spite of all things..

Perhaps the fact that we are able to send you this Price List (utilitarian and simplified though it be) is one of the best indications that our Service continues practically unimpaired.

Deliberately we say "*practically*" unimpaired because it would be foolish and misleading to suggest that there are not restrictions and difficulties.

Prices have gone up . . . because of the higher Duties now in force. A study of the items listed will show how little account is taken of the other increases in cost which have to be met. In particular, the items in heavier type . . . chiefly our own exclusive lines . . . are specially good value.

We have found it essential to economise on the method of delivery of supplies : petrol-rationing enforces this necessity. And we are grateful to those of our customers who (as some already do) now insist upon carrying their smaller purchases home with them. This does not mean we cannot maintain an adequate delivery service . . . we can and do, as you will find when placing your order.

We can supply all Wines, Spirits, Beers, Table Waters and so forth . . . even including German Wines (which, bought long before the War, are still available at pre-War-Budget prices). We have more than 3,000 lines from which you can make your choice. Therefore, please continue to instruct us as before : in spite of all things, we are maintaining the Service which has been a developing tradition during the 74 years since our Founder, William W. Hughes, first supplied Victorian London.

THE VICTORIA WINE CO. LTD.

London's Wine Merchants since the early days of Queen Victoria's reign.

A wartime price list, 1940

Victoria Wine wine catalogues for the 1980s reveal how active the business was in promoting a wider range of products than ever before, through still more expensive advertising and more lively publicity. In 1978/9 the cost of advertising was £300,000, in 1980/1 £426,000, and in 1982/3 £750,000. Indeed, in 1981, leaving aside Christmas advertising, £335,000 was spent on advertising light wines alone. Advertising did not influence the comments of the *Which? Wine Guide* in 1981, however, when it noted a 'tremendous' improvement in the range of wines offered to customers during the previous two years: Victoria Wine, it added, had 'been quick off the mark with exciting new wines' and deserved to be congratulated.[35] And in the following year it began its comments on the wine chain with the sentence, 'If only every off-licence manager employed by Victoria Wine could be persuaded to be as enthusiastic as some of their customers, then the admirable work being done by those who buy wine for this chain could be fully appreciated.'[36]

Top management and managers were aware, of course, of the acuteness of competition, which in a period of growth 'restricted capacity to improve margins' and led to the closure of a number of branches.[37] It encouraged, however, still more sophisticated market research. Current information about customers' profiles was collected assiduously in the most sophisticated fashion: in 1981 over 40 per cent of them came from socio-economic groups C2, D and E, 47 per cent of them were women, and over 43 per cent in age groups below 34. At the same time, the effects of likely changes in taxation were calculated carefully. So too were the figures of 'man hours worked to purchase alcoholic liquor' as compared with those of previous years and of other countries. The future of different drinks was assessed, and particular key geographical areas were chosen for concentrated marketing attention.

Yet for all the sophistication – and the underlying concern for competition, particularly from the grocery trade and the supermarkets, which by 1984 accounted for virtually half of British liquor purchases – there are few entirely new themes for the historian in the recent story of Victoria Wine, except in relation to packaging, grading and marketing. Thus, while one of the latest Grants of St James's wine forecasts sketched 'a picture of light wine buying increasingly enjoyed by all age groups and, very significantly, by all socio-economic groups', it was still echoing

[35] *Which? Wine Guide* (1981), pp. 136–7.
[36] *Ibid.* (1982), p. 154.
[37] Allied/Lyons, *Report and Accounts*, 1983, p. 21. Business grew only marginally 'and an increasing proportion of the business was concentrated into the few hectic days before Christmas'. The Christmas of 1984 was a bumper one.

Gladstone, and it was echoing him also when it insisted that 'it is the new wine drinker who is the key to past and future growth of light wine sales'.[38] Grants were hoping to find him not only in Victoria Wine shops but in the supermarkets and grocery stores. Indeed, in March 1984 European Vintners, specialising in the supply of wines to supermarkets and grocery stores, became a subsidiary of Grants of St James's Ltd, as part of a cluster of wine and spirit interests of Booker McConnell acquired by Allied/Lyons Group, a move described as 'one of the most exciting in the United Kingdom wine trade'.[39] Within the Group Victoria Wine paid special attention to sales conferences at which 'the voice of staff at shop level' was said to be 'coming across as loud and clear' as that of the central and regional management.[40]

It was at the point of sale, of course, that there was direct contact with customers, and perhaps one new theme in the Victoria Wine story was a change in the attitudes of some of its customers. 'The new generation of wine-drinkers has a much more relaxed attitude to wine-drinking', a Grants of St James's Press Release stated in 1983. 'Whilst the majority of wine is still consumed with a meal, the importance of the occasion has declined. Wine has been much more fun and is increasingly being served as an aperitif before or after [sic] dinner, and much of the traditional mystery has disappeared'.[41]

To attract new customers, the actual appearance of wine bottles and packages seemed to matter more and more. The first Nicolas wines had been offered in standard size litre bottles: by 1984 they became available in 'a range of sizes and packing styles to suit all occasions'.[42] Seventy cl carafes had been introduced in 1983, along with 25 cl cans, 25 cl widemouth 'plastishield' bottles and 25 cl tetrapacks. 'The public was more than willing to try out new packaging styles', market researchers suggested, estimating that the market for the 25 cl size would grow to 2 per cent of the light wine market by 1988 and that 36 million cans of wine would be sold in 1990'.[43] 'Our aim', it was stated, was 'to ensure that the wine was good enough to attract repeat purchases even after the novelty . . . had been exhausted'.[44]. For the 'on-trade' there were four styles of ten-litre packs.

---

[38] Presentation of T. Nutt to Seminar, May 1981.

[39] European Vintners was a very young company formed on 1 January 1984 as a holding company for Italvini, France Vin, BWA Deutschwein and Espavino.

[40] Victoria Wine, Conference Special Report, December 1984.

[41] Grants of St James's *News*, October 1983.

[42] 'Grants of St James's Makes a Million', Press Release of May 1984.

[43] 'New Plastishield Bottle for Nicolas', Press Releases of October 1984, January 1985.

[44] *Ibid*, March 1984.

Research seemed to show also that, however knowledgeable a minority of customers might be, customers looking for a bottle of wine usually had only two major considerations in mind – colour and price – so that Victoria Wine in 1984 set about varying its pricing structures and 'making the selection of wines as simple and straightforward as possible'. It appreciated also that it had to counter the advantages supermarkets offered to one-stop shoppers by presenting a specialist service suited to the local 'shopping environments'. Already in 1981 David Bedford had introduced the idea of a 'wine selection system' in order to try to make the choosing of wines easier for the uninitiated. White (and rosé) wines were graded according to sweetness – 'the lower the number, the drier the wine' – and red wines according to body (using the initial letters of the words 'soft' and 'firm'; 'light', 'medium' or 'big'), 'thereby making buying easier'.[45] 'Using our White Wine Selector', customers were told, 'you can choose the white wine that is exactly right for you. (1) denotes very dry, (9) very sweet, with the numbers between indicating the various degrees of dryness and sweetness'.[46] In January 1984 Bordeaux Blanc de Blancs at £2.29 was (1), Wachenheimer Altenburg Riesling Trockenbeerenauslese, 1976 at £32 was (9). Beaujolais, 1982 was SL, Valpolicella FL, Cornas, from the Rhone FB. At Christmas, one white Rioja was offered, along with one German white wine, one Austrian white wine, one United States white wine, one South African white wine, four English white wines and twenty-one French. It was pointed out clearly, however, that 'the great vintage red wines of Bordeaux, Burgundy and the Rhône are not graded as they vary with age'.

When in 1984 important changes were to be carried out in the shops, it was decided that greater flexibility in price patterns should be accompanied by more distinctive forms of display. White wines were to be displayed side by side, ranging from very dry to very sweet. Short descriptions of the different tastes were to be added on the shelf edges, and an explanation of the 'wine selector' system clearly displayed. The red wines and sherries also were to be grouped by taste, with a separate section marked 'Wines for Special Occasions' chosen particularly for 'the

---

[45] 'The white and rosé market is heavily dominated by the irregular drinker whose major concern is how sweet or dry a white wine tastes', *The Grocer* noted, 27 March 1981. Now 'Take a Number' would apply to wine as well as bingo.

[46] 'Now Choosing Wine is as Easy as 1,2,3 ...', Press Release, March 1981. See also, for a critique, *Decanter*, June 1981. The ruling was based on tasting, not on laboratory tests. 'If it doesn't cause some argument, I shall be surprised', Bedford observed. Yet he trusted that his system would educate drinkers. 'If they like a Liebfraumilch, for example, they may be surprised to find other wines with the same degree of sweetness'.

more knowledgeable shopper'. A refrigerated section was to present 'a good range of wines, beers and soft drinks ready chilled' while a dazzling cocktail section 'was to offer a choice of unusual colourful glasses, swizzle sticks and shakers that make delightful browsing'.

'Individual service' was deemed the key to the new style. Every Victoria Wine shop was now to offer free local delivery on all purchases over £25 and a nominal £1 charge on deliveries under that amount; free loan of glasses; cash discounts on wines and beer; and sale or return facilities. In addition, Victoria Wine was now making monthly credit accounts available, as well as accepting all major credit cards. It was also prepared to offer charge accounts. All these services, representing a new approach to business, were to be clearly displayed in the shop.[47] In a 1984 competition for the 'branch of the year', the first time this competition had been held, Wallingford was the winner. It was specially featured in the December issue of *The Victoria Wine Company News*.

Increased 'personalisation' was accompanied by still greater attention to improved staff training and to a more efficient use of management time. These were two of the themes stressed by Lister A. Fielding, who in January 1984 became the new Managing Director of Victoria Wine, with Eric Colwell moving over to the Chairmanship. Fielding was a highly successful 40-year-old businessman who had pioneered a quite different line of business as Managing Director of the European subsidiaries of Mothercare. The emphasis in training was now to be placed on 'training in store', and Dale House, Stockport, was closed in 1985. Six new area managers were appointed in the autumn of 1984.[48] There were also to be experiments in 'district management', a system whereby two or more shops in close proximity would be organised under a single manager, and two new senior sales appointments were made to supervise sales staff in the Northern and Southern divisions.

Meanwhile, as many shops as possible were to be given 'face lifts', so that the *Which? Wine Guide* for 1985 could refer to their 'cool, white-and-green, super-modern look'.[49] And new technology went with the facelift. Electronic data were to be collected from every store at point of sale, part of 'an automatic ordering system with payment with order facilities better to control branch stocks and branch ranging and to eliminate massive quantities of paperwork'. The system, devised before 1984, was intended to provide the Company with 'up-to-the-minute information

---

[47] L. Fielding, 'Note on the future development of Victoria Wine', 3 April 1984.
[48] *Victoria Wine Company News*, April 1985.

In the autumn of 1984 Audrey Twigg was appointed Personnel Officer for the Company at the age of 27.
[49] *Which? Wine Guide* (1985), p. 371.

at all times on stock levels and the flow of sales in all parts of the country'. As Dan Keough had put it in 1983, 'we will be able to measure, and will in turn to be measured'.[50] Three other current Directors who were closely involved in the development of the new policies are Keith Bird, Roger Scott and G.E.J. Phoenix.

Turning to the Victoria Wine lists of the 1980s, with David Bedford as Buying Director,[51] the range of wines available to customers was wider than ever before, although the Olé own-brand series range of sherries was accounting for 45 per cent of the sherry business; own-brand British wines for 50 per cent of the business in these products; and Glen Rossie Whisky for 25 per cent of the whisky business. There were more Italian wines than Spanish wines on the list, evidence of the enterprise of the Italian wine industry, while alongside the clarets and the burgundies, there were now four 'country wines of France' – Blanc de Blanc at £1.65 per bottle, St Chinian Minervois at £1.69, Château Les Palais, Corbières, at £1.88 per bottle, and Latour-de-France, Côte de Roussillon Villages, at £1.92. The least expensive 1970 claret was a Château St Emilion at £5.50 and the most expensive a Pauillac Château Lafite, 1970, at £32. There was also a 1967 Château Latour at £18. One of the most interesting comments came at the end of the 1980 list. 'We also offer many fine chateau-bottled clarets of recent vintage which should be laid down for several years before drinking.' The cellar still counted, therefore, for all that had been said about its disappearance, and owners of cellars figured among the intended readers of Bedford's *Wine Newsletter*.

One new group of wines in the 1980s were the 'varietals', single grape wines selected for the category of grapes used in their making. 'Classic grapes usually make classic wines even if not from the area from which they are best known' was the motto for this group, which in 1980 included a Cabernet Sauvignon from Yugoslavia, a Gamay from France and a Muscat from Spain. These were wines which had been advertised by Grants of St James's on the eve of the decade as 'new wines that shape up to the 80s'. They were expected 'to attract both the knowledgeable drinker who has some awareness of grape variety names, and also the new wine consumer seeking exceptional value for money'.

In line with Victorian drinking habits, the 1980 list of wines could also include at one end of the price range a Château d'Yquem, 1975, at

---

[50] *Drinks*, June 1983.
[51] In November 1984 David Coxon, a former buyer for North West Vintners Retail Ltd., became Buying Controller directly responsible to Bedford. Special attention was to be paid to beers, ciders, minerals, cigarettes and dry goods.

£29.13, four times more expensive than the Château Giraud, Rieussec and Climens of the same year, and at the other a fortified aperitif made from sweet Muscat grapes in the South – a Muscat de Mireval, Domaine des Aresquiers at £3.50. But it was of a sweet wine not from France but from Cyprus, 'traditional' Commandaria, that Geoffrey Jewell of Victoria Wine chose to write lyrically in January 1984. 'Occasionally', he explained, 'a little history adds romance to a bottle of wine, especially when that wine has been made using the same basic methods for some 2,000 years'.[52] Likewise, while an excellent French Blanc de Blanc, Blanc Foussy, was competing successfully with champagne at wedding parties, Bedford was also recommending Codorniu, Grand Corday from Spain, 'constantly popping up at some very grand occasions'. By 1984 Codorniu was selling 40 million bottles a year to more than one hundred countries.[53] The 1984 Beaujolais Nouveau at £2.59 a bottle made its way into a selection of Victoria Wine stores for the 'magic 15 November day', another day in the calendar not known to the Victorians.[54]

The most interesting list for a very grand occasion is a special Royal Wedding Wine List of 1981, which was issued to celebrate the wedding of the Prince of Wales and Lady Diana Spencer. It put the Nicolas Table Wines first, as always stressing the association of Nicolas not with the wine growing regions of France but with Paris, but went on to list no fewer than 66 clarets, the oldest and most expensive of them a Mouton Rothschild, 1970, and a Château Lafite, Pauillac, at £27 a bottle. The Bordeaux region was still producing one third of all French exports of *appellation controlée* wines, and non-vintage claret in 1981 then cost £2.59 – with a Harveys No. 1 at £3.59.[55] The most expensive Burgundy was a 1971 La Tâche at £55. Champagnes ranged in price from non-vintage Mercier Brut Reserve at £6.99 to Dom Perignon at £22.50. Asterisks were placed against some of the special items, cheap and expensive, on a list, with a footnote, 'These are parcels of extremely good and interesting wines which will probably not be repeated, so they are only available while stocks last'.

There were by then seven Australian and eight Californian wines on

---

[52] Victoria Wine, Press Release, 'The Crusader Wine', January 1984.

[53] A Press Luncheon was arranged on 11 July 1984 by Hatch, Mansfield and Company Ltd, Sole U.K. Agents for Codorniu. It was attended by the head of the firm, who was a direct descendant of its sixteenth-century founder.

[54] Victoria Wine, Press Release, November 1984.

[55] In 1984 there was a non-vintage Victoria Wine claret at £1.99. Harveys then cost £3.49. There were seven vintage clarets on the Christmas list costing less than £4 a bottle. The 1982 and 1983 vintages were good in terms of quality and volume.

the list. Each of the five Australian wines on the 1980 list had been described as 'a beaut': their names, however, like those of the ten on offer in 1984, were completely different from the Australian names on the old Victoria Wine lists. The cheapest in 1984 was a white wine (who in Australia would have expected that a half century or quarter century before?), Killawarra Chardonnay, Maclaren Vale, at £2.80, and the most expensive a Wynns Coonawarra Cabernet Sauvignon, 1974, at £18.50. Two were Australian bottled. Equally interesting were a Chilean red, two Lebanese reds, 'very similar to claret and highly praised at the World Wine Fair', three Bulgarians, and one Chinese ('Great Wall' at £4.15). There had been five California wines from the Napa Valley in 1980, all bottled by Christian Brothers, ranging in price from £2.44 for a 'Crystal Dry' white to £2.94 for a Pinot Chardonnay. 'The quality of these wines challenges the best in Europe' the accompanying description had run. Now in 1984 there were 19 United States wines, including five from Washington State. There were five English wines too – Cranmore Müller-Thurgau, 1981 at £3.40, Schoenburger, 1983 at £3.80, Bruisgard St Peter at £4.10, Adgestone, 1981 at £4.80 and Lamberhurst Priory, 1983, at £3.90. The 1983 vintage was said to be the best since the new English vineyards had been opened, with yields ten tons or more per acre compared with two to four tons in 1982 when only half the quantity was produced.[56]

German wines, including Goldener Oktober, were given first place in a list of 'wines from around the world' in 1980, and there were more of them on offer than in the whole Victoria Wine lists of the 1940s and 1950s. A Standard Hock Deutscher Tafelwein cost £2.69 per litre, and among eight Palatinate wines, the most expensive was a Wachenheimer Riesling Auslese 1976, at £7.20. There were seven Rheingau wines, nine Rheinhessen and neighbourhood wines, two Franconian wines, one Baden wine (at £1.95), and fifteen Moselles, including some of the great 1975s and 1976s, among them a Wehlener Sonnenuhr Riesling Beerenauslese at £13.90. By 1984, the price of the standard Hock Deutscher Tafelwein had risen to £3.79 per litre, and there were now only six Palatinate wines, the most expensive a Wachenheimer Altenburg Riesling Trockenbeerenauslese at £32. There were five Rheingau wines, eight Rheinhessen and neighbourhood, one

---

[56] Quality was said to have improved too. John MacGregor, Minister of State for Agriculture, Fisheries and Food praised English wines in the House of Commons in the autumn of 1984. They had just won major prizes in a European competition. (*Hansard*, 25 October 1984).

Franconian wine, three Baden wines (the cheapest at £2.59) and thirteen Moselles, among them three surviving 1976s, the Wehlener Sonnenuhr Riesling now costing £25. At the cheapest end of the Christmas 1984 list Liebfraumilch, 1983, Soave and Valpolicella, at £1.49, were described as 'scoops of the year'. A bad year for the Bordeaux grape harvest did not bode well for claret.

Port, vintage port, madeira and sherry ended the 1984 wine list, the cheapest port, Conference Ruby, at £3.55 and the most expensive a vintage Quinta do Noval, 1966, at £22. 'Please ask your local manager for details of 1978 and 1975 vintage ports which should be laid down until 1990' had been associated advice in 1980.[57] The British were no longer the greatest port drinkers in Europe. There were then only two madeiras on offer, but they were said to be 'enjoying quite deservedly a revival of interest'.

There may be further 'revivals of interest', in cocktails, for example, already well advanced, or in liqueurs. 'We are becoming cocktail crazy', Jane MacQuitty claimed in *The Times* in December 1984, when she gave recipes for cocktails which included liqueurs like Poire William and Parfait Amour.[58]

In general, the wine trade as a whole is not only more competitive in the 1980s: it is more influenced by fashion. Perhaps for these reasons there is a natural interest in trying to look both forwards and backwards at the same time. Thus, Lister Fielding, new to the business, very properly expected that all the changes being made in 1984 'in combination with one another' would 'result in the Victoria Wine Company having a viable and worthwhile future, as befits a business which has survived and successfully developed ever since its foundation in 1865'.[59] No historian could say no.

---

[57] *The Times* also gave seasonal advice. See Jane MacQuitty, 'singled out as Ports of Distinction', 22 December, 1984. See also Avril Groom, 'Passing the Port, but not only at Christmas' in the *Daily Telegraph*, 19 December 1984.

[58] *The Times*, 19 December 1984. In 1984 Warninks Advocaat cost £4.99 a bottle. Grand Marnier was the most expensive liqueur at £12.49. Bailey's Irish Cream cost £5.49 and Malibu £5.99. Advocaat had been taken over by Victoria Wine in 1969.

[59] Press Release, 'Victoria Wine takes up the challenge', April 1984.

Index

Index

Waugh, Alec 14
Waugh, Auberon 16, 174
Weller and Hughes 43
Westcliffe-on-Sea 135
Westminster Wines 141
Weybridge 123
Wheeler, Susan 51
Whisky
  Irish 52, 115
  Scotch 52, 63–4, 93, 96, 99, 106, 107,
    108, 115, 116, 135, 145, 155, 157,
    162, 168
  Welsh 84, 184
  and soda 63
Whitbreads 141
Whiteways Ltd. 131, 161
Whitmore, W.W. 20–1
Willis, T. Lyte 65
Wilson, A. 100
Wimbledon 147, 184
Windsor 123
Wine bars 167, 168

Wine books 13, 76–7, 149, 156–7,
  174–5, 188
'Wine Lake' 179
Wine News Letter, 148
Wine and Spirits Association 16, 66, 67,
  161, 180, 184
Wine and Spirit Trade Defence Fund
  104
Wine (and Spirit) Trade Review 40, 41,
  43, 47, 52, 73, 74, 90, 91, 94, 96,
  97, 98, 103, 127, 154, 155
Women
  as customers 167
  as managers 51, 113–4, 120, 134
Wood, F. 81, 85, 86–7, 90, 110
Wood, F.R. 86
Wood, H.A. 86, 110
Working classes 12, 27, 28ff., 48, 72, 176

Young, G.M. 18, 19, 56
Yugoslavia 141, 156, 168

199